A SHORT HISTORY
OF PAINTING
IN AMERICA

The Story of 450 Years

by E. P. RICHARDSON

Director of The Henry Francis du Pont
Winterthur Museum

THOMAS Y. CROWELL COMPANY

New York • Established 1834

This book is an abridgment, with a
new concluding chapter and other
new matter, of *Painting in America:
The Story of 450 Years.*

Designed by Laurel Wagner

Manufactured in the United States of America

Library of Congress Catalog Card No. 62-12805

ISBN 0-690-73376-3

15 14 13 12 11 10

Contents

Color Plates

Following page 60

One

THE PROBLEM

PAINTING is both an art and a craft. It therefore shares both the unpredictable nature of the imagination which, like the wind, blows where it wills and the social character of an organized skill in human society. These two elements—the one volatile as air or fire, the other earthbound and practical but, like the earth, stabilizing and life-giving—are always present in art. But nowhere is their mutual action and reaction more striking, their interplay more curious, than in their creation of a new national tradition of painting in America.

The story of both art and craft of painting in America is part of the larger story of how Western civilization, after developing through a thousand years in Europe, spread in the sixteenth and seventeenth centuries in the minds and hands of adventurous men to the western shores of the Atlantic, took root there, and developed in a new series of nations on the American continent. Since the American Revolution of 1775-1783 the United States has been politically separated from Europe; but American culture has continued to live its own life within the greater life of the entire Western world, just as have the national cultures of Great Britain, France, Italy, and every other Western nation.

It is written everywhere, across the story of these past centuries, that we have shared with Europe both a common heritage of the past and the climate of the mind which prevails in each successive age: yet this fact is greatly in need of interpretation. One main purpose of this book is to see how American painting appears when observed within the perspective of Western art, seen as a whole. The climate of thought and feeling, and the evolution of forms, familiar in the general history of Western art, have never been brought into relation with the works of American painters. I have tried to tell the story of American painters from their own viewpoint, but in relation also to what was happening in the rest of the world. I do not find that American painting seems less interesting when set beside that of other countries: rather the contrary.

American culture is neither a raw new product nor a borrowed old one. It is the imaginative life of people who share the common inheritance of Western civilization, but live under new skies and feel novel experiences as well as those that all men share. Regard it, then, as one of the broad national traditions which make Western life so varied and so rich: it will provide both surprises and matter for pride.

Two of its stranger elements may call for brief mention here. It is a curious spectacle, for one interested in the life of forms in art, to see how in the colonial centuries, when life on this continent was months away from Europe and still in its rude beginnings, the forms of European painting still made themselves felt. The rich, splendid, complex forms of Baroque and Rococo painting spread outward from their centers, like ripples on a pool, growing fainter as they crossed the broad Atlantic, changing as they broke upon a distant shore, yet still discernible and recognizable, until they vanished into the silence of the forest.

On the other hand, in the vast, centuries-long migration of people and ideas to the New World, talent sometimes outdistanced both the forms and the skills of painting. Notable qualities of art sometimes appear in painters born in frontier cabins, and equipped with most crude or homespun skills, like Winthrop Chandler, or the anonymous New England or Hudson River painters. Or, side by side with those naïfs, one finds another artist, such as West, or Allston, who is a stylist in the extreme forefront of the movement of his times. Skill and perception, imagination and style thus appear in unexpected relations.

To tell this story properly, we must follow (1) the first migration of drawing and painting to the New World, among the explorer artists; (2) the gradual transplanting of the skills, the *craft*, of painting from their old home to the New World, and the growth of its supporting institutions; (3) the changes in the direction of attention, or imaginative interest, that prevail from generation to generation; (4) the evolution of the language of painting, which grows and changes like any other language under the drive of new minds and new ideas; (5) the interaction of American developments with those in other parts of the world; (6) the perceptions, talents, works, and fortunes of many gifted individuals. Most of these will fall into their place as our story develops; but there is one point I feel a need to discuss further here.

Painting on this continent is not like the European schools of art which grew up slowly, almost unconsciously, out of an ancient tradition of craftsmanship, stretching back so far that its origins have been forgotten. Painting sprang up here, in the wilderness, wherever men of Western origin settled, where there was nothing to foster it —nothing but the inner urge, a need of the imagination, a thirst in the soul, that demanded satisfaction and created the art, by sheer force of will, while the forest trees still grew around them.

The *art* of painting came to America in the mental inheritance of the race. But the *craft* of painting is a social product and had to wait upon the slow growth of the tiny European settlements into, first, self-sustaining, then growing and creative organisms. Although painters began coming to America with the first explorers, the earliest professionally trained European artist to settle here permanently was Hendrick Couturier, a Leiden-trained painter who emigrated to the Dutch West India colonies about 1661. A century later, Benjamin West, the first American-born painter to win an international reputation and play a part in the artistic life of Europe, sailed for Italy. In a period of a hundred years, the art was native-born. By the eighteen-thirties, to the eyes of a surprised English visitor, Mrs. Anna Jameson, "the country seemed to swarm with painters." Yet the first academies and exhibitions were established only in the early nineteenth century; the first serious art schools came only in the eighteen-seventies; and for representative collections of great paintings to study, the American artist had to wait until the twentieth century. Both the training of artists and opportunities for self-training were haphazard until late in our history.

The slow development of the technical skills and professional organizations of painting meant that, until relatively recent times, American painters looked to Europe for the great collections of art to study, the leading schools and teachers of art, and the most accom-

plished living practitioners of their craft. As a result American artists
have always been intensely curious (sometimes too curious) to know
what was going on abroad. Style in painting can be studied, but it
cannot be borrowed; for a style is the organic expression of what the
artist has to say.

Because of the special historical conditions under which American art developed, the problem of uniting style with content has
been solved in several different ways. American artists have tended
to fall into two types: Gifted cosmopolitan minds like West, Allston, Whistler, Sargent, Marin, Marsden Hartley, Franklin Watkins,
whose art is nourished by and belongs to the international currents
of art of their day; and solitary individualists like Winslow Homer,
Thomas Eakins, Albert Ryder, Charles Burchfield, Edward Hopper,
Ivan Le Lorraine Albright, who are so concerned with finding a personal interpretation of life that they do not fit easily into the current
of contemporary painting.

There is also a third type peculiar to America and to our historical
conditions of the frontier. In the process of settling the continent,
as family after family left the old, settled districts near the seacoast
to try its fortunes in the wilderness to westward, the population
spread itself very thinly through an immense territory. Gifted individuals with the natural endowments of the artist were born in
lonely frontier settlements, perhaps as often as in the old and settled
regions, but under such conditions that they grew up far from the
established profession of art. Good painters like Charles Willson
Peale, Chester Harding, or Francis Alexander, for example, grew to
manhood before they heard of the existence of the art of painting.
These three, once discovering their vocation, sought teachers and
made themselves trained artists. But frontier conditions prevailed
over a very large part of this country for a very long period; and
not all natural artists were able to find the best training or an opportunity to work in a large city.

Out of these conditions came a kind of artist peculiar to American
painting, whom I call the *untrained professional* artist. There were
many such artists and, untrained though they were, they were often
men of great innate sensibility. The so-called Patroon painters of
the early eighteenth century among the Hudson River Dutch; the
vigorous and interesting back country painters of New England,
especially numerous and prominent in the second half of the eight-

eenth century; some of the anonymous artists of the nineteenth century, all show fine powers of observation, sense of character, and
instinctive sense of style. What is commonly called "folk art" and
which forms the bulk of such collections as Mrs. John D. Rockefeller's at Williamsburg or the Garbisch collection in The National
Gallery, Washington, is more truly amateur art, which also has its
own place and value. Yet exactly what its value is, whether esthetic,
or moral, or social, is more difficult to say. The modern mind tends to
confuse *creation* with *self-expression*: actually they are quite different things. The value of amateur art is a facet of this question.

European historians have tended, owing to an understandable but
almost total ignorance of America, to limit their sympathies to the
American artists closest to European life, especially to such painters
as West, Whistler, and Cassatt, who lived in Europe and played an
active part in European art. Perhaps in reaction, recent American
writers have often seemed to resent any connection with Europe and
have emphasized the opposite end of the scale: the untaught, the
naïf, the artists who never studied or journeyed abroad. This produces what I call the *frontier fallacy*,[1] which tries to identify a "truly
American" note in our art by identifying it with the sturdy, self-
taught independence of the frontiersman.[2] This note exists, and lends
its flavor to our history. Yet the imaginative life of a whole nation is
a vast chorus of a thousand voices, not to be reduced to a single note.

The untrained professionals are only one of a number of types
jumbled together in the omnibus enthusiasm for "primitive" painting or "folk art," which has been so prominent in modern taste.
Various names have been applied to this conglomeration: folk art,
amateur painting, lay painting, primitive painting, Sunday painting. We need, I venture to say, a more exact appreciation of what we
enjoy in these works, and why.

True folk art, in the first place, is an unself-conscious, highly developed, traditional craft. Its makers are not amateurs. They are

[1] Cf. my *Washington Allston, A Study of the Romantic Artist in America,*
Chicago, University of Chicago Press, 1948, p. 13.

[2] Cf. Alan Burroughs, *Limners and Likenesses,* Cambridge, Mass., Harvard
University Press, 1936; Oskar Hagen, *The Birth of the American Tradition in
Art,* New York, Charles Scribner's Sons, 1940; Gordon Washburn, *Old and New
England,* Providence, Museum of Art of the Rhode Island School of Design,
1945.

extremely skilled craftsmen. The element of continuity is important: folk art's products follow an ancient and traditional sense of design. They are also *made for use*. Folk art is a skilled handicraft product intended for the enjoyment of simple people, rather than for the esthetic delectation of the connoisseur. There are such true folk arts in America—Pennsylvania German handicrafts, the *Santos* of New Mexico, cowboy saddlery, the decoration of Mississippi steamboats, the carving of ships' figureheads and sternboards are folk arts. The simplicity and cheerful pageantry of such unself-conscious traditional arts are refreshing in the hyperself-conscious atmosphere of our world, and exert a very strong appeal. Folk art has its own esthetic and human values, but they are not the same values as those of conscious art. In American painting true folk art is found only rarely.

Many passages in the story of painting in America are at the present time very imperfectly explored and documented, many of its biographies unwritten. It is evident that to write such a story in even a cursory way is a vast undertaking and involves the possibility of errors great and small. Anyone in his senses would, no doubt, avoid it. Yet what an interesting problem!

Two

ARTIST-EXPLORERS

AND ARTIST-NATURALISTS

ON SUNDAY, OCTOBER 21, Columbus wrote in the Journal of the First Voyage:

I . . . went forth with my captains and crews to see the island [Columbus called it Isabella; it has been identified as either Fortune or Great Magna Island] and if the others we have seen were beautiful and green and fertile, this one is much more so; with large groves and deep foliage. Here are large lakes, and the groves about them are marvelous; and here and in all the island, everything is green as in April in Andalusia. The singing of the little birds is such, that it seems that one would never desire to depart hence. There are flocks of parrots that obscure the sun, and other birds, large and small, of so many kinds, different from ours, that it is wonderful; there are trees of a thousand species, each having its particular fruit and all of marvelous flavor, so that I am in the greatest trouble in the world not to know them, for I am very certain that they are all of great value. I shall take home some of them as specimens, and also of the herbs.[1]

This is the first record of an experience which Columbus, and many other men in the two or three centuries following, were to feel. Columbus' discovery of nameless islands in the sea, inhabited by brown naked men and filled with unknown trees and flowers, beasts and birds, had to be described to the world at home. But neither in words nor in painting did a style of art exist capable of dealing with this experience. Columbus' excitement and the poetry of discovery

[1] *The Voyages of Christopher Columbus*, New York, 1892, p. 48.

sometimes make themselves felt in the *Letter on the Discovery of America*, but his descriptions end in vague generalizations: the trees are green; the birds are countless; the products of the islands are very good.

We meet here not with a deficiency in Columbus, who was a man of great ability and intelligence, but with the intense concentration of attention then governing European culture. Spain, Portugal, France, the Netherlands, England, the countries looking out upon the Atlantic, which were to carry out the exploration and settlement of America, in 1492 were still medieval countries. Painting and drawing were highly developed in them. But the task of painting had been, up to that date in medieval art, to depict the ideal world of religious faith, the story of Christianity, the lives of the saints. The arts in the medieval world spoke of these ideal subjects in noble, generalized, ideal images. The need for precise and convincing description of this present world had not yet arisen.

During the next two centuries, the sixteenth and the seventeenth, a series of great minds opened a new window upon the infinite reaches of the natural world. This was the age of the rise of natural science. Galileo, Huygens, Newton, and a host of others discovered that profound significance was to be found not only in the books of authority, but in the exact study of the simple things around them —the falling of a stone, the swinging of a hanging lamp, the beams of the sun's light.

In the arts the world of nature was also discovered. The rise of realism (that is, the objective view of nature) is the parallel, in the realm of imagination and feeling, to the rise of science in the realm of the intellect. There is a tradition that the painter Caravaggio, one of the great pioneers of the new approach to nature at the beginning of the seventeenth century, was criticized by the *cognoscenti* of Rome for not studying Raphael and the antique marbles: that is, for not following precedent and authority. Without saying a word, he drew his critic to the door and pointed to the people passing by in the street: then to prove his point, he took a gypsy from the street and painted her in the act of telling the fortune of a young man. It is hard now to realize what is meant to break away from the noble, ideal subjects of medieval and Renaissance art to paint the passing moment of life. The change in the direction of attention, which Caravaggio symbolizes, was like his contemporary Galileo's break from traditional authorities to direct observation of nature. Caravaggio might have accomplished his silent gesture with the words of Cicero's *Dum tacit, clamat,* that Emerson used to express the significance of each moment of life. Though silent, it cries aloud.

The artists who first practiced a descriptive art in America were only on the fringes of this movement. Their part in it is small; they were modest artisans or amateurs. Yet their reports of an age of geographical discovery must have had a part in the rise of the scientific mind and the new realism of Western art during the sixteenth and seventeenth centuries. Men's thoughts were suddenly confronted with a dramatically expanding world, filled with marvels.

The starting point of our story, in more senses than one, is the woodcut title page of a narrative poem written by Giuliano Dati (1493) celebrating the voyage of Columbus (Fig. 2-1). It is the

2-1.   *Columbus' Discovery of America* (wood engraving). (From Giuliano Dati, *The Narrative of Columbus.* Florence, 1493. Courtesy of The British Museum.)

earliest representation of the discovery of America; it is conceived and executed in the medieval narrative style, representing a series of ideas in two-dimensional decorative form rather than an observation of nature. The earliest representation of an American city, the Aztec capital (Fig. 2-2), seen in a woodcut in Cortes' *Praeclara . . . de Nova Maris Oceani Hyspania Narratio* (Nuremberg, 1524) is likewise a decorative ideograph.

The work of the earliest professional painter in the New World illustrates the same all-governing direction of attention. Rodrigo de Cifuentes, a painter from Cordova in Spain, accompanied Cortes on his expedition into Honduras in 1525. The paintings attributed to

2-2.   *Mexico City* (wood engraving). (From Cortes' *Praeclara . . . de Nova Maris Oceani Hyspania Narratio.* Nuremberg, 1524. Courtesy of the William L. Clements Library, University of Michigan.)

him in the Academy of San Carlos, Mexico City, are, however, religious subjects, and a portrait of Cortes and Doña Mariana. He was the first of the religious painters of Spanish America, not an observer of Cortes' conquests.

In New France we may see the same phenomenon. The Jesuit missionaries in Huronia in 1638-1640, thirty days' journey inland by canoe from the last French settlement, had in their bark chapel, built like a long house in the shores of Lake Huron, life-size paintings of Christ and the Virgin, and one of the Last Judgment, to help them convert the Hurons.[2] The life-size figures made an especial impression on the Indians, Father le Mercier tells us in his *Relation*, but they did not seem to care for paintings with small figures. When later the great Bishop Laval wished to make the Canadian church self-sustaining, he founded not only a seminary but an art school to teach the essential skills for making and decorating churches. His academy at Cap Tourment on the north shore of the St. Lawrence River below Quebec (the first art school on the North American continent) and the Séminaire at Quebec itself were schools of *arts et métiers*. Laval brought a sculptor named Jacques Leblond dit Latour from Bordeaux and the school in which he was the leading master taught crafts like joinery, lock-making, painting, woodcarving, and tailoring. Advanced students in letters and theology learned crafts also according to their talents. "They quickly respond, and they cleverly fashion many small articles not only for current use, but also for the altars which they decorate with taste and discrimination," wrote an observer.[3] The arts of painting, sculpture, and wood carving were first established in the New World to serve the need for an ideal, didactic Christian art.

Yet it was not long before other artists appeared in the New World for the purpose of observing and reporting. Of these some were trained, some were amateurs. The leader of an expedition who had to report on the strange lands he had explored, the Indians, animals, and plants he had seen; the governor who wished to describe the

[2] Le Mercier, *Relation des Hurons,* 1637, pp. 175, 176; and 1638, p. 33, in *Relations des Jésuites,* vol. I, 1858. Quoted by Francis Parkman, *The Jesuits in North America,* 1867, p. 201.

[3] Marius Barbeau, "The Arts of French Canada," *The Art Quarterly,* IX (1946), p. 329.

2-3. *Toucan* (wood engraving). (From André Thevet, *Les Singularitez de la France antarctique.* Lyons, 1558. Courtesy of the William L. Clements Library, University of Michigan.)

forts he had built, the harbors he had charted, the battles he had fought—each needed the services of an artist. If the expedition had taken along a trained artist, so much the better; but if no artist was available, the explorer or governor used what skills were available, even his own. In the mid-sixteenth century appeared the first artist-explorers and artist-naturalists, practicing the art of painting in America long before the appearance of the seventeenth-century colonial portrait painters. Today, when the old practical uses for the craft of painting have almost disappeared, we forget how useful it once was for many purposes. For the first three hundred years in America it was a skill which flourished far from the studio, on the decks of ships, in the deep forest, or under the sky. If the explorer-artists were never men of genius, and sometimes not even very good craftsmen, they are nevertheless a picturesque and interesting part of our story.

In 1555 a cheerful French Franciscan monk, named André Thevet, sailed on a French expedition led by Villegaignon to South America. Thevet was a man probably of modest birth and little education, but he had a passionate appetite for knowledge and a thirst for travel. The account of his American voyage, *Les Singularitez de la France antarctique* (Lyons, 1558), contains a number of illustrations of birds, plants and animals done with a shrewd realism that strongly suggests drawings from life. Was the *Toucan* (Fig. 2-3) with his wicked old eye, the first known representation of the bird, engraved from a dead specimen, or does it reproduce a drawing made from life in America? We do not know. However, if Thevet made this and other drawings of the same kind reproduced in his book, he was the first artist-naturalist to work in America.

There is no question about Jacques le Moyne de Morgues (d. 1588) who came to America in 1564 as a member of the Huguenot settlement planted by Coligny at the mouth of the St. Johns River, Florida. Only one original work with American subject matter from Le Moyne's hand is preserved, an exquisite, precise, fresh-colored water-color drawing on parchment, showing *The Indian Chief Saturiba and the French leader Laudonnière at Ribaut's column* (Fig. 2-4), a marker left by a previous French expedition of 1562.[4] Beautiful copper engravings from Le Moyne's drawings were made by Théodore de Bry and his sons to illustrate the artist's narrative, which formed the second volume (1591) of the famous series of voyages published by de Bry at Frankfort-on-the-Main. These engravings became one of the chief sources of information about what America looked like. For two centuries they were borrowed and imitated by other engravers to illustrate books on America.

Another artist-naturalist whose work supplied a basis for de Bry engravings was John White (active 1584-1593) who came to Raleigh's short-lived colony in Virginia in 1585 and returned as governor of the colony in 1587 and 1590. In the British Museum there is preserved an album of sixty-five water-color drawings made by White in Virginia. Many show the life and customs of the Indians; others are studies of flowers and birds, fish and animals of the new land. The album is entitled: *The Pictures of sundry things collected and counterfeited according to the truth in the voyage made by Sʳ· Walter Raleigh Knight for the discovery of LA VIRGINEA. in the 27th year of the most happie reigne of our Souveraigne Lady Queene ELIZABETH and in the year of Oʳ Lord God 1585.* These drawings were engraved by de Bry for the first volume of his *Voyages* (1590).

[4] The Peabody Museum of Archaeology and Ethnology, Harvard University, owns a crayon drawing of *Saturioua, a Timuca Chief*, doubtfully attributed to Le Moyne.

2-4. Jacques le Moyne de Morgues: *The Indian Chief Saturiba and the French leader Laudonnière at Ribaut's column.* (James Hazen Hyde Bequest, Prints Division, The New York Public Library.)

With John White we come to the opposite extreme of art from the Guiliano Dati woodcut. Instead of the general idea, we are given the particular fact detailed with loving interest; in the place of an attractive decorative composition, artistic form is forgotten in an eager curiosity to draw a strange butterfly or "A land Tort[oise] wch the Savages esteeme above all other Torts" (Fig. 2-5). The world of nature has been discovered, its wonder and delight opened to the eye, and the appetite awakened to "counterfeit it according to the truth." In Flanders a great artistic intelligence like Pieter Bruegel had already learned to weave such exact observations into a great interpretative whole. That was beyond John White. But in his own place he is an artist of significance.

A skillful draughtsman was the traveling Netherlander Laurens Bloch, who made the *View of New Amsterdam* in 1650, which is now in The New-York Historical Society (Fig. 2-6). Nothing is known of Bloch but the inscription on this drawing, stating that it was drawn on the ship *Lydia* by Laurens Bloch, son of Herman, in the year 1650. The skills of drawing and painting were so widely diffused in seventeenth-century Holland that it is probable Bloch was not a professional but simply a skilled amateur. This is the sort of drawing that must have been brought home to Holland in numbers and supplied Blaue with the information for the border vignettes of the maps in his great *World Atlas*.

As the North American settlements grew more numerous and important, in the later seventeenth century, the impulse to describe the appearance of the New World became stronger. Among the travelers, soldiers, and priests, French, English, or Dutch, who came out, were some men of inquiring and curious minds who wrote books on their travels. Many of the interesting early volumes on America have illustrations either borrowed from de Bry or simply invented by the engraver in his European workshop. But others have maps, topographic views, and scenes of Indian life of more substantial interest.

Two of the most popular and widely read of these narratives of exploration were the *Description de la Louisiane* (1683) and *A New Discovery of a Vast Country in America, Extending above Four Thousand Miles, between New France and New Mexico* (1698) by that engaging old liar, Father Louis Hennepin (1640-ca. 1701). Hennepin published the first description of Niagara Falls, whose height he

2-5. John White: *A land Tort[oise]* w^{ch} *the Savages esteeme above all other Torts.* (Courtesy of The British Museum.)

2-6.　Laurens Bloch: *View of New Amsterdam* (1650).

exaggerated greatly. The engraving of Niagara in his *New Discovery* is the first appearance of a landscape subject that was to interest artists for nearly two hundred years.

Some readers may wonder if such a fact is of any significance in a history of art. I believe it is significant. Historically, it is one of the steps in the rise of landscape painting. Second, it reveals to us the path by which men's perceptions gradually approached nature. The earliest interest in landscape to appear in America was a naïve interest in the appearance of some great natural wonder, or of a famous work of man like a town or harbor. Down through the eighteenth century this was to be the chief form of original landscape done in America. Nor is this to be dismissed too lightly as raw naturalism or as showing a lack of imaginative power. The topographic landscape or cityscape was the eighteenth century's great contribution to landscape painting, produced by artists of the importance of Canaletto, Guardi, Bellotto, Panini, Hubert Robert, and Vernet. The appearance of the topographic landscape in America belongs to a brilliant chapter in the history of the imagination.

The artist-explorer continued as a type as long as there was a

(Courtesy of The New-York Historical Society.)

frontier, down to the latter part of the nineteenth century. The later examples of the type will be touched on, however, as part of the story of their own times. We will close this chapter on the pioneers of realistic observation in America with Mark Catesby (1679?-1749), the first notable artist-naturalist to work in America. A man apparently of little education but of great natural gifts, he came from England to Virginia in 1712. Slowly the beauty and the wonder of the wilderness continent drew him toward his vocation. Let him tell his discovery of nature in his own old-fashioned and somewhat crabbed words:

My curiosity was such [he relates in his preface] that not being content with contemplating the Products of our own country, I soon imbibed a passionate Desire of viewing as well the Animal and Vegetable Productions in their native Countries; which were strangers to *England*. *Virginia* was the Place (I having Relations there) suited most to my Convenience to go to, where I arriv'd the 23d of *April* 1712. I thought then so little of prosecuting a Design of the Nature of this Work, that in the Seven Years I resided in that Country, (I am ashamed to own it) I chiefly gratified my inclination in observing and admiring the various Productions of those countries,—only sending from thence some dried Specimens of Plants and some of the most Specious of them in Tubs of Earth, at the request of some curious friends, amongst whom was Mr. *Dale* of *Braintree* in Essex, a skillful Apothecary and Botanist: to him, besides Specimens of Plants, I sent some few Observations on the Country, which he communicated to the late *William Sherard*, L.L.D. one of the most celebrated Botanists of this Age, who favoured me with his friendship on my Return to England in the year 1719; and by his advice, (tho' conscious of my own Inability) I first resolved on this undertaking, so agreeable to my inclination. . . .

With this intention, I set out from *England*, in the year 1722, directly for Carolina; which Country, tho' inhabited by *English* above an Age past, and a Country inferior to none in Fertility, and abounding in Variety of the Blessings of Nature; yet its Productions being very little known except what barely related to Commerce, such as Rice, Pitch and Tar; was thought of the most proper Place to search and describe the productions of.

Here, in the words of a man who took part, are outlined the steps in the discovery of the new meaning of nature. First, there is an intense curiosity and a "passionate Desire of viewing" without any clear purpose; then, by the encouragement of a small group of advanced minds, curiosity is crystallized into a purpose—a science or an art. Nature is not merely a source of a few things good for commerce. Its study is an end to which one can devote one's life, and is a source of values as yet vaguely realized but intensely loved.

Such is the origin of *The Natural History of Carolina, Florida and the Bahama Islands* . . . , London, 1731-42, written by Catesby after his return to England and illustrated by him with 100 plates engraved by the author, representing what he considered to be 102 species of American birds. With the birds he drew some of the plants associated with them, thus pointing toward the future ideas of the habitat or ecology.

Catesby's plates, of which the *Ivory-billed Woodpecker* (Fig. 2-7) is a good example, were crudely engraved but are nonetheless strong, decorative, and beautiful. In their rude images is expressed that "passionate Desire of viewing" which during the sixteenth and seventeenth centuries added a new power and a new dimension to the perceptions of the human race. The awakening of this power in the field of intellect made the seventeenth century a great flowering of genius from Galileo to Newton. In the field of the imagination and feeling, in the arts, the development of the sixteenth and seventeenth centuries was a kindred flowering of genius, exploring the world of nature and of light in one of the greatest ages of Western painting. The artist-explorers who brought their art to America were humble representatives on the fringes, but their artistic as well as their documentary value arises from their share in the growth of Western realism.

2-7.   Mark Catesby: *Largest White Billed Woodpecker (Ivory-billed Woodpecker)* (copper engraving, hand colored). From Mark Catesby, *The Natural History of Carolina, Florida and the Bahama Islands . . .* , London, 1731-42. (Courtesy of The Old Print Shop, New York.)

Three

SEVENTEENTH-CENTURY

DUTCH AND ENGLISH

PROVINCIAL PAINTING

THE MEN who settled the first permanent colonies on our Atlantic coast, in the early years of the seventeenth century, brought with them the arts and skills to which they had been accustomed in their homeland. In the hard conditions of pioneer life, all activities had to be purposeful, designed to serve pressing material or spiritual needs. The Dutch and English settlers, sturdy Calvinists all, felt no need for the religious paintings which were the first desire of the French and Spanish missionaries. But family feeling and personal pride were prominent among these strong-willed people; and among the skills which were a normal feature of seventeenth-century middle class life in both Holland and England was that of portrait painting. It accompanied the earliest settlers to America. More than four hundred likenesses have survived of people born in New England and New Netherlands before 1700. The greater part of these were probably painted in America; yet it is characteristic of painting in the seventeenth-century American colonies that the link between the homelands and colonies is still so close that it is impossible to draw a clear line between works painted in the colonies of the Atlantic seaboard and provincial works painted in Europe.

Virginia was also settled early, and life at Jamestown (as revealed by the excavations of the National Park Service) attained a degree of comfort and even elegance rather at variance with our notions of the frontier. Yet the portraits which have come down to us of men connected with the colony seem all to have been done in England, until the last decade of the century. According to Dr. J. Hall Pleasants, "there are in existence a number of unsigned portraits, certainly painted in Virginia as early as the sixteen-nineties and the first decade of the following century" although no painter's name can be assigned to them.[1] By this date, however, they belong in style to the English provincial Baroque, which is described in the next chapter.

In the seventeenth century the cultural center of the Protestant world was The Netherlands which, in the sixty years after the truce of 1614, were at the height of their maritime empire and their intellectual powers. At the end of the century, though losing their supremacy at sea to the English, the Dutch gave a king to England itself. The busy cities of Holland nourished one of the greatest schools of European painting; in contrast, painting in England had no strong tradition, but was carried on chiefly by artists from The Netherlands. It is not surprising that the best painting done in America in the seventeenth century was done in New Netherlands; and that the English colonies, like England itself, were within the ambience of Dutch provincial painting.

At home, in Holland, Dutch artists were giving to the new impulse of realism its first and one of its greatest and most poetic expressions. A new mentality was in flower, a new poetry of nature and life was being explored with immense vigor and imaginative power. Human character, landscape, the charm of daily life, the beauty of cities, of homes and the objects they contain, were studied by artists with love and enthusiasm, sometimes with genius. But in the far corner of the Dutch empire on the Hudson River only a faint echo of Dutch pictorial genius made itself heard.

Several portraits painted in New Amsterdam in the 1660's have been preserved. They represent no special imaginative power applied to the analysis of human character. They have no esthetic flavor beyond the simple, solid craftsmanship of Dutch realism applied to the painting of the human head. The bust portrait, in

---

[1] J. Hall Pleasants, *The Virginia Magazine*, 60 (January, 1952), p. 56.

3-1. *Governor Pieter Stuyvesant* (ca. 1660-1670).
(Courtesy of The New-York Historical Society.)

armor, of *Governor Pieter Stuyvesant* (Fig. 3-1) in The New-York Historical Society shows the virtues of this craftsmanship. It is good direct, solid painting, using a severe color harmony of black, white, and brown to block out the head in broad lights and firm, simple shadows. The sense of character is vigorous and direct and the plastic, atmospheric language of Dutch realism is used in a modest, sober, but competent spirit. Whoever painted this picture observed keenly and knew his business.

We know from documents the names of several of the painters

of New Amsterdam. Hendrick Couturier, who obtained burgher rights in New Amsterdam in 1663 by painting a portrait of Governor Stuyvesant and making drawings of his sons, was, so far as is known today, the first professional European painter to practice in this country. He is recorded as a member of the Leiden guild of painters in 1648; in 1649 he moved to Amsterdam; by 1661, or possibly earlier, he had emigrated to the Dutch settlement of New Amstel on the Delaware River, where he was a trader and public official. He also spent much time in New Amsterdam. In 1674 he removed to England, where he died about ten years later. Several portraits of New Amsterdam at this period have been attributed to him, including the *Peter Stuyvesant* and *Nicholas William Stuyvesant.* (New-York Historical Society) and the *Jacobus G. Strycker* (The Metropolitan Museum of Art); but in the opinion of experts there is no picture that can definitely be assigned to his hand.[2]

Esther Singleton published lists of paintings from documents of this period in *Dutch New York* (1909), which show that the houses of New Amsterdam contained landscapes and other types of painting then found in Dutch houses at home. Except for a few portraits, preserved by family sentiment, nothing has come down to us: at least, nothing that can be recognized. The topographic *View of New Amsterdam* (Fig. 2-6) by Laurens Bloch (1650) is one of only three surviving views of the colony.

Dutch painters of skill and fame found their way to Dutch colonies in Brazil or the Indies. But New Amsterdam was very small, and very poor, compared with the East Indies; and the human race is careless, destructive, and governed by fashion in what it keeps or throws away. Very little has come down to us. Yet the important thing is that the craft of painting was established in the New Netherlands province, and by the early years of the next century there were already native-born painters at work along the Hudson River.

Family feeling and personal pride were as common among the strong-willed New England stock as among their Dutch neighbors. The family portraits they brought with them show the same quali-

---

[2] George C. Groce and David H. Wallace, *The New-York Historical Society's Dictionary of Artists in America, 1564-1860,* New Haven, Yale University Press, 1957.

ties and style as the Dutch provincial portraits. This is hardly surprising, for the portrait style which was brought to New England was a Dutch style transplanted to England. At King Charles's court, after 1624, it is true, taste was dominated by the more courtly and elegant art of the Flemish artists, Rubens and Van Dyck. But among the middle classes, from whom the American emigration came, the virtues of Dutch portraiture—sobriety, directness, and forceful statement of character—were more congenial than Van Dyck's elegant artifice.

Of the New England painters in this taste who worked in America, only one can definitely be identified by name. This is Captain Thomas Smith, a mariner, who came to New England from Bermuda about 1650. Sailor though he was by profession, he was also a painter, for Harvard College paid him in 1680 for a portrait of the *Reverend William Ames*. On this basis rests the assumption that a portrait of *Captain Thomas Smith* is a self-portrait (Fig. 3-2). Indeed it has all the characteristics of a mirror portrait. Smith, if he was the artist, painted in a broad, coarse, vigorous style, cruder than the Dutch idiom he was following, but showing energy and sense of character.

A strong grasp upon the inner life, which is the virtue of all the portraits we have been discussing, was the best characteristic of the Puritan world. One hears its spirit in the verses inscribed on the paper beneath the death's head under Captain Smith's hand:

> Why why should I the world be minding
> therein a World of Evils finding.
> > Then farwell World: Farwell thy Jarres
> > thy Joeis thy Toies thy Wiles thy Warres
> Truth sounds Retreat: I am not Sorye.
> > the Eternall Drawes to him my heart
> > By Faith (which can thy Force subvert)
> To crown me (after Grace) with Glory.
> > > > T. S.

The portrait was the only mode of painting congenial to the seventeenth-century New England painter. His Puritan mode of thought focused his attention upon character rather than beauty. Landscape and genre—which express the interest of nature and human life about us—belong to the transient world of the senses. On the other hand to embody the world of faith and the images of eternity in imagery was distrusted as "papistical."

In these Dutch and English provinces far from the centers of Western culture there was a strong tendency for the language of painting to revert to two-dimensional patterns. Plasticity and atmospheric color—the qualities of the full coloristic tradition of Western painting—were the creation of supremely gifted artists; when

3-2. Captain Thomas Smith: *Self Portrait.*
(Courtesy of the Worcester Art Museum.)

3-3. Freake limner: *Madam Freake and Baby Mary* (ca. 1674).
(Privately owned. Photograph courtesy of the Worcester Art Museum.)

the discipline of a good school of painting is absent, or for any
reason is not mastered, these are the first qualities to disappear.

Yet the absence of a highly developed style does not necessarily
mean the absence of imagination, or instinctive taste, or refined
perceptions. There is a group of paintings, done in New England
about 1670-75 (of which the portraits of *John Freake* and *Madam*

Freake and Baby Mary (Fig. 3-3) are the leading examples) that show how sensitive the work of an "untrained professional" can be. An instinctive sense of elegance, sweetness of sentiment, graceful elaboration of linear pattern, fastidious delicacy in the harmonies of the flat color areas are the virtues of this artist—and these are no small virtues. Painting like this was found in the provincial areas of England itself deep into the seventeenth century (but not perhaps so late as in New England) as a lingering echo of the style of the Tudor period.

But painting in seventeenth-century New England seldom attained this level. Ordinarily it was closer to the ruder amateur level of John Foster, who made a crude woodcut portrait of *Richard Mather*, thus becoming the earliest wood engraver in the United States, and who also probably painted a number of portraits of New England divines, interesting historically but almost totally devoid of any qualities either of craftsmanship or art.

Four

THE BAROQUE IN AMERICA

ABOUT A CENTURY after the first settlements, that is, during the first decades of the eighteenth century, the American colonies began to thrive with a vigorous life of their own. The frontier had been pushed back thirty, forty, even a hundred miles from tidewater. In the settled districts there had grown up the population of yeoman farmers and seamen, led by small groups of merchants, craftsmen, and professional men who were to create the American nation. A new architecture appeared, on Palladian models (the most serene and classical phase of Baroque architecture), adapting the English architecture of Wren and Hawksmoor to simpler American materials and needs. Skilled cabinetmakers and silversmiths replaced the old homemade setting of life with elegant and graceful furnishings, in a colonial version of English contemporary decorative arts.

And, though still remote, the colonies had begun to attract trained artists from abroad. In 1705, an English woman pastellist, Henrietta Johnston, settled in Charleston, South Carolina. In 1708, Justus Engelhardt Kühn, a German painter, was settled in Annapolis, Maryland. In 1711, Gustavus Hesselius, of a distinguished family of Swedish intellectuals, came out with his brother, who was to be the minister of the Swedish colony at Christina (Wilmington) on the Delaware. Hesselius settled at Philadelphia and became the portrait painter of the colonial metropolis and the Chesapeake Bay region. In 1714, a Scot, John Watson, was established at Perth Amboy, then the seat of the proprietors of New Jersey. In 1726, Peter Pelham, an English mezzotint engraver, settled in Boston. In

1729, a traveled and cultured Scot, John Smibert, came to New England in the entourage of Bishop Berkeley. In 1735, Charles Bridges, an old man who "either by the frowns of fortune or his own mismanagement" was "obliged to seek his bread . . . in a strange land" was painting the children of William Byrd of Westover, and remained a few years in Virginia, painting portraits, before going home to die in London. In 1739 a Swiss painter named Jeremiah Theüs settled in Charleston, South Carolina. In 1750, an eclectic German painter and Moravian missionary, John Valentin Haidt, was sent by his Brotherhood to the Moravian mission founded by Count Zinzendorf at Bethlehem, Pennsylvania. These men brought to America a fresh impulse from various European schools of painting.

In the Dutch settlements along the Hudson, however, there were native painters at work; and in New England and the Middle Colonies, in the first decades of the century, a generation of native-born painters appeared, of whom some were to become famous: at Boston, Nathaniel Emmons (1704), Joseph Badger (1708), John Greenwood (1728), John Singleton Copley (1738); on Long Island, Robert Feke (about 1707); in Philadelphia, James Claypoole (1720) and Benjamin West (1738).

The intellectual climate of this century was very different from that of the seventeenth century. King Louis XIV of France, the Sun King, had risen and set; but the grandiose, aristocratic ideal of life at his court had cast its spell over Europe. England and Holland, the keystones of the grand alliance that had pulled Louis down, were themselves captivated by his splendor. Their eighteenth-century culture was now oriented toward the Latin South, rather than the Protestant North. The age of English aristocratic education by a Grand Tour to Italy and of English collections of Italian art had dawned. Alexander Pope, rather than Milton, was the leader of English poetry. The odes of Horace, rather than the Bible and the seventeenth-century theologians, were the favorite reading of the educated. And in the popular *Spectator* papers Addison created, in the character of Sir Roger de Coverley, a new ideal of the country gentleman and of country life.

This ideal world of aristocratic dignity and polite classical learning, seen in terms of the grandeur and elegance of Baroque classicism, became the ideal world of the early eighteenth century in

America. Nor do I imply, by calling it aristocratic, that it was alien, or had no place in America. On the contrary, its political absolutism left behind, it came as a cultural aspiration of great value to the colonies. In place of the Calvinistic belief that this world was evil and man's nature vicious, in place of the menace of hunger and the Indian, it brought an imaginative vision of the dignity and sweetness of life. Houses like Westover and Mount Vernon, for example, are "aristocratic" in the sense that they surrounded life with an atmosphere of spacious dignity, ease, and grace that increases one's respect for man as man. They did not unfit their eighteenth-century owners for hard work and energetic thinking, nor idealism, nor for meeting risk and hardship.

The Baroque style in painting, which originated in Rome about 1600, had given Europe one of its most glorious centuries of painting. For the first time both the inner and outer worlds of consciousness were explored by a profusion of artists of genius. The observation of Nature and the world of ideas, realism, and the capacities of decorative style were carried to heights of splendor and power: Caravaggio and Poussin, Velásquez and Rubens, Salvator Rosa, Van Dyck and Rembrandt—the parade of names goes on and on. By the close of the century, however, the fires of imagination had sunk; and Baroque painting had become a rather eclectic, international idiom, practiced by artists of the second rank. It was this late Baroque style, of little imaginative glow, but still of large and handsome decorative qualities, that was brought to America by the artist-migrants in the early years of the eighteenth century.

It took root first in the middle colonies of Pennsylvania and Maryland, brought there by painters from the Continent rather than from England. Justus Engelhardt Kühn, a German artist who had applied for naturalization at Annapolis in 1708, died there in 1717. A creditor's inventory of his estate, says Dr. J. Hall Pleasants, the authority on his career, "indicates that he was a lover of good books, music and clothes, that he was wont to live beyond his means, and that he augmented his income by painting coats-of-arms."[1] He has left us some naïvely charming portraits with elaborately Baroque scenic backgrounds but technically Kühn was little better than an amateur; he had no followers.

[1] Dr. J. Hall Pleasants, *Two Hundred and Fifty Years of Painting in Maryland*, Baltimore, The Baltimore Museum of Art, 1945, p. 14.

The real founder of painting in the middle colonies was Gustavus Hesselius (1682-1755), a cousin of Emanuel Swedenborg, who settled in Philadelphia in 1711. He was active there and in Annapolis until his death in 1755. In his later years Hesselius was succeeded by his son, John, who lived until 1778. The two Hesseliuses were thus the principal painters in the area of Philadelphia, the colonial metropolis, for half a century.

Philadelphia was the center, in America, of the eighteenth-century spirit of rationalistic science and classical culture that undermined Calvinism. While the Mather family of theologians were the leaders and representatives of New England's intellectual life, the symbol of Philadelphia is James Logan, the deputy of William Penn. Logan was an urbane scholar, owned a rich classical library; and possessed an interest in natural science that led him to publish, in Latin, essays on reproduction in plants and on the aberration of light, as well as on ancient literature.[2]

Philadelphia also attracted from Boston the young Benjamin Franklin, in whom American rationalism flowered into a new philosophy of natural science and democratic common sense. Franklin was the first American writer of international fame, who wrote in the lucid eighteenth-century style created by Addison. His robust rationalism, his intense interest in this world, his lively sense of pleasure were the antithesis of the somber supernaturalism of the seventeenth century. He was the guiding spirit of the American Philosophical Society, formed in the forties, which for the first time made the world aware of an intellectual life in America. Another of Franklin's foundations was the first American magazine, whose success proved that there was need for a new kind of secular reading, in addition to religious books.

The existence in Philadelphia, also, of two of the finest American Palladian churches, Christ Church and St. Peter's, indicates the strength of the Anglican Church in the middle colonies. The English church had no doctrinal distrust of religious painting or of humanistic culture, and commissions for religious pictures were not unknown.

In this atmosphere appeared a modest colonial Baroque art of narrative painting on the Christian and classical themes characteristic

[2] His botanical knowledge was such that his friend Linnaeus named after him a natural order of herbs and shrubs, the Loganiaceae.

4-1. Gustavus Hesselius: *Bacchus and Ariadne* (ca. 1720-1730).
(Courtesy of the Detroit Institute of Arts.)

of the European Baroque. Gustavus Hesselius was trained in Europe, whether in his native Sweden or elsewhere we do not know. Hesselius brought the late Baroque portrait formula to America and painted portraits in Philadelphia and Maryland. But his great interest for us is that we find him painting, probably in the 1720's, elaborate Baroque figure subjects such as *Bacchus and Ariadne* (Fig. 4-1) and a *Bacchanale*, and, in 1721, a *Last Supper*. The two classical pictures, which have survived, are the earliest known paintings by an artist in America of the ideal world of ancient poetry. As such, one looks at them with interest and respect, however modest their attainments.

Hesselius is the pioneer of religious painting and classical mythology in American painting. He was not a strong draughtsman nor was he an expressive figure painter. His gifts were decorative. His color is luminous and simple, his drawing large. His ideal paintings and his portraits have the virtue of dignified and rather pleasing decorations for a Palladian interior. Beyond that he could not go.

In his later years he developed interests significant for other aspects of colonial life. In 1735 he painted for the Proprietor, Mr. John Penn, portraits of the two chiefs of the Delaware or Lenni-Lenape Indians, *Tishcohan* and *Lapowinsa*, who had participated in the so-called Walking Purchase, a notorious and unjust purchase of the Indians' lands. Hesselius made no attempt to give these likenesses the elegance of Baroque portraits, but painted the Indians with a careful realism, as simple men of the Stone Age. These are the first successful and convincing Indian portraits by an American painter. Their sober, documentary character I should call the first artistic indication of the scientific realism rising in the intellectual life of Pennsylvania.

Hesselius, we may say, founded in Philadelphia a tradition of interest in ideal narrative subjects, of scientific realism, and of mechanical ingenuity, which we shall see appear again in Philadelphia painters of greater powers, in Benjamin West and the remarkable Peale family.

The channel through which the late Baroque reached New England and Virginia was the artistic life of London, which, at the opening of the eighteenth century, was dominated by Sir Godfrey Kneller and his school. Kneller was a typical figure of the international late Baroque. He was not a very personal artist; but he painted portraits admirably suited to serve as decorations in the great rooms of English country houses.

Some Americans of the official class, like William and Jeremiah Dummer, Jr., of Boston, had their portraits painted by Kneller in London. At least two representatives of Kneller's school came to America, Smibert to Boston and Bridges to Virginia.

John Smibert (1688-1751) was the more influential. He had come originally from Edinburgh, where he was trained as an artisan; but aspiring to paint, he found his way to London and eventually to Florence. In Italy he met Bishop Berkeley, who persuaded him later to join the faculty of a projected university at Bermuda. On their way to Bermuda in 1729 they put in at Newport, Rhode Island, where Berkeley decided to wait for a parliamentary grant for his university that never came. Smibert meanwhile moved from Newport to Boston. He built a painting room and gallery at the top of the little town, just below Beacon Hill, and supplemented his portrait painting by keeping a shop to sell English engravings, frames, painters' colors, and other goods of an artistic character.

Smibert was a solid, competent, though somewhat monotonous practitioner of the decorative Baroque style. His life-sized group portrait of *Bishop George Berkeley and his Family* (1729), painted at Newport (Fig. 4-2) is a vigorous monumental painting, handsome and luminous in color, imposing in tone, and an admirable expression of the Baroque ideal of personal dignity and elegance.

He also brought with him a small collection of art, including copies made in Florence of Raphael's *Madonna dell' Impannata*, Van Dyck's portrait of *Cardinal Bentivoglio*, Poussin's *Continence of Scipio*, and other pictures whose identity is now lost; also some casts of ancient sculpture, among them the *Head of Homer*, the *Venus de Medici*, and perhaps the *Laocoön*. This gallery, though modest, was in fact a summary of eighteenth-century taste. By good fortune it remained intact for more than a generation after his death, and served as a school of art for New England.

Like Hesselius, Smibert showed a tendency to develop in America, away from the aristocratic ideal of elegance, toward a plainer, blunter realism. This tendency toward frank realism has been attributed with some plausibility to the democratic atmosphere of American life. A blunt realism has therefore been singled out, with a great deal less plausibility, as the characteristic note of American imaginative life. It is one characteristic, certainly. The New England portrait of character is in strong contrast to the more decorative and idealized style of portraiture that flourished in London. That realism called the sole characteristic of our imaginative life, however, is contradicted both by the record of American painting and by the facts of human nature, which are an inextricable mixture of realism and dream, in America as elsewhere.

In the Southern colonies, where plantation life had reached a degree of wealth that was expressed in a handsome Palladian architecture, the late Baroque conception of a portrait as an elegant architectural decoration seemed to find congenial soil, for it struck root in this period and remained the dominant conception of painting until the end of the era of plantation aristocracy, at the Civil War.

Henrietta Johnston (earliest dated work, 1705; d. 1728-1729), the first woman painter in America, practiced the eighteenth-century art of portraiture in pastel in Charleston, South Carolina. Her works are all of small cabinet size, done in a simple, knowledgeable palette of three or four colors, and of a fresh, sweet, delicate character that is most enjoyable in her portraits of young girls; but her men are too girlish to be believable.

4-2.   John Smibert: *Bishop George Berkeley and His Family* (1729). (Courtesy of the Yale University Art Gallery.)

4-3. Charles Bridges: *Maria Taylor Byrd*.
(Courtesy of The Metropolitan Museum of Art.)

The next painter to arrive was Charles Bridges (active in Virginia 1735-after 1740). There are references to him in diaries and other records, but he remains a shadowy figure. Several portraits of the Byrd family have been attributed to him on the basis of a reference to him in a letter of William Byrd. If the *Maria Taylor Byrd* of Westover, Virginia (Fig. 4-3) represents Bridges' work in Virginia, he was a competent painter of the type of courtly and decorative portrait produced in England by Kneller and his school. Through Bridges or other intermediaries, a school of aristocratic portrait painting sprang up in America. There are many portraits from this period of Virginia life. Unfortunately we still know next to nothing about the artists who produced them.[3]

None of the migrants to America were artists of great imagination or artistic power. If they had been, they probably would not have left Europe for these distant colonies. They are more interesting to us historically than artistically. They brought a knowledge of forms, especially the Baroque portrait form, and the solid Baroque painter's craft. They were able to use its coloristic style of solid, plastic forms, rhythmic development of line, simple luminous color, effective contrasts of light and shade. They may have lacked inspiration but they were good craftsmen. The craft is all a teacher can ever give an art student. The qualities of imagination and poetry are born, not taught. The migrants' artistic importance is that they brought the craft of painting to America.

Another source of knowledge of Baroque forms was the engraving. Line engraving, as a means of reproducing paintings, developed in the sixteenth century. In the seventeenth came the mezzotint, far richer in tone. A great development of reproductive engraving followed. The masterpieces of Renaissance and Baroque art, the portraits of French and English court painters, were made widely available in engravings, which offered even more effective examples of Baroque composition than did the work of the migrant artists. During the whole eighteenth century and through the first half of the nineteenth, until the invention of the camera, engravings were the native American painter's chief source of knowledge of the language of European painting. Their influence was omnipresent. Today they are lost or forgotten: it is hard for us to remember that they were everywhere, once, and that their influence was, in some cases, omnipotent.

The point we must now emphasize is that there were native-born painters even before the arrival of Hesselius and Smibert. The

---

[3] The most nearly complete study of Bridges to date is that of Henry Wilder Foote in *The Virginia Magazine*, vol. 60 (Jan. 1952), pp. 3-55.

migrants brought trained craftsmanship; but the impulse to paint was already here.

In the office of the mayor of the City of Albany hangs a full-length heroic portrait of the first mayor of Albany, *Pieter Schuyler* (1657-1724) (Fig. 4-4), which, judging by the sitter's age, must have been painted between 1700 and 1710. His portrait is the work of an unknown artist, who was the first and finest talent of a school of painters active in the Hudson Valley from the earliest years of the century. These Patroon Painters, as Flexner (who was the first to recognize their artistic qualities) has called them, are the earliest significant development of native-born talent in American painting.

The Schuyler painter evidently learned his conception of the portrait from engravings, for he gave us a composition in the lordly Baroque manner. But his style shows the shift toward the two-dimensional—a flattening of the forms, an emphasis on outline and pattern—characteristic of the "untrained professional." Whoever he was, this painter, he was an instinctive painter and observer. The long, firm outlines of his style, the use of lights and shadows, drawn in long, firm strokes to give relief, the simple color scheme of red, brown, blue, gray, and white—all these are singularly knowing and effective. With limited means, he achieved a monumental decorative power. His grasp of character is no less striking: he makes Schuyler's forceful, intelligent, commanding personality so convincing that, to my eye, this is one of the memorable military portraits in American painting.

In the next generation, in the 1720's and 1730's, there were several painters at work up and down the Hudson Valley. One, who painted several portraits dated in the early 1720's, in a flat, rude, harsh style, has been named by Flexner the "Aetatis Suae painter" from his habit of inscribing the age of the sitter and date on the background.

A still more naïve painter (Flexner's "Gansevoort Limner") may have done the gentle, attractive portrait of *Adam Winne* at The Henry Francis du Pont Winterthur Museum, dated 1730. The delicacy of tone shown by these painters is often surprising. Naïve in technique, they betray nevertheless a sweet, untrained sensibility that is the flower of rustic refinement. Another, gayer style, close to the "artisan tradition," appears in the portrait of *Magdalena Gansevoort* of Albany in The Henry Francis du Pont Winterthur Museum, a deservedly famous and popular work, often called "The Girl with the Red Shoes" (Plate I).

These unknown painters of the Hudson Valley, with their bold, flat, effective style, their decorative sense, their varied gifts of mood or character, illustrate a phenomenon that was to appear often thereafter. Artists in the wilderness lacking the developed craft of European painting nonetheless found their way to create works of art that have life and flavor. This interweaving counterpoint of

4-4. Schuyler painter:
Pieter Schuyler
(ca. 1700-1710).
(Courtesy of
the Mayor's Office,
Albany, New York.)

4-5. Robert Feke:
General Samuel Waldo
(ca. 1748).
(Courtesy of The
Bowdoin College
Museum of Fine Arts.)

imagination and craft, of innate sensibility and knowledge, in the story of American painting is to me one of its sources of interest.

There is another native-born painter whose striking portraits and enigmatic career are wrapped in mystery. Robert Feke (ca. 1706-1710 to before 1767) was born at Oyster Bay, Long Island. He is said to have been a sailor, but when he appears in 1741, it is as the painter of a large portrait group, executed in Boston, of the *Family of Isaac Royall*. It is an ambitious, even daring work for an artist plainly without experience, and leans strongly on Smibert's example. Feke was nevertheless a born painter. His full-length of *General Samuel Waldo* (Fig. 4-5), his *Mrs. Josiah Martin* or his *Self-Portrait* of 1750, which show the maturity of his style, reveal a powerful talent. He was only occasionally a student of character. His portraits interest us by their decorative power, their luminosity,

4-6. Joseph Badger: *Mrs. John Edwards* (ca. 1750). (Courtesy of the Museum of Fine Arts, Boston.)

4-7. John Greenwood: *Jersey Nanny* (engraving, 1748). (Courtesy of Henry L. Shattuck; photograph, Museum of Fine Arts, Boston.)

by the bold Baroque rhythm in the flowing folds of his women's costumes, and by the eloquence with which they express the aristocratic ideal of dignity, elegance, and formality.

From 1741 until 1750 Feke was active as a painter; he is documented in Newport and Philadelphia. Then he disappears once more and, according to tradition, died in the West Indies. His fragmentary, wandering, adventurous life, his unknown training, show the difficulties and chances awaiting a painter born into a society without an established craft of painting.

In New England the seventeenth-century limner's style persisted apparently down to the arrival of Peter Pelham and Smibert in the

1720's. The next two painters born in Massachusetts, Joseph Badger (1708-1765) and John Greenwood (1727-1792), were young enough to learn from the example of Pelham and Smibert. In spite of this advantage, the Baroque portrait became, in their practice, an iron-tinctured essence of provincial stiffness.

Badger has a historical importance because Smibert's death left him, perforce, for some years the principal painter of Boston. Artistically, he illustrates the rule that it is the limitations of such painters that make them interesting. He was a house painter, self-taught as a portrait painter, and capable of a wooden amateurishness that should damn him forever as an artist. Yet out of the very narrowness of his talent, out of his inability to achieve the solid, beef-and-bone plasticity of Smibert's figures, comes his own peculiar quality. His *Mrs. John Edwards*, the wife of a Boston goldsmith (Fig. 4-6), is an example of his strangely ghostly style, which gives to his portraits, of the very young or very old especially, a wraithlike charm.

Greenwood is less interesting for his portraits than for his rough

4-8.   John Greenwood: *American Sea Captains Carousing in Surinam* (1757-1758). (Courtesy of the City Art Museum of St. Louis.)

4-9. William Burgis: *A South Prospect of Ye Flourishing City of New York in the Province of New York in America* (engraving, 1716-1718).

humor, which led him to produce the earliest colonial genre painting. His mezzotint engraving (1748) of *Jersey Nanny* (Fig. 4-7) bears the pointed inscription:

> Nature her various Skill displays
> In thousand Shapes, a thousand Ways;
> Tho' one Form differs from another
> She's still of all the common Mother:
> Then, Ladies, let not Pride resist her,
> But own that NANNY is your sister.

Still more vigorous and satirical is the picture, crudely painted in a curious frosty palette, of *American Sea Captains Carousing in Surinam* (1757-1758) (Fig. 4-8). It was painted after Greenwood left New England for Surinam, where he spent several years, and is the only surviving work to remind us that our New England ancestors

were, after all, compatriots of Hogarth. Greenwood ended his days
as a successful art dealer in London.

Such realism was rare in the Baroque period of American painting. The aristocratic ideal of grandeur and repose dominated the
imagination of colonial painters. There were forces in colonial life
working toward realism: there was the spirit of democracy of the
frontier; there was humor; there was the rising spirit of scientific
rationalism. Benjamin Franklin gave form and literary expression
to all three. But the effect of these forces on painting made itself felt
very slowly.

One other aspect of Baroque art has yet to be touched on, that is,
its relation with nature. Mark Catesby, the artist-naturalist, has already been mentioned in Chapter 2. He spent the years 1712-1719
and 1722-1726 roaming the forests of the South. But what of landscape painting?

There is a common supposition that landscape painting arises, inevitably and automatically, wherever there are people living among woods, rivers, hills. Nothing could be further from the truth. Landscape painting arises from an imaginative impulse notably rare in the history of civilization. In the seventeenth century Europe had seen the first great outburst in the landscape art of Rome and the Low Countries, but this was followed by a prolonged lull during most of the eighteenth century. The urbane and decorative interests of the late Baroque transposed the seventeenth-century realistic landscape into graceful decorations for walls, tapestries, or overdoor panels.

The decorative landscape with figures appeared in America perhaps for the first time when William Clark built a fine Palladian house in the old north end of Boston, about 1712-1714. In the main parlor the eleven wall panels were filled with landscape compositions, some time before the death of Mr. Clark in 1742; four of these still exist, rather crude but effective examples of Baroque decoration of a type more familiar to us in the form of tapestry. Decorative landscapes on walls or overmantels or even on canvas are not uncommon thereafter, generally on a very modest level of craftsmanship; an excellent survey of them has been published by Nina Fletcher Little in *American Decorative Wall Painting* (1952).

The cityscape however, appeared in America with William Burgis (documented in New York 1716-1718, Boston 1722-1730, New York 1730-1732). Burgis' imposing drawing of New York, engraved in London by I. Harris, appeared as the rare and beautiful engraving entitled: *A South Prospect of Ye Flourishing City of New York in the Province of New York in America* (Fig. 4-9). Drawn about 1716-1718, engraved 1718-1721, it is the earliest and most celebrated of eighteenth-century views.

Other engravings of colonial cityscapes are preserved from the 1730's; cityscapes in oil are much more rare. In the possession of the Library Company of Philadelphia is a long narrow canvas representing *The South East Prospect of the City of Philadelphia* about the years 1718-1720. It is signed by Peter Cooper. At either end are the arms of the city and the province; beneath is a descriptive panel identifying various buildings. It seems to be the earliest cityscape in oil from the middle colonies that has come down to us. Its long narrow shape strongly suggests the overmantel of a public room and its crude but effective style is that of an artisan. A similarly rough but decorative view of New York harbor during the last French war is preserved in The New-York Historical Society, called *British Privateers with French Prizes in New York Harbor* (ca. 1756-1761). It, too, is artisan's work, executed with the flat colors and conventionalized brush stroke that, in the eighteenth century, were reserved for signs and showboards. It is more spirited work than Peter Cooper's and better deserves the title of landscape. These two show, at least, that the painted cityscape existed in America.

The first half of the eighteenth century established the art of painting as an element in the life of the American colonies. Migrants from Europe, native-born talents, skilled craftsmen, humble artisans, all took part in achieving this. The institutions which form and strengthen an artistic life were still wholly lacking. But the thing planted then, took root.

In retrospect, the native-born painters of the colonial Baroque seem often the more interesting. The migrant painters were competent craftsmen but they were rarely inspired performers. The native-born were poorly trained; their faults are often glaring; their knowledge of European forms was limited. But they became painters because they were driven by the urge of talent and passionate interest. The contrast between their sensibility and their primitive means appeals to our imagination, and gives vitality and personal character to their work.

Five

THE ṚOCOCO IN AMERICA

THE GRAND AND SPLENDID FORMS of Baroque painting changed, in Europe, into the lighter, gayer, more intimate final phase known as the Rococo, almost as insensibly as one season of the year changes into another. In France the Rococo appears, in the genius of Watteau, as early as the second decade of the century: by 1730 its luminosity and easy grace were visible in England in the early conversation pieces of Hogarth, in Venice in the decorations of Tiepolo and the cheerful views of Canaletto, in Vienna in the cupola of the Hofbibliothek frescoed by Daniel Gran.

In the American colonies, the Baroque portrait style reigned undisturbed until two English painters arrived in the colonies, bringing with them the English Rococo, John Wollaston in 1749 and Joseph Blackburn in 1753. Both were craftsmen-painters rather than artists, practicing their art with skill rather than feeling, using a decorative portrait formula which varied little from one sitter to another. But they brought something of the idyllic note of the Rococo, with its pleasing artificialty and delicate movement, which artists like Highmore and Hudson were practicing in London; their portraits made attractive decorations for the Georgian mansions that were now rising in all the colonies along tidewater; and they spread the new style, Wollaston from New York City southward, Blackburn through the provincial capitals of New England.

Trained in London, Wollaston learned there a solid, competent portrait formula: he was essentially a London "drapery painter," one of those specialists in costume who, in the London studio practice, executed clothes and background on a canvas upon which a "face painter" had done the face. This practice, so contradictory to modern notions of painting, was a legacy of the Van Dyck-Kneller tradition of workshop production, and both Wollaston and Blackburn illustrate its peculiar merits and limitations. Wollaston could paint heads solidly, if somewhat coarsely and without much individuality, but imposing on each a curious mannerism of slanting, almond-shaped eyes, one slightly higher than the other. What his portraits lacked in characterization was made up by his skill in painting laces, silks, and satins (Fig. 5-1).

This was enough to win Wollaston immense success in America. He was the first painter of fashion to show himself in New York City, and his success was immediate. Before he left the colonies he had painted some three hundred portraits (equal to the total production of Smibert, Feke, and Blackburn together), and the example of his bold, coarse, confident pictures was the strongest influence upon colonial painting in the middle colonies and the South before the Revolution.[1]

Joseph Blackburn introduced a somewhat more delicate version of Rococo elegance and artifice into New England (Fig. 5-2). He arrived at Boston from Bermuda in 1753 and extended his practice from there to Newport, Salem, and Portsmouth, until 1774, when, perhaps finding the competition of Copley too formidable, he returned to England. He, too, was a drapery painter. His works seem today so thin and lacking in characterization that one finds it hard to believe they once seemed fresh, gay and fashionable and exerted an immense influence.

Yet wherever they went in the colonies, Wollaston and Blackburn found sitters eager to be painted by them and young colonial painters eager to adopt their new manner. In part, their success was one of fashion: they brought the new mode from London to the colonies. Thus they illustrate not only the importance of forms in art but the fact that forms are diffused by means easily forgotten afterward, by men of very modest talent or by teachers who are not successful painters, or by engravings, small carvings, photographs, or mediocre reproductions. The migration of ideas can

[1] The authority for Wollaston is George C. Groce, in *The Art Quarterly*, XV (1952), pp. 132-149.

5-1. John Wollaston: *Mrs. Perry and her daughter Anna*
(ca. 1758).
(Courtesy of the Philadelphia Museum of Art. Photograph by
A. J. Wyatt, staff photographer.)

be very baffling in the history of art if one forgets how modestly they
travel and looks only for great personalities and obvious sources of
influence.

Wollaston and Blackburn were, in their time, an improvement.
When one sees a pair of Blackburn's portraits in their fine Rococo
frames, such as those of *Timothy Fitch* and *Mrs. Fitch* in the dining

room of the Pingree House, Salem (now part of the Essex Institute), one discovers the secret of his success. However unsatisfactory as studies of character, these portraits are pretty and graceful decorations in a Georgian interior.

There were other migrant artists who brought a faint touch of Rococo graces to America without exerting so wide an influence. William Williams, an English painter, was active in 1746-1747 in Philadelphia, where he befriended Benjamin West as a boy.

5-2. Joseph Blackburn: *Mary Warner* (ca. 1760). (Courtesy of Warner House, Portsmouth, N.H.)

Williams was a curious figure of varied talents: sailor, painter-novelist, musician, and wanderer. He was one of the *petits maîtres* of the English conversation piece, and of them all perhaps the most naïve. His conversation pieces painted in America, such as the *Husband and Wife in a Landscape* (Fig. 5-3), are sensitive in color, bold and even impressive in design, and absurd in drawing to the point of caricature. The aristocratic ideal in Williams' hands becomes a conventional but sweet and flowerlike sentiment.

With Benjamin West (1738-1820) and John Singleton Copley (1738-1815) we come to a new stage in the development of painting

5-3.   William Williams: *Husband and Wife in a Landscape* (1775). (Courtesy of The Henry Francis du Pont Winterthur Museum.)

in America. It is an error to believe (although it has often been so stated) that painting appeared in America because there was a colonial aristocracy that wanted portraits. It was the other way around: painting appeared because there was an impulse to use the imaginative language of vision, and the painters adapted themselves as best they could to the world they lived in. One might say the history of American painting proves that a certain number of individuals out of the population are born with a predisposition to paint, as there are a certain number with a predisposition to be professional men or craftsmen or soldiers. This impulse showed itself very early in the American colonies and flowed naturally into the kind of painting and direction of attention prevailing. From the first it had to struggle against limitations of environment. Now the time had arrived when talents were to appear too great to be contained within the limits of colonial life.

John Singleton Copley was seventeen when Blackburn arrived in Boston in 1755. His mother had married as her second husband Peter Pelham, the English-trained mezzotint engraver whose work had been influential in New England since 1726. Copley therefore grew up in an atmosphere of prints, pictures, and music that must have been helpful to a youth very hesitant and self-doubtful by nature; it helped him find his vocation early and without hesitation. He had studied Smibert's works and the copies of Poussin and Van Dyck in his painting room; he had learned what he could from Badger and Greenwood. But the luster of Blackburn's color, the flash of his textures, the charming artificiality of his poses were both captivating and stimulating. In 1756 he used one of Blackburn's Rococo poses, a shepherdess with her lamb, in a portrait of *Ann Tyng* (Boston, Museum of Fine Arts). Yet the young painter's Rococo shepherdess in her white dress, seated on a green bank, is more richly painted, more plastic, more effective than anything done by Blackburn.

This is a clear illustration of the relation of forms to imagination in art. Painting is a language; and to use it well one needs to know the language in all its forms. The language itself, however, may be used and passed along by painters of little creative power. Copley, seizing upon the empty Rococo forms of Blackburn, poured into them an imaginative power to observe and to experience reality that filled them with the glow, vitality, and mystery of life. In the ten

5-4. John Singleton Copley: *Mary and Elizabeth Royall* (ca. 1758).
(Courtesy of the Museum of Fine Arts, Boston.)

years after his first contact with Blackburn, Copley created the most
brilliant and convincing expression of the aristocratic ideal that
American eighteenth-century painting was to produce. His double
portrait of *Mary and Elizabeth Royall* (ca. 1758) (Fig. 5-4) shows
two little girls on a couch. One, in a blue dress, holds a humming-
bird on her fingertip; one, in white, holds a puppy; swathed around

5-5. John Singleton Copley: *Mrs. Sylvanus Bourne* (1766).
(Courtesy of The Metropolitan Museum of Art.)

5-6.   John Singleton Copley: *Mr. and Mrs. Thomas Mifflin* (1773).
(Courtesy of The Historical Society of Pennsylvania.)

5-7. John Singleton Copley: *Ezekiel Goldthwait* (ca. 1770).
(Courtesy of the Museum of Fine Arts, Boston.)

and enframing them, wine-colored and golden draperies flow to the
floor. The picture has all the elegance and artifice of Rococo taste,
infused with the natural animation of two happy little girls.

Copley also made powerful use of another Rococo form which he
may have seen in Blackburn but which he undoubtedly studied in
engravings also. This was the portrait of a person in the setting of

his daily life—what the French call the *portrait d'apparat*. He learned to use this so well that there leaps to the mind's eye, when one thinks of Copley, a crowd of people caught in the midst of life, speaking with characteristic expression and lively gesture—*Mrs. Sylvanus Bourne* (Fig. 5-5), who has laid down her book for a moment, her face alight with wisdom and good humor, as if to say, "There, the man has sense . . ."; *Mr. and Mrs. Thomas Mifflin* (The Historical Society of Pennsylvania) (Fig. 5-6) talking pleasantly during an afternoon at home; the shrewd old town clerk of Boston, *Ezekiel Goldthwait* (Fig. 5-7) who has swung around in his chair, quill pen in hand, to answer an inquiry or settle a point of discussion; and a crowd of other unforgettable characterizations. Within the discipline of the aristocratic ideal Copley became a penetrating master of human character.

The effort it cost Copley to create an art of such force and authority, unsupported by any comparable craft or tradition of art around him, is impossible to estimate. He had an instinct, one may say, for the large movement in drawing, for plasticity, for luminous color. He very early learned from Blackburn the eighteenth-century painter's method of painting flesh in three simple tones of green, rose, and cream-white; and he could study chiaroscuro in prints. As one follows his development one sees many unsuccessful pictures, many awkward experiments, that reveal the difficulties through which he struggled. The one quality of the coloristic style he failed to master was atmosphere, although the hard, clear quality of his figures is very handsome in its own way and as uncompromising as his drawing of character. That he was able to achieve a style of first quality, by the standards of any school in light, form, drawing, expression, far beyond anything in the artistic life or in the pictures around him, is evidence of extraordinary powers.

Benjamin West's evolution in Philadelphia was more meteoric than Copley's in Boston. West (1738-1820) had supreme self-confidence: Copley was hesitant, self-distrustful, timid. West gained his first knowledge of painting from the painters he could see in Philadelphia, from William Williams, from Gustavus Hesselius, perhaps later from Wollaston. West's portrait of the young *Thomas Mifflin* (ca.1758-1759) (Historical Society of Pennsylvania) shows that he, like Copley, had powers that his predecessors lacked. Crude and immature as this picture is in many ways, it has a boldness of composition and luminosity of color such as one does not find in Wollaston. But, happening on a *Saint Ignatius* of the school of Murillo, taken from a Spanish prize ship, West realized that there were forms of art which he could study only abroad. He determined to go to Italy and, in order to earn passage money, set out for New York, where he thought he could charge higher fees for his portraits. Instead, a group of Philadelphia merchants subscribed the necessary funds. "It is a pity," one of them wrote, "such a genius should be cramped for the want of a little cash." So in 1759 West became the first of a long line of American art students who were to go to Italy to study the great masters of their profession.

After three years in Italy, spent chiefly in Rome, where he enjoyed a great social success, he journeyed north to London, arriving June 20, 1763. There he met with such encouragement that he remained the rest of his life: Philadelphia could offer no such opportunities for his talents.

At first Copley tried a different method of self-improvement. At the urging of a sea-captain friend, he sent a painting, *The Boy with the Squirrel,* to the exhibition of the Society of Artists in London (1766) and wrote to ask Sir Joshua Reynolds and West for criticism. Reynolds praised it highly but criticized its lack of atmosphere: "A little hardness in the drawing, coldness in the shades, an overminuteness. . . . If you are capable of producing such a piece by the mere efforts of your own genius, with the advantages of example and instruction you would have in Europe you would be a valuable acquisition to the art and one of the first painters in the world, provided you could receive these aids before it was too late in life, and before your manner and taste were corrupted or fixed by working in your little way in Boston." Copley's response was to paint the portrait of *Mary Warner* (1767) (Toledo Museum of Art) in which he tried to imagine what the aerial richness of color recommended by Reynolds might be. But Reynolds found the second picture less successful than the first; and so did West.

West urged him, as Reynolds had done, to study in Europe before it was too late. But in that direction lay the possibility of financial difficulties. He wrote to West, January 17, 1768:

I should be glad to go to Europe, but cannot think of it without a very good prospect of doing as well there as I can here. You are sensable that three hundred Guineas a Year, which is my present income, is a pretty living in America, and I cannot think You will advise me to give it up without a good prospect of something at least equel to it . . .[2]

And he begged West to tell him frankly what possibility there was for him to become as successful in London.

The dilemma of the man with a family to support, the craftsman with a skill to be learned, and the artist obscurely aware of powers within himself that demanded their rights also, could hardly be more clearly stated than in these letters. Another gnawing sense of discontent is hinted at in an undated and unaddressed draft of a letter (in the Copley-Pelham letters):

A taste of painting is too much wanting in Boston to afford any kind of help; and was it not for preserving the resemblance of particular persons, painting would not be known in the place. The people generally regard it as no more than any other useful trade, as they sometimes term it, like that of carpenter, tailor, or shoemaker, not as one of the most noble arts in the world, which is not a little mortifying to me. While the arts are so regarded, I can hope for nothing either to encourage or assist me in my studies but what I receive from a thousand leagues distance, and be my improvements what they will, I shall not be benefited by them in this country, neither in point of fortune or fame.

In point of fortune Copley was doing very well: but in point of fame—what was it to be the leading painter of Boston, where people thought his art no more than a trade? Another American, West, had left America for London and became a celebrity, even a favorite of the king. West was famous; Copley no more than the portrait painter of a remote provincial town. Jealousy of West haunted Copley throughout his life.

Ultimately, after seven more years in America, during which he rose to the heights of his American style, Copley reluctantly left America to study abroad. In June, 1774, he sailed for London, on the road to Italy, leaving his family in Boston. He had not decided to leave America for good; that decision was made for him later by circumstance. He made the Grand Tour of Paris, Rome, Florence, Parma, Mantua, Venice, Amsterdam, Brussels, Antwerp, studying his art voraciously, and writing homesick letters to America. In the

[2] *Letters and Papers of John Singleton Copley and Henry Pelham, 1739-1776.* Boston, The Massachusetts Historical Society, 1914, p. 68.

PLATE I. Unknown, early eighteenth century: *Magdalena Gansevoort.*
(Courtesy of The Henry Francis du Pont Winterthur Museum.)

PLATE II. Charles Willson Peale: *James Peale (The Lamplight
Portrait)* (1822). (Courtesy of The Detroit Institute of Arts.)

PLATE III. Charles Burchfield: *Black Iron* (1935). (Courtesy of
Mr. and Mrs. Lawrence A. Fleischman, Detroit; color plate courtesy
of the Archives of American Art.)

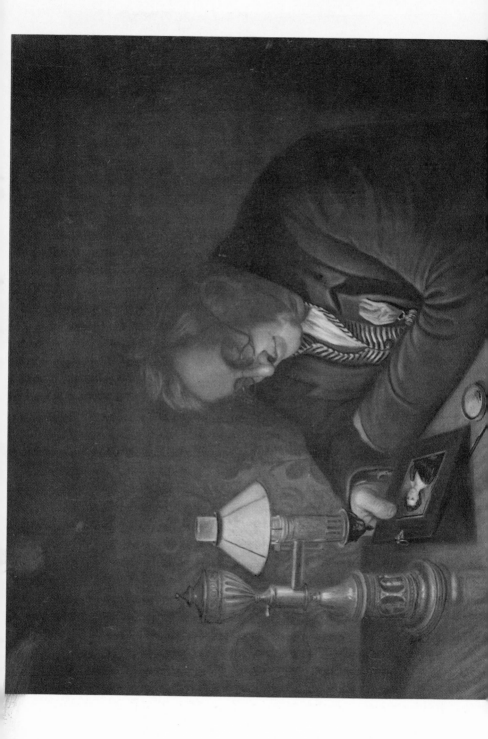

PLATE IV. James Abbott McNeill Whistler: *Nocturne in Black and Gold—The Falling Rocket*. (Courtesy of The Detroit Institute of Arts.)

meantime the American Revolution had begun; Massachusetts was the seat of war. Boston was no place, he saw, to support a family by portrait painting. He wrote for his wife to join him in London and settled where fate had directed that he could practice his art and support his family, but his heart was with the colonies.

A disparity had grown up between the talents and aspirations of the artists born in America and the primitive state of their profession. There were neither teachers nor collections of art for them to study in America. There was no sale for anything but portraits. Both Copley and West were too big for their limited setting. They went abroad to learn more of their art, and, in the end, remained there. This has frequently been treated by American writers as an act of deplorable moral weakness, as if they had been untrue to themselves—which is to read the emotions of later times into the eighteenth century. Copley and West loved their native land. When the colonies revolted against the absolute rule of Britain, their sympathies were American. But art, proverbially a jealous mistress, led them elsewhere. The opportunities and rewards for their talents were so much greater in London that they could not afford to come back to America. The careers of other American artists in their own and in the next generation confirm the wisdom of their course. This disparity between talent and environment was to trouble the course of American painting for a long time. In this period, it split the artistic life of America into two.

Benjamin West was born under a fortunate star. In spite of the crowd of talents in London, there was no one to compete with him in the style of historical painting he had learned in Rome. Within five years he had attracted the attention of King George III, and his fame and future were assured. As the first American artist established in Europe he served as a magnet to attract others. Almost as soon as he was settled in London, other American painters came to join him. He was a man of great generosity of character, unfailingly kind and helpful to all young artists who sought his aid. As his career gained momentum, he received commissions for enormous historical canvases in which he could give small parts to assistants. He also became a collector of art, so that his house was a gallery (both of his own pictures and those of greater, earlier masters) which was

5-8.   Matthew Pratt: *The American School* (1765).
(Courtesy of The Metropolitan Museum of Art.)

open to art students. In those days there was no public gallery in London. His studio and home thus became the art school in which a whole generation of young Americans studied.

The Americans who came first, in the 1760's, were West's own contemporaries in point of age. Matthew Pratt stayed four years with West, from 1764 to 1768. Abraham Delanoy of New York was there from about 1766 to 1770. Henry Benbridge, of Philadelphia, stayed there the winter of 1769-1770 on his way home from Italy. Charles Willson Peale also was there in 1766-1767.

The effect of these studies in London was not to bring to America West's neoclassic style (which was hardly as yet formed) but the English provincial Rococo style, such as was practiced by the men

we think of as the *little masters* of the English conversation piece,
like Arthur Devis or Benjamin Wilson. These English artists did not
paint with Reynolds' full-loaded brush and rich compositional
imagery. Their art was simpler and more direct than that of the great,
fashionable portrait painters of London: they drew with precise,
clear outlines and painted with clean, fresh, luminous colors, in a
style not unlike what the Americans were used to. In fact the painters
of this simple and idyllic school, with its combination of realism
and delicate formality, were close, in many ways, to American taste.
They found their chief patrons among the British merchants, professional classes, and country gentry who were, of all the English,
closest in temperament to their American counterparts.

The most famous of American conversation pieces is *The American School* (1765) (Fig. 5-8), painted by Matthew Pratt (1734-
1805). It represents a group of young American painters working
together in West's studio. At the left, West is criticizing a drawing
by Pratt; the other two artists have not been identified. This is a

5-9. Charles Willson Peale: *Peale Family Group* (1773).
(Courtesy of The New-York Historical Society.)

5-10.   John Durand: *The Rapalje Children* (ca. 1768).
(Courtesy of The New-York Historical Society.)

typical eighteenth-century conversation piece—a group portrait of figures, represented smaller than life, and engaged in the activities of their daily life. The precise, slightly naïve drawing and the luminous color are characteristic of Pratt. After his return to Philadelphia Pratt painted a few modest portraits, but found it necessary to supplement these by painting signs. Both Dunlap and Neagle speak of these with enthusiasm, saying that he made the city remarkable for the beauty and skill displayed in its signs.

5-11.   Winthrop Chandler: *Mrs. Samuel Chandler.* (Courtesy of Colonel and Mrs. Edgar W. Garbisch.)

Henry Benbridge (1744-ca.1812) brought home a richer, more sophisticated style than Pratt's, capable of large and skillful group portraits like the *Gordon Family* (painted in Philadelphia in 1771). Later in the year 1771 he moved for the sake of his health to Charleston, South Carolina, where, after this promising beginning he settled down as the local portrait painter. He seems to have settled down all too well.

Another life-size conversation piece, by one of West's pupils of the sixties, is the famous *Peale Family Group* (Fig. 5-9) (1773 with later additions) showing the artist giving a drawing lesson to his brother, St. George Peale, who is sketching their mother at the other end of the table. Seven other figures and a dog complete this cheerful and animated scene "emblematical," as Peale said, "of family concord." Charles Willson Peale's pupil and brother, James, subsequently became the most prolific painter of conversation pieces in America.

With the exception of Peale, the careers of the Americans who studied in London in the sixties with West and returned to try to practice their art in America during the troubled years of the Revolution are fragmentary and meager. One should consider the problem that faced Copley and West in the light of the record of those who returned. The urge toward painting at this moment of our history was far greater in America than were the resources of American society to reward or support its artists.

Other painters were developing who had no chance to go to London and enjoy the benefit of West's encouragement. Their work shows the variations in technique to be expected of the "untrained professional."

John Durand (fl.1767-1782) came of a Huguenot family settled in Connecticut. Like all untrained professionals, he saw in terms of outlines and flat areas of color, rather than of solid shapes surrounded by airy space; yet within his limits he was an artist of innate elegance and style. His portrait group of *The Rapalje Children* (ca.1768) (Fig. 5-10), a work both charming in its style and diverting in its naïveté, is his most ambitious painting.

Connecticut was to produce a surprising number of painters in the next half century. Winthrop Chandler (1747-1790), born near Woodstock, Connecticut, was trained in a tradition of craftsman-

5-12. William Bartram: *A Beautiful Fly of East Florida*. (Courtesy of The British Museum, Natural History.)

ship which extended from heraldry to house painting, and from limning portraits to japanning and gilding. In experience and in training Chandler could hardly have been more limited; yet his innate powers were those of an artist. He had a gift for the *portrait d'apparat*, for color, for vigorous linear pattern, and for seeing character—and those are no small equipment for any artist. His portrait

of the *Reverend Ebenezer Devotion*, seated among his books (1770)
(Brookline Historical Society), or of *Mrs. Samuel Chandler* (ca.
1775-1785) (Fig. 5-11), seated in her parlor, enframed in a strange
arrangement of drapery, are extraordinary pictorial documents. They
are works of skill—but it is an unlettered skill; whereas the intuitive
sensibility that speaks through them has power.

In this period also came the second important artist-naturalist,
William Bartram (1739-1823), the son of the great botanist John
Bartram of Philadelphia. William was a born plant hunter and artist.
In 1755 his father wrote: "Botany and drawing are his darling de-
light: am afraid he can't settle to any business else." He wrote, and
illustrated with his own drawings, one of the most famous and in-
fluential American books of the eighteenth century. *Travels Through
North and South Carolina, Georgia, East and West Florida, the
Cherokee Country, the Extensive Territories of the Muscogulges, or
Creek Confederacy, and the Country of the Chactaws; Containing an
Account of the Soil and Natural Productions of Those Regions, Together with Observations on the Manners of the Indians*, published in
Philadelphia in 1791, had seven European editions within ten years:
London (1792-1794); Dublin (1793); Berlin (1793); Haarlem
(1794-1797); Paris (1799-1801). The charm of its description of
tropical forests and the life of the wilderness made it eagerly read
by poets like Coleridge and Southey, while its information was wel-
comed by scholars. Drawings by Bartram, such as *A Beautiful Fly
of East Florida* (the imperial moth and a marsh pink) (Fig. 5-12)
are delicate and exact in line, often quite without composition, but
vital and graceful. They have the artless spontaneity of things seen
in excitement for the first time.

In the Rococo age, painters emerged on a level of unquestioned
skill; and it becomes clear that a new national temperament and life
were finding voice. American painting had not the inherited grace
of the French, the gaiety and grandeur of the Italian, nor the aristocratic decorative tone of the English Rococo painting. Yet it had its
own integrity. The people of America were something new. They
breathed a new air. Their art was that of a strong, earnest, intelligent,
middle-class society, somewhat sober and limited in its interests, but
thoughtful, and of deep, earnest feelings.

Six

NEOCLASSICISM: THE IDEAL

AND THE REAL

WITH THE SECOND HALF of the eighteenth century the aristocratic ideal began to disappear. The democratic rationalism of Americans like Franklin and Jefferson was inspired by the ideas of the French encyclopedists, who, inspired in turn by English thought of the period of Newton, Locke, and Hume, put an end to the theory of divine right and the aristocratic ideal of society. As that ideal faded, the eighteenth century's other enthusiasm for the classical world of Greece and Rome grew. Political rebels searching for a new form of government found their model in the republics of antiquity. Moralists searching for a new theory of society to take the place of rank and birth found it in the ideal of *citizen*, the responsible individual member of the *civis* or city-republic of the ancient world. Theorists of art searching for a new form to replace the Rococo found it in the imitation of antiquity.

The excavations at Pompeii and Herculaneum, begun in the second quarter of the eighteenth century, had opened a world of marvels. Archaeology now resurrected the long-lost physical appearance of that vanished world of classical antiquity in enchanting completeness. At the same time, the mental image of the past was transformed by writers like Gibbon and Voltaire who, instead of writing a mere chronicle, used a comparative and critical study of sources to build up a living portrait of civilization.

In the arts, historical eclecticism became the new direction. In

France a series of powerful talents, beginning with Jacques Louis David in the 1780's and ending only with the death of Ingres in 1867, tried to make modern art the reconstruction of an antique world. In Germany, after the transition figures like Mengs and J. H. W. Tischbein, the friend of Goethe, there came a generation of passionate, idealistic neoclassicists. These artists sought to live in an ideal world where only antique sculpture, Homer and Plutarch, Michelangelo and Raphael existed. To the men of the eighteenth century the past was a tool of liberation, the key to the future. It is impossible for us to comprehend today how vivid, fascinating, and important the dream of Greece and Rome was to men in the later eighteenth century.

The capital of that dream world was Rome. There a new theory of art was developed in the 1750's and 1760's by a German art critic, Winckelmann, and by the artists Raphael Mengs and Pompeo Batoni, expressing the urge of their generation to transform the arts into an image of classical beauty. Their theory may be summarized as the doctrine of Ideal Beauty. Beauty—ideal, impersonal, universal Beauty—the neoclassic theory held, is found not in the world of nature, but in the mind. Nature, which is diverse and constantly changing, is the object of sensation, a lower form of human response; but Beauty, which is ideal and universal, is the conception of Reason. Art must therefore turn its back upon Nature and create an Ideal Beauty out of the mind.

To this Winckelmann added two other notions, derived from his love of the antique sculpture in the Vatican, which distinguished the neoclassic dogmas from more recent theories of ideal art. The stable and intellectual elements of art, he said, are drawing and form. These represent the geometry of the mind and are therefore the primary elements of art. Color, which is variable and makes its appeal to the emotions, is secondary. And, since classical sculpture had attained the perfection of ideal nobility, modern artists should model themselves upon it. Neoclassic painting on the continent rejected the technique of painting in light and color that had prevailed since the Venetian sixteenth-century painters. Drawing and simple local colors became its new technique, while an episode from history, drawn from antiquity and treated in a style based upon Roman sculpture, became its subject matter.

The first painters to achieve a style based on Winckelmann's theories asserting the superiority of classical subjects and antique sculpture as models were neither German, French, nor Italian but Scottish and American, Gavin Hamilton and Benjamin West. Gavin Hamilton spent most of his life in Florence and his works have passed into obscurity. West, after three years in Italy which enabled him to absorb the atmosphere of the dawning neoclassic idealism, migrated to London where his new style made him one of the most celebrated painters of his age.

West's *Agrippina with the Ashes of Germanicus* (1767) fully illustrates the new style. It illustrates also the difficulty we have today in appraising West. The grandeur and solemnity of the conception strike the observer today, as they did in the eighteenth century. The color is excellent, the chiaroscuro interesting. Yet it has also in the figures the woodenness and mawkishness that are the failings of West's art. We, to whom West's good qualities have lost their novelty, are apt only to see his weaknesses; the eighteenth century, to whom his art was all new, found his good qualities fresh and invigorating.

The neoclassic style of West differed in two important respects from French and German neoclassicism. He continued to use the coloristic technique of the eighteenth century instead of abandoning glazes and aerial tone for bare earth colors; and his conception of history included not only Greek and Roman history, but the Bible, English history, even recent events. In *The Death of Wolfe* (1771) he represented a contemporary deed of heroism in contemporary costume. His *William Penn's Treaty with the Indians* (1772) was drawn from the history of his own Pennsylvania. Generous, noble, patriotic actions—the antique virtues—whether in ancient or modern life, were his subject matter.

Penn's Treaty is an example of West's large and simple drawing, the pleasing color, and well-handled chiaroscuro which always make his pictures effective decorations, whatever we may think about their sentiment. His unfinished *Conference of the American Commissioners of the Treaty of Peace with England* (Fig. 6-1) shows his monumental powers in spite of its small size.

Another American to paint the ideal world of antiquity was John Vanderlyn (1775-1852), whose story is typical of the problems of artists in America at that time. At the age of twenty he attracted the interest of Aaron Burr who, believing him a genius, paid the

6-1. Benjamin West: *Conference of the American Commissioners of the Treaty of Peace with England* (1783). (Courtesy of The Henry Francis du Pont Winterthur Museum.)

expenses of a year of study with Gilbert Stuart in Philadelphia and then five years in Paris (1796-1801). He was apparently the first American artist to study there. From his teacher, Vincent, he absorbed the fine draughtsmanship, the enamel-like color, the firm sculptural style of the French neoclassic school. His early portraits and portrait drawings are admirable (Fig. 6-2). But he also absorbed the French neoclassic notion that only great, ideal, historical compositions were worthy of an artist: portraits he looked down upon.

During a three-year stay in Rome (1805-1808) he did some charming drawings and painted his first classical subject, *Marius on*

the Ruins of Carthage (1807), representing the fallen Roman hero
brooding in exile on the ruins of the fallen city. In Paris again, Vanderlyn painted his best work, *Ariadne* (Fig. 6-3) (1812) a dignified, handsome picture of monumental size, which is the most successful ideal nude produced by American neoclassicism. In 1815,
at the age of forty, he returned to New York, having spent half his
life abroad. He was well trained. His talents had been recognized
by Napoleon's gold medal, which shone with great luster in American eyes. Life had gone well for him. But it had not prepared him
for the difficulties he must face in the New World.

   The situation of a painter in New York, to one accustomed to the
proud atmosphere of art in Paris, was chilling and depressing. There
was no Emperor to distribute honors, no Louvre to lend prestige to

6-2.   John Vanderlyn: *A Lady and Her Son* (1800).
(Courtesy of the Senate House Museum, Kingston, N. Y.)

painting, no Salon to attract the attention of society. The torpid
American Academy of Fine Arts, for which he had bought casts of
antique sculpture twelve years before, was almost dead and its collections were in storage. Colonel John Trumbull, who came back
from England the year after Vanderlyn's arrival, claimed and secured
the only great public commission for historical painting offered in
the United States: four murals for the Rotunda of the Capitol in
Washington. Trumbull no doubt deserved the commission, yet Vanderlyn felt himself the better painter and much ill-feeling ensued
between the two men. When the City of New York commissioned
Vanderlyn to paint a portrait of *General Jackson* for the City Hall,
it did not satisfy his feeling of injured pride and neglect.

Unfortunately for Vanderlyn, he had absorbed along with the
technique of French neoclassicism its grandiose ambitions, which

6-3. John Vanderlyn: *Ariadne* (1812). (Courtesy of
The Pennsylvania Academy of the Fine Arts, Philadelphia.)

he was neither able to carry out by his own unaided strength nor to find a foundation for in American society. Monumental paintings imply a monumental architecture which can house them and calls for enrichment. In America there was as yet hardly any monumental architecture; there was no king or emperor; no owners of ducal palaces; no apparatus of state patronage, no tradition of church art. The neoclassic architecture then taking shape was monumental in feeling but usually not in size. Poor Vanderlyn's bitter, thwarted career is that of a man who wished to paint great historical murals in a society that could not use them.

Yet we cannot blame all of Vanderlyn's troubles upon external factors. The neoclassic theory was focused upon ideal historical subjects, which he executed slowly and hesitantly. His admirable early portraits suggest that his natural gifts were for an art of observation, rather than fancy. A conflict between what he was born to do and what he thought he ought to do might account both for his small production and his unhappy nature.

Neoclassic painting in its strictest form, as David or Cornelius practiced it, and as Vanderlyn tried to practice it, fed upon the great collections of antique sculpture in the Vatican, the Louvre, and the British Museum. Removed from those, it could hardly flourish. Vanderlyn's *Marius* is an illustration. The head of Marius was painted from a marble bust in Rome; the body is a pastiche of other ancient sculptures; the temple and ruins were painted from a model constructed in his studio. The method of production was so laborious and tedious that it alone might have been enough to paralyze the man's power to create. Without abundant models, without ancient sculpture and archaeological remains at one's elbow, such art was impossible. The first move of the little academies and athenaeums organized in America after 1800 was to purchase casts of the most celebrated antique statues: but this was not enough. Painters in America other than Vanderlyn experimented with neoclassic subjects. Yet these efforts were of necessity desultory and ineffective.

Antiquity also presented itself, however, to eighteenth-century minds in another guise—their own better selves. Generous and noble actions, courage, self-sacrifice, elevation of character exist in the present as well as in the past. American painters of the first years of the Republic saw about them a world made memorable by cour-

6-4. John Singleton Copley: *Watson and the Shark* (1782).
(Courtesy of The Detroit Institute of Arts.)

age, patriotism, and devotion, by the antique virtues enacted in their own times. Here were the ancient themes of classicism alive and breathing. The heroic narrative pictures of Copley and Trumbull, the portraits of Stuart and Peale and their contemporaries apply classical vision and its style of firm drawing and clearly lighted plastic forms to subjects from the world of reality rather than of fancy. As a re-creation of the antique past, American neoclassic painting was uncertain, fitful, and unhappy; as a celebration of antique virtues in modern life, it was energetic, profuse, varied, and assured.

Neoclassic realism has received less attention than the ideal narratives. It is my opinion that neoclassic realism produced in America an admirable national style, full of character and solid in achievement. It is important, if I am right, to describe its chief works and try to delineate its character.

Let us take Copley's development after 1774 as an example. Copley, it will be remembered, had gone to Europe to escape from an environment that limited him to portrait painting. As soon as he was settled in London, he turned his gifts for penetrating observation and robust, objective creation to narrative subjects on the large Italian scale. *Watson and the Shark* (Fig. 6-4) (a composition which exists in several different versions) is an episode in the life of a friend, Brook Watson, who, swimming as a boy in Havana Harbor, had one leg bitten off by a shark. He was rescued, however, by his shipmates and lived to become a great merchant and Lord Mayor of London. The contemporary subject had in it the elements of courage and loyalty in a moment of supreme danger that the classical artist wished to honor.

In *The Death of the Earl of Chatham in the House of Lords* (1779-1780) (Tate Gallery, London) he painted the last act of Pitt, a patriot as devoted as Regulus, who used his final strength to denounce in the House of Lords the government's policy toward the revolted colonies (1778). In *The Death of Major Pierson* (1783) (Tate Gallery, London) he chose the self-sacrifice of a gallant officer. These pictures show Copley's growth. He had left America to master the larger language of painting; now he had done so. In dramatic force, in convincing expression of life, in sweeping movement, in monumental disposition of lights and shadows, these are among the remarkable paintings of their times. Not until Baron

Gros painted Napoleon's campaign in Egypt, a generation later, was there to be again such dramatically effective narrative painting.

Another important American narrative painter of the period was John Trumbull (1756-1843). Like the other American artists of this century, he was born with a strong innate urge to paint, for which one can see no cause in his environment. The portraits of his early years are those of an "untrained professional" of great natural gifts.

Son of the governor of Connecticut, Trumbull served during the first year of the Revolution as an aide-de-camp to Washington. In 1785, after a year of study in London with Benjamin West, he produced his first independent neoclassic composition, a subject from Homer: *Priam Returning with the Body of Hector* (Boston Athenaeum). Then abandoning the Homeric wars, he turned to the wars of his own day and the story of the American Revolution. He knew personally most of the men, in America and abroad, who had played the leading roles. He resolved to paint likenesses of the principal actors, while they were still living, and to incorporate these into the twelve large narrative subjects, thus making them a historical record as well as works of art. The eight small studies completed in the next ten years, and the many miniature portraits in oil of the American, British, and French actors in the story (most of which are preserved at Yale University) are both a unique historical record and a notable artistic achievement.

Trumbull was, fortunately, no dogmatic theorist in the neoclassic manner. The painter he admired most was Rubens (whom the neoclassic theorists detested) and he learned much from Baroque narrative painting. The *Death of Montgomery Before Quebec* and his *Washington at the Surrender of the Hessians* (Yale University Art Gallery) show in their spirited action, their composition in depth, their luminous chiaroscuro, and psychological force, how well he had absorbed the lessons of Baroque painting.

Trumbull thought, not without reason, that engravings after his twelve historical pictures would be popular in America. Unfortunately, when he returned there in 1789 he found the country still exhausted from the war and preoccupied with political and economic problems. After a first encouraging reception, interest lagged and subscriptions for the engravings ceased. Deeply discouraged after a few years of struggle, in 1794 he dropped the project and gave up art to accept a diplomatic post in London. When that post came to an end he stayed in London and, taking up painting once more,

6-5. John Trumbull: *Sortie of the British Garrison from Gibraltar* (1789).
(Courtesy of The Boston Athenaeum; photograph, Museum of Fine Arts,
Boston.)

spent the next years working as a rather unsuccessful portrait
painter. When he returned finally to America in 1816 and Congress
voted to commission (1817) four of his Revolutionary subjects in
heroic size for the Rotunda of the new Capitol in Washington, thirty
years had passed since he first conceived the series. His pictures in
the Rotunda are handsome and imposing decorations. Yet they lack
the ardor of his youthful work and also lack some of the plasticity.

Trumbull was an artist of great gifts, an excellent colorist, a master
of expressive movement and chiaroscuro. His miniature portrait
studies made in preparation for the Revolutionary pictures are admirable observations of character. For the dramatic subtlety of expression one might have expected to find in the large pictures, had
he executed them during the freshness of his inspiration, look at the
row of officers' heads in the foreground of his *Sortie of the British*

Garrison from Gibraltar (1789) (Fig. 6-5). I regard a passage such as this as worthy of the greatest Baroque narrative painters. Trumbull was criticized by Americans for painting this picture, which celebrates a British feat of arms. He answered the criticism in his *Autobiography*: he chose the subject, he said, "to show that noble and generous actions, by whomsoever performed, were the objects to whose celebration I meant to devote myself." The statement breathes the spirit of the classical period, with its conscious choice of lofty, healthy, and universal values.

The last chapter of Trumbull's long, changeful, gifted, but unhappy life was the most unfortunate. In 1817 Trumbull became head of the American Academy of Fine Arts in New York, organized to afford that city a gallery of art and an art school. By selling his own works at high prices, Trumbull ruined the finances of the gallery. And instead of rising to his position as the leading figure of his profession in America, Trumbull became the enemy of his fellow painters and a caustic discourager of the young. The first war between generations waged in the story of American painting was fought by the young New York painters to rid themselves of the incubus of this bitter old man.

The direction of attention of the classical period was focused very largely upon the merits and the rights of the individual human being. Its political revolutions, its ethical and social ideas, its humanistic culture were all expressions of a profound interest in and respect for the individual. This interest made it also one of the rich periods of portrait painting.

The most celebrated portrait painter, and the creator of a distinctive American classical portrait style, was Gilbert Stuart (1755-1828). He began painting portraits in his teens, in Newport, in a very attractive if naïve style. Cosmo Alexander, the Scottish migrant painter, was interested by the talented boy and took him to Edinburgh to study in 1772. Alexander's death left him stranded in Scotland and he worked his way home as a sailor, suffering hardships he never liked to discuss afterwards. He went again to London (1775-1787), where he became eventually a successful portrait painter. But Stuart was a gay, carefree, extravagant fellow. Debts drove him to Ireland (1787-1792) and again from there to America (1793). He returned, he said, to paint the portrait of Washington. He did so in a way which left a profound mark upon our painting.

In London Stuart experimented with the portrait formulas of English painting. He composed portraits like Reynolds, like Gainsborough, even like Van Dyck; he painted people in action, in the setting of life, without setting. But gradually his portraits grew simpler, quieter; an air of remoteness, of detachment from the stir of existence settled over his characters. When he returned to New York in 1793 his portraiture had assumed the bland stillness, the steady unflickering glow of life that were to be his peculiar note.

Washington Allston observed, "Stuart knows how to distinguish very well the accidental from the permanent." It is the permanent and timeless aspect of a human being that Stuart's portraits give us and of which the "Vaughan" type of *Washington* is perhaps the perfect example. All the accessories of daily existence of the eighteenth-century *portrait d'apparat*, all the fleeting gestures and expressions that Copley had used to create a moment of life were eliminated by Stuart. Stuart knew very well what significant gesture was and what accessories could do. If he used them, it was to build an individual into a type. His *Washington at Dorchester Heights* (Fig. 6-6) (1806) is a type of Washington as Soldier Hero, as his *Athenaeum* (1796), *Vaughan* (1795), and *Lansdowne* (1796) portraits, or the seated *Washington* of 1797 are types of Washington as Elder Statesman. His portraits of private individuals wear the same remote and timeless air. Almost without exception Stuart eliminated all detail to show the man or woman in his permanent aspect. The bone structure of the head, the glow of life in the skin and eyes, an expression of calm and well-being, an exquisite freshness of color, these were what interested him and all that, in most cases, he allowed to enter the disciplined perfection of his art. After he had created this very personal classical form, he practiced within these narrow limits for thirty years.

Charles Willson Peale (1741-1827), the most interesting artist of Philadelphia, was not only an admirable portrait painter but a man of generous enthusiasms and fertile intellectual curiosity. If West and Trumbull and Vanderlyn are examples of how the disembodied Ideal of Art could send its enchantment out into remote frontier regions of a new continent to inspire youths with ambition to become an Apelles or a Raphael almost before they had seen such a thing as a picture, Peale came into painting by way of skilled handcraftsmanship. He believed accordingly that anyone could paint, that art was only a matter of training and taking pains, a view that must have been irritating to minds filled with Winckelmann's lofty theories of Ideal Beauty. Peale's belief in training made him the organizer of the first art school in America. And his encyclopedic interests, his ingenious, experimental nature illustrate how closely allied the objective, realistic imagination of the artist may be to the interests of the scientist.

6-6.   Gilbert Stuart: *Washington at Dorchester Heights* (1806). (Courtesy of the City of Boston; photograph, Museum of Fine Arts, Boston.)

Born in Queen Anne's County, Maryland, Peale was early apprenticed to a saddler. The boy was a natural craftsman and, having an
eager, curious mind, not only learned his own craft, but tinkered
readily at any other that presented itself—watch and clock repairing,
silversmithing, casting in brass. At the age of twenty-one, he saw
at Norfolk some landscapes and a portrait by an amateur artist. The
idea of making pictures now took hold of his mind. Getting paint
and brushes into his hands, and buying in Philadelphia a book called
The Handmaid to the Arts, he discovered a natural aptitude for
painting. Yet it was not until a Maryland planter paid him ten pounds
for portraits of himself and his lady that Peale (married by this
time and with a child on the way) realized he might support his
family better by this skill than by his other trades. He got a little
instruction from John Hesselius in return for one of his best saddles;
went to Boston, where Copley lent him a picture to copy; and made
such progress that his friends raised money to send him to study in
London. There West received him kindly and he spent two years
in the metropolis, 1767-1769.

Ardent, hopeful, enthusiastic, Peale was a creature
of what the eighteenth century called sensibility. His career, told
with insight and wit in Charles Coleman Sellers' two-volume biography (1947) is a most entertaining mirror of his age. The generous
enthusiasms and hopes of its liberal thinkers, the optimistic rationalism of the philosophers stirred him deeply; the nascent natural
sciences appealed to his insatiable curiosity. After Copley's departure in 1774, Peale was the leading portrait painter in the colonies; but his art was only one aspect of his long, indefatigably active,
and influential life.

Adding an exhibition gallery to his Philadelphia studio in 1781,
he launched on a project of painting the principal leaders of the
Revolutionary War, both civil and military, the outstanding diplo-
mats, and the foreign ambassadors to the young republic. By 1784
there were forty-four such likenesses in the gallery. In 1786 a museum of natural history was added. The collection outgrew Peale's
gallery, and in 1794 was transferred to Philosophical Hall, the new
building of the American Philosophical Society; finally, in 1802, to
the upper floor of the State House (now known as Independence
Hall). There it remained until the collection was dispersed in the
eighteen-fifties, and there some of the portraits still hang today.

Peale understood his own strength and limitations in the field of painting. The Ideal World of neoclassic theory, of which he had had a glimpse in Benjamin West's studio, was not for him. Three years after his return to America, he wrote to his old friend, John Beale Bordley (1772):

A good painter of either portrait or History must be well acquainted with the Grecian and Roman statues, to be able to draw them at pleasure by memory, and account for every beauty, must know the original cause of beauty in all he sees. These are some of the requisites of a good painter. These are more than I shall ever have time or opportunity to know, but as I have variety of characters to paint I must as Rembrandt did make these my Anticks [Antiques], and improve myself as well as I can while I am providing for my support.[1]

The best of his portraits painted in the 80's and 90's can stand comparison, in all but color and the sensuous use of paint, with the best of contemporary work. How he arrived so early and unaided, cut off from artistic contacts, at so interesting a parallel to the neoclassic portrait style worked out in France by David, I cannot explain. By the early eighties, Peale's portraits had lost all traces of Rococo pose or elaboration, and emerged in a severely simple, neoclassic style, never wholly free from naïveté and provincial awkwardness, but cogent, amiable and, at its best, of penetrating candor.

Peale was profuse and unpredictable. He did silhouettes with the physiognotrace, a machine to record the profile; he painted admirable miniatures; one of his finest works was a life-sized *trompe l'œil*. *The Staircase Group* (Fig. 6-7) (1795), showing his sons Raphaelle and Titian Ramsay Peale going up a narrow stair, was shown at the Columbianum Exhibition of 1795 as a *trompe l'œil*, framed in an actual door frame and with a wooden step projecting out below to complete the illusion.

After 1786 his energies were drawn more and more into his other great activity, the creation of the first American scientific museum. Peale's museum was the first in the United States and one of the earliest in the world to pass beyond the primitive stage of a gathering of curiosities, in order to represent a scientific concept. Its greatest achievement was the excavation and mounting of the first mas-

[1] Charles Coleman Sellers, *Charles Willson Peale, Vol. I, Early Life (1741-1790)*, Philadelphia, the American Philosophical Society, 1947, p. 113.

6-7. Charles Willson Peale: *The Staircase Group* (1795). (Courtesy of the Philadelphia Museum of Art.)

todon skeleton (1801), of which Peale himself left an amusing record in the painting, *Exhuming the Mastodon* (Peale Museum, Baltimore). Peale's dream of making his institution a National Museum was half a century ahead of its time; the museum had to exist on admission fees. In midcentury, unable to compete with more commercial amusements and Barnum's type of showmanship, it went to the wall and its collections were dispersed. Yet it was, in its heyday from 1800 to Peale's death in 1827, an extraordinary achievement and it entitles the artist to a singular place in our intellectual history.

At the age of seventy-four the old man, whose interest in painting had been secondary for twenty years to the creation of his museum, took up his brushes and colors to enter another and in some respects his most interesting period as a painter. In his middle years, his best trait of style was his sensitive, expressive draughtsmanship: now he was interested in light, which he used with true subtlety. His portrait of his brother, *James Peale (The Lamplight Portrait)* (Plate II) (The Detroit Institute of Arts), was painted in 1822, when the painter was eighty-one years old. It is a subtle composition of half-lights and shadows sensitively observed: one could say without exaggeration, such a composition was beyond the capacity or even the conception of most of the younger American painters at that day.

A gifted, ardent, ingenious, practical, idealistic man, who lived to carry out every idea that came to him, from mounting a mastodon to inventing porcelain false teeth, Peale is one of the most entertaining and remarkable characters in our art. During his lifetime Philadelphia was the cultural center of the country. Peale, incessantly active, curious, and alive, was one of the figures who made it so.

All of these American neoclassical painters—Copley in his later development, West, Trumbull, Stuart, Peale—worked in a more linear style, more precise in drawing, thinner in pigment, than that of the English neoclassicists like Romney and Hoppner. The Americans seem never to have liked the thick impasto and the generalized, idealizing drawing characteristic of the English school from Reynolds' time. On the other hand, their painting, though firm, was fresh and luminous, a more coloristic style than that of the French neoclassicists.

6-8.   Ralph Earl: *Roger Sherman* (ca. 1777-1779).
(Courtesy of the Yale University Art Gallery.)

Around these leaders there grew up a school of neoclassic portraiture that is one of the solid achievements of American painting.
Each of the major cities on the eastern seaboard had an active
group of artists. The back country towns had their artists, too; and,
as the tide of settlement pushed into the wilderness which still
waited close even to the oldest settlements, both the idea and the
craft of painting was swept along with it. This was a period prolific
in both trained and untrained professionals.

6-9. William Jennys: *Mrs. Constant Storrs.*
(Courtesy of The Pennsylvania Academy of the
Fine Arts, Philadelphia.)

Ralph Earl (1751-1801) may be taken as either the most notable
of "untrained professionals" or the most unskilled of the professional
painters, as you prefer. He was born in one of the hilly interior
townships of Connecticut, which were at this time prolific in painters. His early training is unknown, yet six years in England made
scarcely any impression upon the archaic severity of his Connecticut
style. *Roger Sherman* (ca.1777-1779) (Fig. 6-8), painted before
Earl's journey to London, already shows his mature manner in essence. The gaunt Connecticut lawyer is painted life-size, in dark
russet suit and black stockings, seated in a Windsor chair. The
figure and chair achieve a maximum effect of pattern against a bare

brown background. The effect is one of monumental, rather flat outline and deep tones of russet, black, and brown, with only the face
and hands as light accents. John Adams, who observed Roger Sherman closely in the Continental Congress, noted in his diary that he
was one of those men whose movements are "stiffness and awkwardness itself." Earl's awkward strength of style and the sitter's character combine to make a striking portrait.

Connecticut was full of untrained professionals at this period.
Richard Jennys (active in Boston in the 1770's; in the West Indies;
in Charleston, South Carolina, 1783-1784; and in Connecticut in the
1790's) and William Jennys (active ca.1800-1810) are a confusing

6-10. Reuben Moulthrop: *Bradford Hubbard*
(ca. 1785). (Courtesy of the New Haven Colony
Historical Society, New Haven, Conn.)

6-11. Jacob Eichholtz: *Self-Portrait* (ca. 1805-1810).
(Courtesy of Mrs. James H. Beal, Pittsburgh.)

family of painters known to have been active in the Connecticut Valley. Both seem to have used rather a muted palette, and to have painted human beings with a kind of rigid, psychological intensity of character that is most convincing. The sculptured, melancholy face of *Mrs. Constant Storrs* (Fig. 6-9), painted by William Jennys, seems like the earnest soul of New England looking out at us from the canvas.

Another Connecticut painter of striking psychological power was Reuben Moulthrop (1763-1814). His grave, thoughtful figures, like the portrait of *Bradford Hubbard* (ca.1785) (Fig. 6-10) look upward from under level brows at the observer. Their bodies are drawn in steep perspective, as if the sight of some old Tudor or Dutch sixteenth-century portrait had helped to form the artist's notion of his art.

Such artists were most abundant in New England but are not confined to that region. One finds them in New York State and Pennsylvania—and in the towns along the Ohio River where the population of New England and the Middle States was beginning to pour over the Alleghenies into the empty continent.

In the Middle States Jacob Eichholtz (1776-1842) (Fig. 6-11) of Lancaster, Pennsylvania, represents the art of the back country in contrast to the metropolis. Like Peale, he came into painting by way of the crafts (he was a tinsmith before turning to portrait painting) and his work always retained the flavor of slightly archaic simplicity and severe honesty of spirit that we associate with the untrained professional. Yet he was nearer to the atmospheric style than Earl, for example—as a young painter he went to Boston to learn what he could from Stuart and he was a friend of Sully—so that he occupies a separate niche. His art shows a good sense of character in portraits of the old, an innocent sweetness in portraits of children, and a hard, clean, fresh, luminous style that neither fades nor grows dingy—qualities of an excellent craftsman and an unsophisticated, natural sensibility.

Artists continued to be drawn to America from Europe. The confusion of the French Revolution and the Napoleonic Wars sent many fleeing to the young republic of North America. The story of the migrant painters becomes at this time very picturesque and touching: enthusiasts for Liberty, refugees from the Terror, hapless political exiles, terrified and destitute families escaping from the horrors of the revolt in Santo Domingo, they came for many reasons, both willingly and unwillingly; some remained, others returned to Europe. Among them were many of superior talents and intellectual power: Englishmen such as Robert Edge Pine, Francis Guy, George Beck; Frenchmen such as Pierre Charles L'Enfant and Charles B. J. F. du Saint-Mémin; the Swedish painter Adolph Ulrich Wertmuller; the Swiss Pierre Eugène du Simitière. It is significant of the growth of a native artistic life, however, that these migrants, although interesting and sometimes attractive figures, were now marginal to the

main stream of American painting. The energies and talents of a
new American nation had begun to flow into painting. It is the
fortunes and difficulties of the American-born artists which now
make up the story that concerns us.

In the neoclassic artists' period they became numerous enough to
create an artistic life, for the first time, in an American city. The
city where this took place was Philadelphia. It was not only the
largest city and the first capital, but it had an intellectual life and a
humane tradition of culture. It was, to the neoclassic period, what
New York became with the rise of the romantic movement, the center

6-12.   W. R. Birch: *The Sun Reflecting on the Dew, a Garden Scene,
Echo, Pennsylvania, a Place Belonging to Mr. D. Bavarage* (stipple
engraving). (From Birch's *The Country Seats of the United States*, 1808.)

of activity and focus of talent. The concentration of attention upon human beings, upon their character and their actions, which had characterized the eighteenth century, gradually widened. Men began to look at the earth around them, not solely as the background of their own activities, but as something interesting in itself. After the Revolution, an increasing number of magazines were published in America (apparently we have always been a nation of magazine readers) and there appeared in these, after 1800, a steadily increasing number of landscape engravings. As one looks through their pages, one can watch the topographic interest of the subject slowly recede in importance until the simple contemplation of nature becomes motive enough for an illustration, and the name of the artist is Thomas Doughty or Alvan Fisher.

At about this same time the technique of engraving, which had been very crude, was raised to a new level by a migration of well-trained English engravers, acquainted with both line engraving and aquatint, drawn by the opportunities of the new world. They came to Philadelphia immediately after the close of the War of 1812 and began to lift the standard of reproductive engraving to a good level. One of the first landscape artists of interest was William Russell Birch (1755-1834), a miniature painter and engraver who settled in Philadelphia in 1794. In 1799-1800 Birch issued a series of twenty-eight plates of Philadelphia, a delightful record of the most beautiful of American eighteenth-century cities. In 1808 he brought out *The Country Seats of the United States.* One plate of this bears a significant title, *The Sun Reflecting on the Dew, a Garden Scene, Echo, Pennsylvania, a Place Belonging to Mr. D. Bavarage* (Fig. 6-12). Suddenly we are in a new world. It is no longer the country house but a moment in the life of nature itself that interested the artist: and we are on the threshold of the romantic age.

Landscape engraving, in fact, bridges the gap between classicism and romanticism in American perceptions and, in a land where so few paintings were to be seen, formed an influential source of style for many of the early landscape painters.

The prince of American topographical draughtsmen and aquatint engravers was, however, William James Bennett (1787-1844), who migrated from England in 1816. His nineteen colored aquatints of American cities (issued 1831-1838) were called by I. N. Phelps Stokes the finest series in existence. Bennett's work was done with the transparent realism, the clear lighting and even accent of the classical style, but certainly helped to popularize a taste for landscape that the romantic landscapists were to profit by.

At the same time, wood engraving, to which Bewick had given an entire new impetus in Great Britain, was lifted to a new importance in the United States by Alexander Anderson (1775-1870). Anderson re-engraved Bewick's cuts (*Quadrupeds* and *Emblems of Mortality*) and was a most prolific craftsman. The New York Public Library has his old scrapbooks, containing something like eight thousand proofs of his wood engravings. He made every kind of illustration, from sheet ballads and business cards to scientific treatises and large Bibles. Wood engraving, which could be printed with the letter press, inexpensive, and capable of producing a large number of impressions, was thus started on its great period in America. It was to have countless and often delightful results in the books and magazines of the nineteenth century. With the rise of wood engraving came the rise of illustration.

The widening of the field of attention brought with it genre painting, which is the art of observation of daily life.

The pioneer of genre painting in Philadelphia was John Lewis Krimmel (1787-1821). He was a modest, genial painter with a pleasant humor, who had time to do only a few good pictures, of which a typical example is *A Fourth of July Celebration in Center Square, Philadelphia* (1819) (Fig. 6-13). His career was cut short by accidental drowning at the age of thirty-four.

In Boston another painter also made a beginning at genre. He was Henry Sargent (1770-1845). He painted portraits, did a number of large historical and religious pictures, which he exhibited from town to town and, in the same large scale, painted two interesting genre scenes of Boston upper-class life, *The Dinner Party* (Fig. 6-14) and *The Tea Party* (ca.1815-1820). They are too large in scale either for the subject or for his powers as a painter, but show nonetheless a sensitive perception of light and a good feeling for architectonic composition. These abilities might have led to interesting results had Sargent been surrounded by an active artistic life in Boston to sustain and encourage him. But Boston had at this time only a fragmentary and disorganized artistic activity and most of Sargent's energies were devoted to other things than painting.

6-13. John Lewis Krimmel: *A Fourth of July Celebration in
Center Square, Philadelphia*, 1819. (Courtesy of The Pennsylvania
Academy of the Fine Arts, Philadelphia.)

There had been an interest in still-life painting among the artists
of the latter part of the eighteenth century. Very few pure still
lifes of this early period have been preserved but from about 1810
onward there are many. A Philadelphia school of still life appears,
deriving, as did so many other things, from the unpredictable energies of the Peale family. The two miniature painters, James Peale
(1749-1831) (the brother of Charles Willson) and Raphaelle Peale
(1774-1825), Charles Willson's eldest son, were both active painters
of still life in their old age. Their pictures followed the Dutch and
Flemish model closely; their subjects were a dish overflowing with

6-14. Henry Sargent: *The Dinner Party* (ca. 1815-1820).
(Courtesy of the Museum of Fine Arts, Boston.)

fruit, and a few other objects, set on a tabletop whose fore edge runs across the bottom of the picture, and lighted from one side. Their still lifes combined precise drawing, bright, clear colors, and simple effects of luminosity.

This period also saw the career of one of the greatest of American artist-naturalists, Alexander Wilson (1766-1813). Wilson was an impecunious Scot who emigrated to Philadelphia in 1794 and subsequently developed a passion for the great spectacle of nature in this wild continent. In 1805 he began work on the drawings of birds which became his *American Ornithology* (9 volumes, 1808-1814), both text and illustrations provided by himself. It was his ambition to make it not only a complete record of one phase of nature, but the most beautiful book ever produced in America. This was an enormous undertaking for the slender resources either of the man or of the times. He had to discover, study, draw the birds, and to write their descriptions; then sell subscriptions; see each volume through the press; and pay the bills. Alternately, he would set off on foot across half the continent to make his drawings and to sell his subscriptions; then he would return to Philadelphia to prepare another volume for the press.

As an artist Wilson has been overshadowed by his great successor Audubon. The difference between them is not only one of precedence in order of time, but of temperament and artistic period. Wilson drew with a clear, nervous precision. His plates are arbitrarily composed, but with an admirable sense of pattern, as one may see

6-15. Alexander Wilson: *The Little Owl, or Saw-Whet Owl* (pen and water-color drawing). (Courtesy of the Academy of Natural Sciences of Philadelphia.)

in the plates of *The Nighthawk* or *The Little Owl* (Fig. 6-15). The cool clarity, the freshness, the objectivity of his art are typical of the American neoclassic taste, of which his book is one of the notable productions.

The independence of the United States from Europe, first won by the Revolution, was confirmed by the War of 1812. Peace, coming again in 1814, brought with it an upsurge of national pride and self-confidence. The Federal government, states, and cities rehoused themselves in newly built public buildings. American painters for the first time received official commissions for portraits, or historical subjects, to decorate these public structures.

The greatest demand was for portraits of national heroes. Laurence Park lists 111 likenesses of Washington by Gilbert Stuart; G. A. Eisen in his *Portraits of Washington* (1932) lists 175. Although most of these were bought by individuals, portraits of Washington were also popular as decorations of public buildings. The portraits of military and naval heroes of the War of 1812 commissioned of Jarvis, Vanderlyn, Waldo, and Sully by the city of New York for its beautiful new city hall still hang there, giving an idea of such an ensemble at its best.

The first Federal commission came in 1817. Congress voted $32,000 to Col. John Trumbull to make four enlarged versions of his Revolutionary subjects for the Rotunda of the Capitol in Washington. The subjects chosen were in a pictorial sense the least interesting of the series: *The Declaration of Independence* (1818), *The Surrender of Cornwallis at Yorktown* (1817-1820) (Fig. 6-16), *The Surrender of Burgoyne at Saratoga* (1817-1821) and *General Washington Resigning His Commission* (1824). These are by no means bad decorations: large in scale and pleasing in tone, they are better than popular opinion credits them. But the public had expected too much. There was a great deal of petty, carping criticism of historical details as well as his failure to recapture the freshness of the sketches (now at Yale) made thirty years before. He was not asked to complete the four remaining panels and his failure to please gave a serious check to the ambitions of his fellow painters.

American artists have always longed for public subjects and monumental commissions, partly from a desire for a recognition of their art, partly from artistic ambition. Conflicts with unsym-

6-16. John Trumbull: *The Surrender of Cornwallis at Yorktown* (1817-1820). (Courtesy of the United States Capitol.)

pathetic public opinion were not the only obstacle met by this first wave of mural painting. American Federal architecture, though often monumental in feeling, was not in actuality large in size; it had not as yet created buildings which offer either the need or the opportunity for large-scale decoration. When Benjamin West sent over his *Christ Healing the Sick* in 1816 as a gift to the Pennsylvania Hospital, Philadelphia, a special building, known as the West Picture House, had to be erected for it.[2] Sully's *Washington at the Passage of the Delaware* (Fig. 6-17), painted for the Capitol of North Carolina, proved too large for any wall in the building.

These experiences did not encourage other states to try their luck with anything more ambitious than portraits. It may be, also, that American life was too individualistic to demand a public art: the

[2] An admission fee was charged to see the picture and fortunately not only paid for the building but brought the hospital a profit.

portrait, not the mural, was the form instinctively adopted to commemorate public as well as private memories and affections.

Artists had by this period become numerous enough to attempt to form academies, the institutions created by their profession in the Old World. The Academy in Europe was a professional organization to train young artists and to show its members' work to the public. Charles Willson Peale launched just such an organization, The Columbianum, in Philadelphia. In spite of political dissension among the artists, the Columbianum set up an art school and held one exhibition in the spring of 1795.

Ten years later the Pennsylvania Academy of the Fine Arts was organized. Though formed by a mixed group of artists and laymen, its board of control was dominated by laymen and had the purposes congenial to the community mind: a public building and

6-17.   Thomas Sully: *Washington at the Passage of the Delaware* (1819).
(Courtesy of the Museum of Fine Arts, Boston.)

a collection of great art. These were aims inspired, not by the professional needs of the artist, but by the example of the Louvre, into which had been gathered, in Napoleon's time, not only the magnificent collections of art of the dethroned kings of France but the artistic spoils of Italy and Flanders. A new institution had appeared in Western life, the art museum. The trustees of the Pennsylvania Academy of Fine Arts began its permanent collection by purchasing casts of the classical sculpture in the Louvre and paintings by West, Lawrence, Allston, and other contemporary artists.

It was not then realized (as it is not clearly understood today) that the needs and wishes of the artists are not always identical with the needs and wishes of the public. In Europe academies had been composed of practicing artists, under the patronage of the ruling prince but otherwise independent. An academy dominated by the laymen of the community was a new pattern for such an institution, or rather it was a move toward a new kind of institution serving the public, the art museum, whose nature and function were as yet only dimly realized. This academy, however, took on the sponsorship of a school and an annual exhibition and has continued to fulfill these functions until today.

Philadelphia was then the most active center of the arts, but other cities also formed academies during the first quarter of the nineteenth century—the American Academy of Fine Arts was founded in New York with John Vanderlyn commissioned to buy casts of classical sculpture for it in Paris; the Athenaeum in Boston, a combined art collection and library; the South Carolina Academy of Fine Arts in Charleston. These were all dominated by lay interest and not all survived the inexperience and the lack of resources of the times.

In the neoclassic period American painting assumed a shape and direction it had never possessed before. American energies and talents flowed less into the recreation of an ideal past than did those of European neoclassicism and more into depicting the people and actions our artists saw around them. If neoclassic realism outweighed neoclassic idealism, it is a sign that American painters were at one with their own world. Instead of an artificial and rhetorical art they gave the new American nation so vivid an image of itself, its great leaders, its heroic actions, that to a very large extent we still see ourselves through their eyes. This I regard as imaginative achievement of the first order.

Seven

ROMANTICISM:

THE FIRST GENERATION

THE NEOCLASSIC PERIOD in America began about 1780 and continued until about 1820; but its last two decades overlap the first romantic generation. Vanderlyn, born in 1776, was the youngest and last of neoclassic painters. The generation born in the decades 1775 to 1794, who made their appearance as artists between 1800 and 1820, belong, with the exception of Vanderlyn, to the first generation of romanticism.

Romanticism was a world-wide movement and one of the most creative periods of Western art. It is a protean thing, this affair we call romanticism. Taking a thousand different forms in a thousand energetic minds, it is like the jinn that filled the sky and refused to go back into the bottle; it defies us to compress it into a formula. Its true source was a shift in the direction of attention from the ancient world to other parts of our inheritance, from the clear neoclassic vision of the world to a many-colored and often deeply shadowed perspective. Neoclassicism may be defined as a focusing of attention on logic, clear thinking, and the robust, healthy norm of humanity. It was also a concentration upon order and authority, an esthetic dogma of Ideal Beauty, a preoccupation with antique sculpture and Graeco-Roman mythology at the expense of everything that had happened since the fall of Rome.

In Britain and America, where theoretical rules were never very powerful, the change from one period to the other came as a gradual

alteration of the climate of the mind. There was never occasion for
a war of styles such as occurred in France between neoclassicists
and the men of 1830; for only in France was the problem formal
and stylistic rather than intuitive. In Britain, classical purity of outline became the vehicle of Blake's mystical visions; Flaxman found
the models and poses for his illustrations of Homer in the streets of
London rather than among the sculptures of the Vatican; Lawrence
created the romantic portrait of mood, and Turner the landscape
of mood, within the framework of the Royal Academy. Among
Americans, West was a leader of neoclassicism in the seventeen-
sixties and of romantic melodrama a few years later; Copley's
dramatic narratives present some revolutionary breaks from tradition; while, on the other hand. Allston had his studio full of casts
of classical sculpture and never lost the imprint made by Rome
upon his art.

If this intermingling of two movements within the same period
of time, and even the same men, seems illogical and confusing, it is
not the first time that life and men's dreams have seemed so.

"Poetry," said Byron, "is the expression of excited passion." This
was the mood in which the romantic impulse detached itself from
classicism. Subject matter of the most dramatic kind demanded a
different style, also, from the clear and sculpturesque groupings of
neoclassic art. A new mood and a new manner of painting developed
together.

One of the first painters to lead the way was Benjamin West. With
his usual facility and sensitiveness to new impressions, West, as
early as 1777, painted *Saul and the Witch of Endor* (Fig. 7-1), a
haunting masterpiece of protoromanticism, embodying its fantastic
subject in highly dramatic effects of color and light. Such subjects
gradually become more important in his work. An enormous *King
Lear* (1788) (Boston, Museum of Fine Arts), filled with wild turmoil
on a heroic scale, is one of his most powerful romantic melodramas.
By 1800 this had become the predominant mood of his work.

The subjects of romanticism—excited passions—were in the air.
They crop out in most unexpected places. One might perhaps argue
plausibly that Vanderlyn's *Death of Jane McCrea* (Hartford, Wadsworth Atheneum) is more romantic than neoclassical. And Copley,
the most objective and realistic intelligence in American painting

7-1. Benjamin West: *Saul and the Witch of Endor* (1777).
(Courtesy of the Wadsworth Atheneum, Hartford.)

at that age, drew on one of romanticism's most fruitful sources, Spenser's *Faerie Queene*, for the theme of his curious, dreamlike family group called *Una and the Red Cross Knight* (Washington, National Gallery of Art). There was thus within later eighteenth-century painting a protoromantic movement of fantasy and melodrama. The first generation of romanticism, from 1800 to 1830, inherited its highly wrought mood.

The most important figure of the first romantic generation was Washington Allston (1779-1843), a South Carolinian whose life was spent in Boston, except for two long periods of study and work abroad.

In London, where he studied from 1801 to 1803, Allston learned the coloristic technique of the London studios: the use of under-paint and glazes, of light and color, which was the key to the stylistic development of romantic painting. When he went on to Paris (1803-1804) and Rome (1804-1808) he had a technical instrument that, during the ascendency of neoclassicism, Continental painting had forgotten how to use.[1] In Napoleon's Louvre and in Rome he dis-covered what he wanted to do with this technique. Years later he summed up his impressions of the Venetian sixteenth-century painters in a passage so significant that it is worth quoting here:

Titian, Tintoret, and Paul Veronese absolutely enchanted me, for they took away all sense of subject. When I stood before the *Peter Martyr, The Miracle of the Slave* and *The Marriage of Cana*, I thought of nothing but the gorgeous concert of colors, or rather of the indefinite forms (I cannot call them sensations) of pleasure with which they filled the imagination. It was the poetry of color which I felt; procreative in its nature, giving birth to a thousand things which the eye cannot see, and distinct from their cause. . . . They addressed themselves, not to the senses merely, as some have supposed, but rather through them to that region (if I may so speak) of the imagination which is supposed to be under the exclusive domination of music, and which, by similar excitement, they caused to teem with visions that "lap the soul in Elysium." In other words they leave the subject to be made by the spectator, provided he possessed the imaginative faculty—otherwise they will have little more meaning to him than a calico counterpane.[2]

This passage, with its conception of a picture as an evocation of reverie, is a perfect description of his own later paintings. At first, however, he was governed by the grandiose and dramatic mood. His aim before 1818 was to use the Venetian language of the radiance of light and the resonance of tone, to express visions of the magical, the terrifying, and the mysterious in nature and in the soul of man.

These visions took shape first in a series of landscapes, *The Rising of a Thunderstorm at Sea* (1804) (Fig. 7-2), *The Deluge* (1804)

---

[1] A number of anecdotes told by both Allston and other painters, revealing the novelty of his technique in the eyes of painters in Paris and Rome, are in my *Washington Allston*, Chicago, University of Chicago Press, 1948.

[2] Quoted from a letter to William Dunlap in *A History of the Rise and Progress of the Arts of Design*, New York, George P. Scott and Company, 1834, vol. II, pp. 162-163.

and *Diana in the Chase* (1805), which lifted American landscape painting from the level of simple topography to that of the dramatic landscape of mood. Nature is no longer a backdrop for human life, but a vast experience of tremendous imaginative meaning within which human life exists as an element.

In Allston's figure paintings likewise the clear light, the objectivity, the calm and repose of neoclassical art gave way to a mood of magic. He loved to draw from the Old Testament subjects that lay on the border between the known and unknown, where out of the darkness something makes itself felt upon our psychic life. Two of the most famous of these pictures are scenes from the legends of the Jews, *The Dead Man Revived in the Tomb by Touching the Bones of the Prophet Elisha* (1811-1813) (Fig. 7-3) and *Belshazzar's Feast* (1817-1843) (The Detroit Institute of Arts).

7-2.   Washington Allston: *The Rising of a Thunderstorm at Sea* (1804). (Courtesy of the Museum of Fine Arts, Boston.)

7-3. Washington Allston: *The Dead Man Revived in the Tomb by Touching the Bones of the Prophet Elisha* (1811-1813). (Courtesy of The Pennsylvania Academy of the Fine Arts, Philadelphia.)

7-4. Washington Allston: *The Moonlit Landscape* (1819).
(Courtesy of the Museum of Fine Arts, Boston.)

The aspect of Allston's art most appealing to modern taste is his landscape reveries upon nature. It was his theory, clearly stated in the letter to Dunlap already quoted, that a picture should be full of suggestion: be so rich in overtones of feeling, and so poetic in its use of light and tone, that the observer will find it the starting point for long meditation. As his art grew quieter, the mood of his landscape changed: after the drama of the early works came in his old age a quieter reverie on the notes of wonder and solitude. To achieve this, in pictures like *The Moonlit Landscape* (1819) (Fig. 7-4) or *The Flight of Florimell* (1819) (Fig. 7-5) (The Detroit Institute of Arts), he developed a style of controlled luminosity and deep resonances of tone that set new standards of subtlety and atmospheric richness in American painting. He learned in these pictures to do

7-5. Washington Allston: *The Flight of Florimell* (1819). (Courtesy of The Detroit Institute of Arts.)

what he admired in Venetian painting: to work with atmospheric tone which was also light. He thus found his own way to the new mode of perception which, between 1820 and 1830, became the problem of creation for the most advanced minds in painting—for Constable and Corot, Delacroix and Turner. Allston developed his own technique, a use of underpaint and glazes, to create a diffuse glow of color which is both light and tone, filled with many accents, but fused into an over-all unity.

Allston was not an active teacher: he preferred to live in retirement among his memories and dreams. Yet through the example of his work and through one of his early pupils, Samuel F. B. Morse, who became the first head of the National Academy of Design in New York City, his influence made itself felt. He was the pioneer of an art of mood in America. The note of grave, brooding reverie which he struck became one of the characteristic tones of American painting: in Page and Quidor, Rimmer and Fuller, LaFarge and Vedder, it is heard throughout the nineteenth century. The vein of feeling opened by him proved to be a rich one.

He made still another important contribution when, after wining a distinguished reputation in London, he returned to practice his art in Boston. Stuart had returned, but to practice the art of portraiture, which was already well established here. Vanderlyn and Trumbull had returned from Europe with another, wider conception of painting, but to become bitter, complaining old men, discouragers of the young rather than leaders of a rising profession. Allston's production after his return in 1818 is tragically small, yet he remained a courageous, dignified figure, who lived and worked as an imaginative artist, and gave stature to the profession of painter in American life.

The portrait remained the staple of American painting, both as an economic base and as a disciplined craft, throughout the early nineteenth century. The public wanted portraits and would pay for them: and for the most part would pay for no other kind of painting. When artists painted other types of subject matter, it was to please themselves.

The stylistic development of the portrait was away from the calm, statuesque, clearly lighted neoclassic portrait toward a portraiture of mood. Allston created a highly original portrait form, suggested to him by the gravity and mystery of Titian's portraits. But his mysteriously luminous portraits were done only to please himself, as records of his family and intimate friendships, and had no effect on the general practice. The chief influence came from English romantic portraiture, especially that of Lawrence: dramatic contrasts of light and dark, a graceful flowing movement in the pose, a new interest in touch or brushstroke, and especially the suggestion of a flash of fleeting expression by the emphasis given to the eyes and the corners of the mouth were its chief characteristics.

Thomas Sully (1783-1872) was the leading portrait painter of this generation in Philadelphia. He was in the United States what Lawrence was in England, the creator of a romantic portraiture of mood, elegant, reflective, tinged with sweetness and melancholy, and immensely popular. His masterpiece is perhaps the full-length of *Col. Thomas Handasyd Perkins* (Fig. 7-6), the great China merchant and philanthropist, painted for the Boston Athenaeum in 1831-1832. Sully never surpassed the mingled grace and dignity of this figure. In addition to portraits, Sully painted some five hundred subject pictures, historical compositions, and landscapes during his long life. Many of these are what his own age called "fancy subjects" and appear to us exactly that, for romantic sentiment declined easily into the sentimental. Sully was at his best as a portrait painter. His portraits were always large, easy and decorative in style, sometimes highly perceptive (especially in his earlier years), often romantically pretty. The high level of his portraits and their sheer number (about two thousand) make him the dominant figure in his generation of American portrait painters.

Rembrandt Peale (1778-1860) a son of Charles Willson Peale, was a more complex character. His early work starts from his father's neoclassic style but has an ease and grace of its own. In 1812, piqued by criticism of one of his pictures, he abandoned painting, moved to Baltimore, built the Peale Museum there, and established the first illuminating gas works in that city, thus continuing his father's dual interests. When he returned to painting again in 1820 he produced the most popular painting of the decade, a huge picture (11 feet 6 inches by 23 feet 5 inches) entitled *The Court of Death* (1820) (Fig. 7-7). It is what the artist himself called a "Moral Allegory," based upon a poem by an English clergyman, Bishop Portuns. Death is represented enthroned in a gloomy cave, his feet resting on the

7-6. Thomas Sully: *Col.
Thomas Handasyd Perkins*
(1831-1832).
(Courtesy of The Boston
Athenaeum, Boston.)

body of a man stricken in the prime of life; surrounding him, to right
and left, are his principal agents—War, Conflagration, Famine and
Pestilence, Pleasure, Intemperance, Remorse, Delirium Tremens,
Suicide and an array of deadly diseases. Before the throne Old Age,
supported by Faith, resigned but unterrified, greets the figure of
Death.

This moral allegory was so well addressed to the taste of its time
that the artist earned, in the first year he exhibited it, over $8000 in

admissions; it continued to be exhibited in various cities for half a
century. Although allegory by nature lacks psychological cohesion,
The Court of Death is by no means an inconsiderable painting; it is
monumental, graceful in detail, subtle in its chiaroscuro. Rembrandt
Peale's talents are more easily grasped, perhaps, in the *Self Portrait*
(1828), painted at the age of fifty, to leave with his wife, before his
departure on a voyage to Italy. Sober, incisive, full of life, it shows
Peale's qualities as a romantic realist. Yet his was an uneven talent,
for he produced also some of the worst pictures of his generation.

Samuel F. B. Morse (1791-1872), like Vanderlyn, illustrates the
tragedy of an observer, a realist by temperament, who was carried
away by the theory of an ideal art. Morse brought back from his
years in London an excellent coloristic technique; yet he wandered
unhappily from city to city, up and down the Atlantic coast, in
search of portrait commissions, finally settling in 1824 in New York
city. He was tormented by the feeling that the only work worthy
of a true artist was to create great imaginative compositions. No
one ordered such pictures, however; nor did they come out of
Morse's own mind. He had time and opportunity, during the in-

7-7.   Rembrandt Peale: *The Court of Death* (1820).
(Courtesy of The Detroit Institute of Arts.)

tervals between portraits, to paint whatever he wished. Instead of pouring forth a stream of imaginative compositions he sat idle, and felt unhappy.

Congress Hall (1822) (Fig. 7-8) (Washington, Corcoran Gallery of Art) and *The Gallery of the Louvre* (1832) (Syracuse University, Syracuse, N. Y.), his two large pictures, are vigorous, interesting, sensitively observed examples of documentary realism, and in their own way truly original. He professed great distaste for portrait paintings; yet he could paint delightfully observed and sparkling portraits, like *Mrs. Daniel De Saussure Bacot* (The Metropolitan Museum of Art). His travel sketches of Italy (1832-1834) are pleasing in their transparent romantic realism; the pictures painted from them in the studio tend toward an operatic sentimentalism.

Ultimately his restless mind turned to scientific invention. The idea for the telegraph came to him on his return voyage from Italy in 1832 and, seizing upon it, he exhibited the unhesitating, self-

7-8.   Samuel F. B. Morse: *Congress Hall (The Old House of Representatives)* (1822). (Collection of The Corcoran Gallery of Art.)

confident drive of the man who knows what he wants to do with his
life. After 1837 his invention completely superseded painting and
became the great achievement of his life. Yet he has a place in painting as a romantic realist; in photography, as one of the first Americans to seize upon Daguerre's invention; and in the social history
of art, as the leader of the young romanticists of New York city in
their revolt against Colonel Trumbull.

The first annual exhibition of painting, in 1811, at the Pennsylvania Academy of the Fine Arts, contained not only plaster casts of
antique statues, portraits, and still lifes, but landscape paintings. The
decorative and topographical branches of landscape had been practiced by a number of migrant neoclassic painters from the 1790's
on. The first development beyond these is associated, first of all with
Allston's landscapes of mood, secondly with the beginnings of romantic realism in Thomas Birch (1779-1851), Alvan Fisher (1792-
1863), Robert Salmon (ca.1785—after 1840), and Thomas Doughty
(1793-1856).

The last-named and most important of this group, Thomas
Doughty, was born in Philadelphia and began to draw at fourteen,
but at sixteen was apprenticed to a leather merchant. He taught himself to paint, as an amateur, and did not abandon his leather business
to devote himself to painting as a livelihood until about 1820. Like
Constable, he began to paint because of an intense love of nature.
He was an enthusiastic hunter and fisherman, who found something
in the wooded hills and lonely streams of this country that had to
be expressed. His art never lost the impression of its origin. Each
of his pictures is built out of the emotion of communion with nature.
Usually, although not always, it contains a solitary wandering figure
—a fisherman casting his line in the lonely river, a hunter with a gun,
or a single traveler on the road—which is a symbol of the artist's
own relation to nature. Like the sage gazing at the mountains in a
Chinese landscape, these little figures say to the imagination: it is
good to be here, in this solitary valley, lingering by this stream,
looking at these hills. Whatever else Doughty lacked as a painter
(and he lacked many obvious things), he had this one gift of utter-
ing the poetry of solitude. He was never a strong or well-trained
painter. His style was monotonous in color and naïve in composition.
His pictures are small, unassuming, easily overlooked among the

7-9.   Thomas Doughty: *In Nature's Wonderland* (1835).
(Courtesy of The Detroit Institute of Arts.)

works of later, more attractive, more brilliant men. Yet they have, at
their best, a very personal flavor compounded of their luminous
skies and gentle solitude. A picture such as *In Nature's Wonderland*
(1835) (Fig. 7-9) has something of the quality of Bryant's poem,
"To a Waterfowl," and Doughty, like Bryant, was one of the first
to see this wild and lonely continent as a theme of art.

The landscapes of the early romantic realists are as direct and
transparent in style as they are in sentiment. A simple perspective
from near to far, a development from warm dark foreground to cool
blue distance is their compositional method: their richest develop-

ment is in range of tone. But for the uncomplicated, affectionate contemplation of nature which is their source and reason for existence, these means suffice.

The still-life tradition founded by James and Raphaelle Peale grew and expanded in Philadelphia. Another kind of still-life appeared with Charles B. King (1785-1862) whose *The Vanity of an Artist's Dreams* (1830) (Fig. 7-10) introduced the *thematic* or *story-telling*

7-10.   Charles Bird King: *The Vanity of an Artist's Dreams* (1830). (Courtesy of the Fogg Art Museum, Harvard University.)

still life which was to have an interesting development in the nineteenth century.

When the romantic sense of wonder was turned upon nature, immense vistas were opened to the imagination. John James Audubon (1785-1851) is a peak in the long line of artist-naturalists beginning with Abbé Thevet. Born of French parentage in Haiti and educated in France, in 1804 he came to the United States where, in the fertile, teeming wilderness of the New World, to study and draw birds became an uncontrollable passion. The ruin of his career as a frontier merchant in Kentucky was inevitable. The family migrated to Louisiana, where the idea of basing a new career upon his drawings of birds gradually crystallized.

Audubon had developed his passionate interest in birds in solitude, by instinct. When the scientists of Philadelphia rejected his work in 1824, he realized that there were exacting scientific standards of which he was as yet hardly aware. The hostility of the late Alexander Wilson's successors was a further good fortune for him, for it sent him to England where there was wealth, taste, and interest in nature enough to support him. In 1826 he sailed for Great Britain, with a few letters of introduction and a portfolio of watercolor drawings of American birds as his only capital. The story of what he accomplished in the next ten years—of how he won support for his book, found engravers to produce the plates, sold the subscriptions, acted as his own publisher, painted replicas of his pictures to sell for living expenses, wrote the scientific text and the enchanting essays that lighten it, traveled back and forth to America to complete the series of birds, oversaw the engraving, colored the first plates, and finally brought out, in double elephant folio, *The Birds of America, from Original Drawings, With 435 Plates Showing 1,065 Figures*—is one of the most fantastic instances of talent and energy in the history of American art. *The Birds of America* appeared in four volumes from 1827 to 1838; the accompanying text as the *Ornithological Biography* in five royal octavo volumes, 1831-1839. Taking writings and paintings together, it is a monumental work whose like does not exist (Fig. 7-11).

It is as an artist, not as a scientist, that Audubon is remembered. Scientists distrust the force of emotion one feels in his great plates: they point out that he discovered few new species and had little

7-11.   John James Audubon: *Purple Grackle* (water color).
(Courtesy of The New-York Historical Society.)

interest in classification. But as an artist he drew with a splendid
energy of line to which his clear, fresh, water-color tones give handsome support; his oils are only a translation of this technique into the
richer medium. His aim was to depict fact—the birds of America,
life-size, with scientific accuracy—but his love and enthusiasm for
these strange, wild, lovely creatures, his delight in the splendor and

mystery of nature, make his pictures the most dramatic ever published of birds. Birds, one might say, are his subjects: but his theme is nature—wild, grand, multiplex, and infinitely beautiful.

The generation of 1800-1825, the first of the romantic movement, when compared with the preceding neoclassic generation, seems uneven and inconsistent. It had great ambitions and wide variety of interests (too great and too wide, say its critics), remarkable achievements, great failures, great personal tragedies.

The achievement of this generation is best shown by its two great figures, Allston and Audubon. Worlds apart in their temperaments, ambitions, and styles—the one an explorer of the soul, the other of the world of nature—they are alike only in the excitement, the adventurousness, and the poetry of discovery that filled their vision. It was no inconsiderable generation that produced these two artists and had, in addition, excellent portrait painters and the pioneers of romantic realism in landscape.

Eight

ROMANTICISM: THE SECOND

GENERATION, 1825-1850

THE ROMANTICISTS OF 1800 in all Western countries had been linked still to the neoclassicists by their interest in a monumental and ideal art and by lingering classical enthusiasms. Love of the past and rivalry with it were strong inspirations among the first romanticists; they merely changed their minds about which part of the past it was desirable to revive. For the neoclassicists, the antique sculpture in the Vatican and the Louvre had been supreme. The first romantic painters, with equal passion and delight, studied the great European painting of the sixteenth and seventeenth centuries: this was the past which Delacroix, or Turner, or Allston wished to revive and surpass. To the romantic realists of the next generation the tradition of art meant little. They wished to paint what was before their eyes. And if some of the new men—Cole, Page, or Quidor—were also inspired by the past, as we shall discover, they saw it from a different perspective.

There were potent new elements and inspirations in the America of 1825 making for change. The tone of life itself was radically altered. It was not merely that the old leaders of the republic were dying out and taking with them the lingering traces of eighteenth-century elegance and colonial memories of the days when the United States had been part of the Old World. By 1830 the great tide of settlement was pouring westward. About a third of the American people now lived beyond the eastward face of the Appalachians.

8-1.   George Catlin: *One Horn. A Dakota (Sioux) Chief* (1832).
(Courtesy of the Chicago Natural History Museum.)

In the vast Mississippi Valley, cut off by the mountains from the
eastern seaboard, there had developed a rough frontier society of
pioneers, Indian fighters, and river men; its hero, Andrew Jackson
of Tennessee, was in the White House, the first President to represent the coonskin democracy west of the mountains.

The plantation aristocracy of Virginia, which provided four of
our first five Presidents, had lost the leadership of the South to the
new power of King Cotton in the deep South. In New England and

the Middle States, the families which had made their wealth in ships and overseas trade were transferring it now into factories and mines; the perspective of the manufacturer replaced that of the importer from overseas. And now the terrible issue of slavery arose to dominate the thoughts and inflame the passions of men. Everything seemed to combine to replace the international interests and the classical culture of the past by new and local interests.

The generation that matured men like Lincoln and Emerson cannot be said to have failed to meet the challenge to create a new imaginative life in the vast new land which was growing increasingly remote from European traditions of culture. The country poured its energies into painting, to such a degree that the English critic, Mrs. Anna Jameson, traveling here in 1837-1838, found painters literally everywhere. Most of them were romantic realists, interested to discover and paint the character of what lay before their eyes.

One of their discoveries was the wilderness. To the eighteenth century nature seemed only a background to human life and was most admired when most humanized in gardens or neat plantations, just as human life was admired in its most civilized form, in the classical hero or the polite citizen of the world. In the 1820's a young portrait painter in Philadelphia, George Catlin, saw a delegation of Western Indians passing through on their way to the capital. Twenty years later he looked back upon the impression they made upon him:

In silent and stoic dignity these lords of the forest strutted about the city for a few days, wrapped in their pictured robes, with their brows plumed with the quills of the war-eagle, attracting the gaze and admiration of all who beheld them. After this, they took their departure for Washington City, and I was left to reflect and regret, which I did long and deeply, until I came to the following deductions and conclusions.

Black and blue cloth and civilization are destined, not only to veil, but to obliterate the grace and beauty of Nature. Man, in the simplicity and loftiness of his nature, unrestrained and unfettered by the disguises of art, is surely the most beautiful model for the painter,—and the country from which he hails is unquestionably the best study or school of the arts in the world: such I am sure, from the models I have seen, is the wilderness of North America.

"And," he went on,

the history and customs of such a people, preserved by pictorial illustrations, are themes worthy of the lifetime of one man, and nothing short of the loss of my life, shall prevent me from visiting their country, and of becoming their historian.[1]

Thus, instead of the centers of art in London and Paris, the wilderness had become the inspiration of the artist (Fig. 8-1).

Catlin's career was one expression of a new enthusiasm. Nature, in all senses of the word—landscape, the wild and untamed earth, the life of animals and plants, the instinctive life of primitive men close to earth—came to have a new meaning and fascination.

In 1825 three landscapes in the window of a New York shop caught the eye of old Colonel Trumbull. He bought one for twenty-five dollars; the others were bought by William Dunlap and an engraver by the name of Asher B. Durand. They had been painted in the Hudson Valley by a young artist named Thomas Cole (1801-1848). The older artists were thus the first to recognize the talent of the man who was to be the most conspicuous and popular figure of the new generation.

Before 1825 Cole had been a wanderer. Born in England, he migrated as a child with his family to the frontier in Ohio. An itinerant portrait painter had given him his first impressions of painting; but he was really wholly self-taught. He drifted to Philadelphia, then to New York. In the scenery of the Hudson River he found, at last, the reason for his life. In 1826 he moved to the village of Catskill, on the west bank of the Hudson, where he made his home for the rest of his life on a bluff looking out upon the blue heights of the Catskill Mountains and the grand river sweeping past below. But he ranged widely on foot over the northeastern states with pencil and sketchbook, from the White Mountains to Niagara, making pencil studies from which he painted in the studio in winter. Partly as a result of this method, which makes an artist rely upon memory, and partly from temperament, Cole's pictures struck a new note of both romantic realism and dramatic mood. Each was a lyric of the wild and solemn beauty of the American wilderness. Their success was immediate and extraordinary. In 1829 Cole was able to go abroad and spend three years in England and Italy. On his return he found himself the most conspicuous figure, after Washington Allston, in American art.

[1] George Catlin, *Letters and Notes on the Manners, Customs and Condition of the North American Indians*, New York, Wiley and Putnam, 1841.

One of the best examples of Cole's treatment of the American landscape is *In the Catskills* (1837) (Fig. 8-2), a picture which he never surpassed either in imaginative realism or lyric sentiment. It is based upon his favorite evening walk along the road leading westward from the village, beside Catskill Creek, toward the mountains and the sunset. Tiny figures of a woman and child in the foreground suggest his own wife and baby. It is a picture large in scale, rich in tone, and suffused with reverie, excitement, and inner happiness. The brushstroke is minute in detail, but the details fall into place in a luminous and spacious whole.

Cole belongs to romantic realism but his mind was also saturated with romantic literature. His artistic attitudes were profoundly literary and his greatest popular success came from paintings that express a mood of sentimental melancholy derived from books. This elegiac note of meditation upon the flight of time and the brevity of human life was a fundamental of the romantic spirit. Remember the somber eloquence of Bryant's *Thanatopsis* (1816):

> Go forth, under the open sky, and list
> To Nature's teachings, while from all around—
> Earth and her waters, and the depths of air—
> Comes a still voice—Yet a few days, and thee
> The all-beholding sun shall see no more
> In all his course . . .
>
> So live, that when thy summons comes to join
> The innumerable caravan, which moves
> To that mysterious realm, where each shall take
> His chamber in the silent halls of death,
> Thou go not, like the quarry-slave at night,
> Scourged to his dungeon, but, sustained and soothed
> By an unfaltering trust, approach thy grave,
> Like one who wraps the drapery of his couch
> About him, and lies down to pleasant dreams.

A vaster theme, the death of civilization itself, was expressed in a book which had immense fascination for that day, Volney's *Ruines, ou Méditations sur les révolutions des Empires* (1791). Volney was one of the first European intellectuals to go beyond Italy, or even Greece, and to visit Egypt and Syria where enormous ruins of vanished civilizations stood in solitude among the sands. His reflections

8-2.   Thomas Cole: *In the Catskills* (1837).
(Courtesy of The Metropolitan Museum of Art.)

upon these spectacles, embodied in a now forgotten book, were
one of the elements in popularizing a new attitude toward the past
throughout the Western world.

It had seemed an easy thing to neoclassic thinkers to revive the
forms and the virtues of antiquity, because the ancient world of
Greece and Rome was regarded as continuous with our own. The
world was very young—after all, had it not been created in 4004
B.C. according to the chronology of Bishop Ussher? Therefore, when
Charles Willson Peale in 1801 excavated the first mastodon skeleton,
the men of science had to be convinced with difficulty that it represented an extinct species. The notion that the Creator could allow
one of his own creations to disappear was at first resisted by even
so advanced a mind as Jefferson's. Volney, however, with impas-
sioned eloquence, drew a picture of entire civilizations, dead, vanished, swept away upon the stream of time. The immensities of
time past, the immeasurable perspectives of the earth's history are

today an accepted part of our consciousness. It is difficult for us to conceive with what resistance and revulsion, with what shuddering awe and fearful delight, such ideas were received by men of 150 years ago.

Cole returned from his years 1829-1832 in England and Italy, not only enriched by memories of European scenery but in love with the haunting poetry of past time. In rapid succession he produced a series of allegories based on Volney's theme of the passage of time. *The Course of Empire*, in five scenes, painted for Luman Reed; *The Departure* and *The Return*, painted for William van Rensselaer; *Past* and *Present*, painted for P. G. Stuyvesant; *The Voyage of Life*, in four scenes, painted for Samuel Ward (Fig. 8-3); the last, *The Cross of the World*, was left unfinished at his death. These elaborate allegories were undertaken as commissions for some of the most intelligent and discerning men of that day. They were engraved and, in this form, enjoyed a national popularity. There is no question that

8-3.   Thomas Cole: *The Voyage of Life: Manhood.*
(Munson-Williams-Proctor Institute, Utica, N. Y.)

they were the most popular and successful expressions of Ideal sentiment painted in this generation.

To our minds, after the heroic vision of antiquity of the neoclassicists and the tragic images drawn from the Bible or Shakespeare by the early romanticists, these melancholy allegories of the flight of time seem sentimental and obvious. In comparison with Cole's landscapes they have grave faults; their multiplicity of detail makes them small in scale, instead of monumental as their themes require. Yet *The Voyage of Life* (Fig. 8-3) is a landmark in our cultural history, and landmarks, even if of outmoded design, are not to be ignored; Moral idealism, a brooding upon the mystery of time, the image of life as a dream, were very deep currents in the mental life of the nineteenth century. It was Cole's achievement to feel them and to invent images that expressed them so simply and forcibly that, once seen, they are never forgotten.

The image of life as a dream haunted him. He stated it boldly

8-4.   Thomas Cole: *The Roman Campagna* (1843).
(Courtesy of the Wadsworth Atheneum, Hartford.)

and eloquently in *The Architect's Dream*, painted for the neoclassic architect Ithiel Town. The practical-minded architect did not care for the picture but to the poet's mind of William Cullen Bryant it was a dream-image of the past "such as might present itself to the imagination of one who had fallen asleep after reading a work on the different styles of architecture." It is a striking piece of romantic melodrama and fantasy.

The reverie upon the past is perhaps expressed most sympathetically, for our taste, in what I should call his elegiac landscapes. In 1843, after his second visit to Italy, (1841-1842), he painted a pair of landscapes, *The Roman Campagna* (Fig. 8-4) and *An Evening in Arcady* (Wadsworth Atheneum, Hartford), which are to my eye at the summit of his art. The one represents the long line of the Claudian aqueduct at sunset, stretching across the plain to the Alban Hills. A solitary goatherd pastures his flock beside it in the rosy evening light. The other is a singular fantasy upon the ancient, inexhaustible theme of the Golden Age, set in the evening of a golden day. Both are large, simple, luminous pictures, rich in the deep cello tones of reverie.

Another artist who made a large contribution to the new taste was Asher B. Durand (1796-1886), by his two careers as engraver and as painter. He was older than Cole and had made himself first the outstanding line engraver of his day before turning to painting as a new career.

All through the twenties and thirties, in the pages of the magazines and gift annuals, there appeared numerous plates inscribed "Engraved by Durand," reproducing vigorously and sympathetically the works of Cole, Doughty, Fisher. These engravings, carried through the country in the pages of popular journals, did much to popularize the new landscape school. But perhaps his greatest achievement as an engraver was a projected serial publication called *The American Landscape* (1830) with plates by Durand after American landscape painters (including himself) and text by William Cullen Bryant. Only one number of six plates appeared. The public was not yet ready to support so ambitious a project; but though a financial failure it was an artistic success. The copper line was never used more vigorously by an American nineteenth-century engraver than by Durand in the plates of *The American Landscape*. In feeling

8-5. Asher B. Durand: *Kindred Spirits* (1849).
(Courtesy of the New York Public Library.)

also Durand had left topographic inspiration behind and the theme of his plates became the contemplation of nature for its own sake.

The note of his painting, both in portraits and landscapes, is a romantic realism so simple and transparent as to seem artless, at least to the complex standards of modern taste. *Kindred Spirits* (1849) (Fig. 8-5) is one of his most attractive works and a revealing document for the spirit of romantic realism. It was painted in memory of Thomas Cole in the year after his death and shows Cole, with the poet William Cullen Bryant, standing on a cliff over a stream in the Catskill forest. It is as direct in spirit as Bryant's poetry of nature and although, like the latter, limited in means, it is unforgettable.

Since Durand was trained as an engraver, it is natural that a fine, precise line and a sense of tone should be the basis of his art; yet he had a painter's eye for light. Durand was one of the first Americans to advocate painting out-of-doors, in face of nature; the practice led him toward luminism. His exploration of space and light drew him ultimately to the airy vacancy of *Kaaterskill Clove* (1866) (New York, Century Association), remarkable for its headlong plunge into green-gold airy space and for its joy in solitude.

Durand showed himself an effective genre painter and also did a few allegories in the vein of Cole. But his true gift was for observation. What observation meant to the romantic spirit was, however, poetry. "Nature is a language," said Emerson in his *Journal*, "and every new fact that we learn is a new word; but rightly seen, taken all together, it is not merely a language, but the language put together into a most significant and universal book. I wish to learn the language, not that I may learn a new set of nouns and verbs, but that I may read the great book which is written in that tongue."

In such an atmosphere landscape painting flourished. New York City had the largest group but it was only one of many centers; decentralization was the character of the age. The professional artist, the amateur, and the untrained professional appeared wherever the population spread in its westward course: in raw new cities on the rivers of the interior; in small towns where no artist could earn a living today; in remote corners of the backwoods. It was a period of remarkable flowering of the imaginative impulse, remarkable in its profusion although (understandably enough) not always remarkable in its quality.

One great discovery of romanticism was that nature was an imaginative experience valuable for its own sake, irrespective of a notable or picturesque subject. The second, parallel discovery was that the study of the simple, the humble, the familiar in human life was equally rewarding. It was not necessary to seek for moments of antique grandeur or of thrilling drama: "The meal in the firkin; the milk in the pan; the ballad in the street" were also wonderful to the discerning eye. A fresh, varied, attractive school of genre—the painting of human beings in their daily life—was the fruit of this perception.

American life was never richer in materials for the observer of the humors and flavors of life. The country was extraordinarily diverse,

8-6.   William S. Mount: *The Painter's Triumph* (1836). (Courtesy of The Pennsylvania Academy of the Fine Arts, Philadelphia.)

8-7. William S. Mount: *Eel Spearing at Setauket* (1845). (Courtesy of
The New York State Historical Association Museum, Cooperstown, N. Y.)

for local differences had not been flattened out by ease of travel and
communication. The New England Yankee, the Southern planter,
the Western riverman ("half horse, half alligator, a little touched
with the snapping turtle"), the farmer, the frontiersman, and the
untamed Indian retained their strong individual character.

One of the first and most characteristic traits of romantic genre
was humor mingled with affection; but a strange kind of grand and
solemn poetry is also found, as unexpected as it is noteworthy.

The mixture of humor, affection, and graceful style, which makes
Washington Irving's descriptions of country life on the Hudson River
so enduring, has its parallel in the art of William Sidney Mount
(1807-1868). Mount was born on Long Island and in 1826 he was

one of the first students in the drawing class opened by the National Academy of Design. His early paintings were portraits and religious subjects, but when an illness sent him back to his home, he discovered, as a theme for painting, the charm of the rural life in which he had grown up.

Mount, in Virgil Barker's happy phrase, was an artist singularly at ease in his time. He felt no need to study abroad, no restless craving to see Italy. All that he required for his life's work was what he saw around him in his own little corner of the earth. This does not mean he lacked ambition in his art. He worked hard to discipline his hand and brush to an effective and distinguished style. To expressive drawing he added the charm of luminosity and a transparent simplicity of statement. The result is a series of little pictures that sum up, genially and sympathetically, a moment of life. *Bargaining for a Horse* (1835) (New-York Historical Society), two men talking and whittling beside a tethered horse; *The Painter's Triumph* (Fig. 8-6) (1836); *The Banjo Player* (The Detroit Institute of Arts), in which the only action is the slight, self-absorbed movement of the musician's figure; *Music Hath Charms* (1847), a more elaborate group of four different people enjoying the music of the banjo; or the famous *Eel Spearing at Setauket* (1845) (Fig. 8-7). In each of these, a human being or a group of people act a passing moment of their lives before our eyes. They are not isolated figures: their lives are drawn together psychologically into the unity of an action which they feel and share. This is a very rare achievement in genre painting. Minor genre painters make up for its lack by sentimentality or exaggeration or obviousness of anecdote. Mount, like Irving, was never obvious. He was simple, natural, easy, with a lucidity of style that conceals his skill.

New York City had a number of genre painters who painted the rural life of the East or the streets of New York, although no other of Mount's artistic caliber.

The westward migration of the nineteenth century that peopled this continent and created most of the states and cities of the present United States was a unique experience which has left its traces upon every aspect of American life. A whole group of artists made this national experience of the frontier their theme. The greatest is George Caleb Bingham (1811-1879), whose achievement is one of the mysterious phenomena of the age. Born in Virginia, he migrated at the age of eight with his family to the outer edge of a settlement in Missouri. He had his first glimpse of an artist in the following year when the genial giant, Chester Harding, passed by in search of Daniel Boone, whose portrait he wished to paint. The boy Bingham very early began to copy engravings and to paint with homemade pigments; but he met the obstacles natural to the frontier.

In 1837-1838 he studied for a few months at the Pennsylvania Academy of the Fine Arts in Philadelphia. There he could learn something of the atmospheric style. There were good pictures by West, Allston, Lawrence, Sully to be studied and he evidently absorbed their lessons. He painted portraits in Washington for a few years and returned finally across the mountains to his home in Missouri about 1844. The first fruits of his return to the frontier was one of the most original and striking works of its age, *The Fur Traders Descending the Missouri* (The Metropolitan Museum of Art) with its archaic strength of drawing, its strange smoky yet brilliant color, its air of solitude and mystery. Bingham seems to have had, at a very early date in his career, the idea of becoming the painter of what he later described as "our social and political characteristics." He looked around him in his frontier region and saw what was original yet typical in the life of America: a pair of wild *coureurs de bois* coming down the river with their furs from the Rocky Mountains, bound for St. Louis (he painted this a second time, on a different scale, in a picture in Detroit) (Fig. 8-8); raftsmen playing cards as they floated downstream (Fig. 8-9); a steamboat crew camped on a sandbar, guarding the cargo of their stranded vessel; a farmers' shooting match, or a game of checkers at a crossroads tavern. He delighted in scenes of political campaigns or elections, where the crude, vigorous democracy of the frontier brought out the excitement and passions of these country folk, when they met to organize themselves as communities and to decide the issues of the day.

It is interesting that he should have had the desire to make himself the social historian of his own place and people. His subjects, which now seem beautiful and original, were then as commonplace as is the sight, today, of a filling station attendant putting ten gallons of gas in a car or changing an inner tube. But Bingham saw the grand meaning of the commonplace. What is more extraordinary,

8-8. George Caleb Bingham: *The Trappers' Return* (1851).
(Courtesy of The Detroit Institute of Arts.)

he was able to create, out of his meager experience of pictures and
his own sensibility, a style of great visual poetry—a large and almost
archaic severity of drawing, brilliantly luminous, yet smoky in color,
and extremely subtle in its gradations of light and air. And over all
there is a mood of grandeur and solemnity in his work, as if he
would say to his fellows: This is a heroic age.

Bingham had a remarkable sense of what was grand, essential,
typical. None of the other painters of the frontier could approach
him, either in sobriety and freshness of observation or in talent as
a painter. He was a part of the life he painted. The other painters
of the frontier were Easterners like George Catlin (1796-1872),
whose discovery of the Indians in the streets of Philadelphia has
already been told. They were drawn to the West by the lure of the

picturesque; and the picturesque was what they painted. None the less, their work forms a valuable and entertaining historical record.

One of the most important social changes of the nineteenth century was the rapid increase in the reading public. The birth of popular education and the rise of literacy and political democracy went hand in hand with the rise of the popular newspaper, the periodical magazine, and the novel. But popular reading was also illustrated: the graphic arts were transformed to meet a constantly larger use. Wood engraving began a rapid development. About 1835 lithography took the place of the beautiful but difficult medium of aquatint; and steel engraving came to supplement, but did not wholly replace, engraving on copper. The new techniques, if less rich in tone, were more suited than the older media to the larger editions and more rapid printing of nineteenth-century periodicals.

8-9.   George Caleb Bingham: *Raftsmen Playing Cards* (1847).
(Courtesy of the City Art Museum, St. Louis.)

Like the reading habit, the appetite for illustration grew with what it fed on. Engravings reproduced and popularized the work of serious artists such as Bingham and the romantic landscape painters of the 30's and 40's. At the same time the illustrator, the humorist, the satirist flourished. A broadening flood of black-and-white illustration and chromolithography spreads through the last three quarters of the century. The phenomenon is so familiar that we hardly

8-10.   John Gadsby Chapman: *JGC in His Studio, Rome* (etching, 1881). (Courtesy of The Valentine Museum, Richmond, Va.)

8-11. David Claypoole Johnston: *The Militia Muster* (ca. 1829).
(Courtesy of the American Antiquarian Society, Worcester, Mass.)

notice it: yet it has both artistic results and social implications of
very great interest.

The first notable figure in American illustration was John Gadsby
Chapman of Virginia, whose chief achievement was to make more
than 1,400 of the 1,600 illustrations of Harper's *Family Bible* (1846),
a landmark of American wood engraving whose wood blocks were
engraved with such firmness and delicacy by J. A. Adams that they
seem like copper plates. One sees his qualities in his *JGC in His
Studio* (1881) (Fig. 8-10) (Richmond, Virginia, The Valentine Museum), a late print, showing the genial old artist at work in his
studio in Rome. It is a characteristic example of the mellow, sharp-
eyed spirit that makes Chapman one of the most attractive of our
romantic illustrators.

8-12.   Currier and Ives: *"Rounding a Bend" on the Mississippi.*
(Courtesy of The Old Print Shop, New York.)

David Claypoole Johnston (1799-1865) is noteworthy for his satirical engravings. The drollery of his water-color drawing *The Militia Muster* (about 1829) (Fig. 8-11), for example, wears very well—at least I can never look at it without laughing.

On the most popular level of illustration, the lithograph reigned. The great name here is Nathaniel Currier (1813-1888), who in 1835 established his own shop in New York in association with J. H. Bufford, and brought out his first topical print, *The Ruins of the Merchants Exchange*, after a drawing by Bufford. This was the first of the series of popular lithographic prints on topical, landscape, genre, or sporting subjects, which continued for nearly seventy years. In 1850 he took into partnership an artist, J. Merritt Ives (1824-1895), and after 1857 all the prints issued by the firm bore the imprint "Currier and Ives." Although seldom of very high quality, either as drawings or as lithographs, they form an incomparable storehouse of scenes of American life and the events of the day (Fig. 8-12).

From 1830 to 1860 Italy was the goal of all American artists wishing to study the tradition of their art. They found no strong con-

8-13. William Page: *Mrs. William Page* (1860). (Courtesy of The Detroit Institute of Arts.)

temporary school at work there. They found instead a landscape of great beauty, an atmosphere stimulating and congenial, galleries filled with the inspiring masterpieces of their art, a spur of emulation in the companionship of other artists, a soil rich with the creative life of centuries past. Even in an age of predominant romantic realism there were many artists who needed this experience of tradition.

William Page (1811-1885) was the most complex personality and the most original, experimental stylist of this generation. Page was always an unpredictable and a controversial figure, praised and ridiculed by other artists, attacked and defended by critics. He took up again, through Morse (under whom he studied at the newly

8-14.   John Quidor: *The Devil and Tom Walker* (1856).
(Courtesy of Mr. and Mrs. Lawrence A. Fleischman, Detroit.)

founded National Academy of Design from 1826 to about 1828) Allston's interest in Venetian color and monumentality, to which he added his own peculiarities.

One of his theories was that monumental paintings of ideal subjects should be based upon sculpture—in which nature was already transposed into a new key—rather than upon life. It was a theory that had been a dogma of the neoclassicists in Paris and Rome; and it had been held and practiced with great success by some earlier painters like Poussin and Tintoretto. By Page's generation it had become highly unfashionable: Page not only believed it but gave it his own original twist. At a time when direct painting and a general lightening of the palette were coming into favor, he painted dark, rich pictures like the *Self-Portrait* and *Portrait of Mrs. Page* (Fig. 8-13), of 1860. This, too, was flying in the face of fashion: yet such works show a capacity for original conception and a style of such rich, solemn, monumental gravity as to set Page completely apart from the mass of nineteenth-century portrait painting.

The dreaming, brooding tone of Page's work at its best is gravely impressive. It is a tone heard often, hereafter, among the most solitary and original of our artists, and may be taken as one of the characteristic notes of American painting.

A dreamer of another sort, even more solitary, John Quidor (1801-1881), never enjoyed Page's degree of acceptance. A simple, eccentric soul (by the few accounts we have of him), he earned his livelihood as an artisan-painter, doing banners and fire-engine panels in New York City, while his imagination lived in the earlier New York of Washington Irving's books. The odd, humorous characters of Irving's invention were transposed by Quidor's fantasy, however, to another plane. Irving's imagination was genial: Quidor's pictures have a pungent flavor, compounded of riotous, uncouth *grotesquerie* and the remoteness of dreams. Contrary to modern notions of illustration, the dramatic energy of his drawing and his fantastic invention are so unlike the tone of Irving's art that his pictures are more like independent inventions than literary illustrations.

Quidor the craftsman must have used the flat, bright, ornamental colors of the artisan-painter; yet Quidor the artist used the same technique of underpaint and glazes that Allston and Page had used. His earliest works, in the 1820's, use fairly light color and even tonalities. By the 1850's he was working in the deep brown-gold tonality and the vague, soft glazes of *The Devil and Tom Walker* (Fig. 8-14). As he grew older, he drew further and further into an ideal world of shadows.

The tendency away from the monumental interests of the previous generation is very well shown by the second series of decorations in the Capitol at Washington. Trumbull had filled four of the eight panels in the Rotunda (1817-1824). The remaining four blank walls were a mute challenge to complete the set; and eventually they were assigned, in 1836, to John Vanderlyn, R. W. Weir, J. G. Chapman, and Henry Inman. The panels of the first three were installed in 1846. Both artists and public received Vanderlyn's *Landing of Columbus* (1842-1844) with disappointment. Weir's *Embarkation of the Pilgrims* (1837-1840) and Chapman's *Baptism of Pocahontas* (1837-1842) were respectable but did not capture the imagination. As one looks at them today, the change in scale and conception between Trumbull's works and these is striking. Trumbull's panels are decorations by a man who had at least some notion of monumental painting. The next three look like romantic book illustrations blown up to gigantic size.

Ill health and the pressure of portrait painting prevented Inman from doing his panel: after his death in 1846 there was a scramble for the vacant commission. Congress gave the contract to William H. Powell (1823-1879), a young man of twenty-four, whose qualifications were that he hailed from Ohio, a populous state whose congressmen thought that the artists of the Queen City of the West, Cincinnati, should get one of these commissions. Powell went to Paris and spent five years, 1848-1853, on *The Discovery of the Mississippi River by De Soto*, which, although it hangs in the Rotunda and clearly represents a great deal of trouble, has not caused anyone to remember his name. This ended that chapter in the public patronage of painting by Congress.

In spite of the variety of new interests which enriched American painting in this generation, portrait painting remained the staple and main support of the painters' profession. The sheer bulk of work makes it difficult to report, for, in great numbers, portraits are monotonous and their merits tend to be lost in the mass. How-

8-15. Henry Inman: *Self-Portrait* (1834). (Courtesy of
The Pennsylvania Academy of the Fine Arts, Philadelphia.)

ever the significant portraits of the time may be divided into groups:
on the one hand those done by professional painters in the great
centers, like New York, Boston, Philadelphia, Baltimore, or Richmond, who were distinguished craftsmen and produced a portraiture
of solid character and decorative dignity; the work of the untrained
professionals; finally, the naïf painters.

In New York City, Henry Inman (1801-1846) was looked on in
his own time as the leading American portrait painter. He was
active in New York City except for three years in Philadelphia
(1831-1834) and a visit to England in 1844. Inman was a broad,

8-16. George Peter Alexander Healy: *Mrs. John Church Cruger*
(1842). (Courtesy of The Metropolitan Museum of Art.)

rapid, direct painter. One of his most attractive portraits is the *Self-Portrait* (1834) (Fig. 8-15) in a yellow top hat, painted at a single sitting to show three young Philadelphia artists how he worked. Inman was a good-humored man and his genial view of humanity is evident in the calm and amiability of his portraits; that of *Georgianna Buckham and Her Mother* (Boston, Museum of Fine Arts) is an excellent example.

8-17.   William J. Hubard: *Horatio Greenough in His Studio in Florence*
(1838-1839). (Courtesy of The Valentine Museum, Richmond, Va.)

After the death of Inman, Charles Loring Elliott (1812-1868) became the leading portrait painter of New York City. He was an excellent observer of character and a painter who used oils in a solid, free, painterly way. His work is interesting and often distinguished, forming an invaluable gallery of the Knickerbocker poets, painters, and celebrities.

William Page's portraiture, the most distinguished of all, has already been discussed.

In Boston also there were men capable of distinguished portraiture. One who belongs by date of birth to an earlier generation was Chester Harding (1792-1866). Harding was a genial giant of a frontiersman, renowned (like Lincoln) as an axeman, barely able to read, and ignorant of any book but the Bible. Yet having once discovered his art, he made himself an able (if uneven) painter whose portraits have the bluff, objective honesty one might expect. His full-length portrait of the great New England philanthropist, *Amos Lawrence* (Washington, National Gallery of Art), is perhaps his masterpiece.

George Peter Alexander Healy (1813-1894) was a precocious youth who established himself as a portrait painter in Boston at the age of eighteen. Healy's success as a portrait painter was extraordinary: he painted most of the great and famous people of two continents during his lifetime but his best work was done in the first half of his life, before the influence of the camera made itself felt in a disagreeable dryness of drawing and insipidity of color. At his best, Healy could paint the grace of a young woman, as in the *Mrs. John Church Cruger* (1842) (Fig. 8-16), or the force of a masculine personality, as in his *John Tyler* (dated 1864 but based on a study of 1842) (The White House), with very happy eloquence. But he was uneven; the bulk of his work is dry and tiresome.

In Philadelphia, John Neagle (1796-1865), who married Sully's stepdaughter, was, with his father-in-law, the chief portrait painter of the city before the Civil War. His admiration for Gilbert Stuart was a strong influence upon his art: but Neagle was, alas, a monotonous painter.

In Richmond there was a much more interesting personality, William J. Hubard (1807-1862). Born in England, he came to the United States as a boy, and first appeared as a child prodigy, cutting silhouettes "by the hundreds in the Hubard Gallery in Boston" (1825-

1826)[2] under the management of a man named Smith. In 1830 Hubard was in Philadelphia and later he traveled in Italy. A souvenir of this trip is the portrait of *Horatio Greenough in His Studio in Florence*, painted about 1838 or 1839 (Fig. 8-17), in which the sculptor, then at the height of his fame, appears as darkly romantic as the hero in a tale by Edgar Allan Poe.

This generation gave us a strong, firmly drawn and plastic portraiture, whose aim was character. For the most part it was an art of romantic realism marked by an admirable lucidity and directness. William Page, on the other hand, and occasionally other portraitists such as Hubard created a romantic portraiture of mood.

[2] Swan, *The Athenaeum Gallery,* 1827-1873.

8-18.   Jeremiah P. Hardy: *Catherine Wheeler Hardy and Her Daughter* (1842). (Courtesy of the M. and M. Karolik Collection, Museum of Fine Arts, Boston.)

The phenomenon of the *untrained professional* continued to lend its distinctive note also. An example of a true and sensitive artist outside the norm of the professional painter's practice is Jeremiah P. Hardy (1800-1888) who worked as a portrait painter in the towns of Hampden and Bangor, Maine. In the Karolik Collection of the Museum of Fine Arts, Boston, are two of Hardy's portraits of his own family. *Catherine Wheeler Hardy and Her Daughter* (Fig. 8-18) (1842) shows his wife and little girl on a sofa before a window looking out upon the Penobscot River; *Mary Ann Hardy* (1821) shows a little girl in a white dress with a moss rose clutched in one small hand. These pictures have little to do with the atmospheric-plastic technique of Samuel F. B. Morse, from whom Hardy is said to have had a little instruction in New York. Along with a certain flatness and a tentative quality of technique that marks the untrained, his pictures have certain very positive esthetic qualities: very exact observation, expressed in a curiously beautiful quality of outline; luminosity of tone; and a strange mood of loneliness, and melancholy.

There were a great many other untrained professional portrait painters throughout the country working on Hardy's level of professional skill—too many to attempt to mention—but none who show the same degree of poetry.

But what is really most extraordinary in these decades was the popularity of the visual image. This showed itself most strikingly in the immense wave of portrait painting, yet was by no means confined to it. Painters like Thomas Cole became national figures: his untimely death was spoken of as a public calamity. Illustrated books and magazines became more and more popular. Framed engravings or lithographs were on every wall. Painting was practiced not only by well-trained professional painters in the larger cities, but by the untrained professional, the self-taught, the amateur, in every corner of the land. In sheer mass and enthusiasm, the production of self-taught and amateur painters reached its highest point in the decades from 1825 to the Civil War; although it never quite reached the level of artistic quality attained by the untrained professionals of the preceding fifty years.

Two conclusions may be drawn. One is that the intuitive, undogmatic nature of romanticism produced a very favorable climate for the growth of popular art. Its inspirations rose spontaneously. No esthetic dogma separated the leading professional artists from the interests of the general mass of men; consequently the amateurs and the gifted naïf could feel the strong, warm, magnetic pull of active and gifted minds drawing them generously onward. Romanticism spoke to, and stirred, our whole population as no esthetic or imaginative movement has done since. Secondly, it is clear that painting, after a slow, difficult growth of generations, had struck root. It flourished as a craft; it filled a deep-seated need for the visual image; it was a popular enthusiasm.

It is beyond the perspective of this study to offer a survey of American naïve and popular art. This is predominantly an anonymous phenomenon. A great many of even the most interesting canvases are by unknown makers.[3] In this field, however, there are two men who throw light upon deeper bases of popular feeling.

Edward Hicks (1780-1849) was born of Quaker stock in the fertile farming country of Bucks County, Pennsylvania, in the bend of the Delaware River north of Philadelphia. He was a sign and carriage painter by trade. In his trade he learned the artisan's technique of painting, the flat decorative colors and careful lettering and the use of gold leaf; he had also the artisan's attitude toward originality, that to follow a design by some other hand was natural and normal. But his art sprang from his inner life rather than from his craft.

Hicks's popularity today rests largely upon his *The Peaceable Kingdom* (Fig. 8-19), illustrating the prophecy in the book of Isaiah, Chapter 11, of the lion lying down with the lamb. More than a hundred of these exist, often with scriptural texts carefully lettered across the bottom or around all four sides. He painted them to give to his friends as expressions of his simple Quaker faith in the peace of God, and hope for Peace on Earth. He devised stock patterns of all the animal types mentioned by Isaiah (arranging them differently in each picture); and paraphrased Isaiahs' prophecy in verses, which he had printed on cards, for presentation with the pictures. Probably no one would be more surprised than Hicks, if he were alive today, to find that these pictures expressing his gentle Quaker piety and

[3] The reader must consult the specialists, such as Holger Cahill, Jean Lipman, Edith Halpert, Nina Fletcher Little, Alice Ford, and the numerous excellent picture books and museum catalogues in the field for a detailed survey.

intended for his rustic fellow religionists on the farms of Bucks county, a hundred years later fitted exactly the taste of the advanced artists of the 1920's and should become collectors' items in the thirties and forties: yet naïveté, intense conviction, and decorative charm are true artistic qualities and the taste for stylized forms and for the childlike in feeling found an appealing forerunner in Hicks.

While Hicks spoke for the earnest piety of rural America, Erastus Salisbury Field (1805-1900) spoke for its love of the American Republic. He was a rustic portrait painter of the untrained professional sort, in the Connecticut valley. His portraits were no better than a hundred others; the Biblical subjects he occasionally painted were as naïve as Hicks's. But in the 1870's, when the centennial of Independence came around and the Centennial Exposition in Philadelphia became a landmark in American life, the old painter produced his own celebration. On a canvas nine by thirteen feet, he painted a *Historical Monument of the American Republic* (1876) (Springfield Museum of Art), an architectural fantasy so strange, so ingenious, so labored and absurd that it succeeds in expressing, with a genuine and touching eloquence, the love and visions of grandeur that filled his simple mind.

Another sign that painting had struck root in American life was the growth of public institutions devoted to art.

The Pennsylvania Academy of the Fine Arts in Philadelphia was the first to be successfully established. From 1775 to 1825, Philadelphia had been the creative focus of American art. It was the home of the activities of Charles Willson Peale and his family, the organization of the first successful academy (1805) and annual exhibitions (1811), the rise of still life, genre, and landscape, the center of the best engravers.

After 1825 New York began to assume an importance in the arts it had never possessed before. The best of the younger artists, who were to be the leaders of American painting from 1825 to 1850, were there. The rise of New York as a port of entry for European goods was paralleled by its rise as a point of traffic in ideas. The opening of the Erie Canal in 1825 made it the gateway to the interior of the continent. Journalism and book publishing more and more were deserting their old home in Philadelphia; the muse of painting for the most part deserted Boston after the death of Allston. The book

8-19.   Edward Hicks: *The Peaceable Kingdom*.
(Courtesy of Mrs. Holger Cahill, New York; photograph courtesy of
The Museum of Modern Art.)

and magazine publishers carried the engravers with them to New
York: and painting, in the second generation of romanticism, was to
become very closely linked to engraving. The men, the organizations,
and the opportunities in painting after 1825 were increasingly to be
found concentrated in New York City.

The American Academy of Fine Arts had been revived in New
York City in 1816 with most laudable motives. When De Witt Clinton
retired as president in 1817, it seemed natural to elect the dignified,
famous Colonel Trumbull, lately returned from London. But Trumbull's irritable temper led to difficulties with the younger artists.

In the spring of 1826, a group of the younger men organized themselves as the National Academy of Design, with Morse as president,

and held their first exhibition of painting. The group gradually established themselves as the first strong, progressive institution managed wholly for and by artists in the United States. The National Academy of Design attracted all the best of the younger men: for they found in it not only a school but an annual exhibition in which they could make their reputations. The older American Academy struggled on for a few years, but finally collapsed. A fire completed the ruin of the institution; its remaining casts were bid in by the National Academy of Design. An attempt to turn Luman Reed's collection of paintings into a New York Gallery of Fine Arts also failed, and the idea of a permanent public gallery of art was not revived until after the Civil War.

In Philadelphia, The Pennsylvania Academy of the Fine Arts carried on its three-part program of school, gallery, and annual exhibition with dignity and success. The artists resented its control by laymen and in the 1840's attempted to form a rival organization of their own. After a few years this disintegrated, leaving the field once more to the Academy. But Philadelphia, although still the home of good painters, was no longer the leading center of the art.

Some of the small cities also made a beginning: Hartford, in Connecticut, acquired the Wadsworth Atheneum in 1844 as the gift of Daniel Wadsworth. The Albany Gallery of Fine Arts was founded in 1846. The Trumbull Gallery at Yale College, in New Haven, opened in 1832, owed its existence to the enthusiasm of a single individual, Trumbull's devoted nephew-in-law, Professor Benjamin Silliman. Moved partly by a just estimate of the historical significance of Trumbull's life work, partly by sympathy for the man, he raised funds to give the old painter a life annuity, in return for which all works of art in Trumbull's possession were given to Yale.

In the West, beyond the Appalachians, new cities were rising overnight along the great riverways. The extraordinary diffusion of the arts meant that artists of some sort were at work in every state, every city, almost every county. But although Cincinnati and St. Louis had little colonies of painters, the artists were on the whole too widely scattered through the vast distances of the interior to create and support institutions of their own.

Distance, lack of population, lack of means, are old, familiar enemies, which Americans have constantly throughout their history used their ingenuity to overcome. The answer for a time, so far as painting was concerned, was found by one original and highly successful device that grew almost overnight into our first national institution of art.

James Herring, an engraver in New York City, began as a commercial venture what was first called the Apollo Association (1838) and afterward the American Art Union (1842). In essence, it was a lottery, open to all who paid a membership fee, the prizes being works of art. The winners of the drawing, which was held with some ceremony once each year, received one of a number of oil paintings purchased by the Art Union for that purpose; while every subscriber received an engraving made from some American painting of popular interest, such as Bingham's *Jolly Flatboatmen* or Cole's *Voyage of Life*. The Art Union's success was enormous. Its subscribers rose to nine thousand (sixteen thousand in the year that *The Voyage of Life* was distributed) and were found in every remote corner of the land. Before it went out of existence, the Art Union distributed some 150,000 engravings and 2,400 paintings, by more than two hundred and fifty artists. It also published a *Bulletin* and *Transactions*, sent to the members, which may be called the first journals of art in this country. The impact of its activity was very great. It created for the first time a national audience for the artists of America. Philadelphia, Boston, and Cincinnati started Art Unions upon the same lines, which were also successful on a smaller scale.

This prodigiously successful institution was ended by the jealousy of artists. The National Academy of Design, although it did not formally protest, felt that its success was threatened by this rival; certain artists, who felt that they were not so much favored as others, helped initiate a legal suit which led to a court decision, outlawing the Art Union as a lottery. All the Art Unions thus came to an end in 1852; and once again artists were dependent on sales from their studios, or from the three annual exhibits in Philadelphia, New York, and Boston, until the rise of the art dealer's gallery in the second half of the century.

Nine

THE CLOSING PHASE

OF ROMANTICISM:

THE GENERATION OF 1850.

LUMINISM, NATURALISM, AND

SENTIMENTALISM

AMERICAN PAINTING was, in the true sense of the word, a popular art in the generation of 1850. Its interests—landscape, genre, portraiture —were those of its public. Its style was simple, transparent, and easily grasped. The esthetic problems that interested painters led toward heightening and deepening the common consciousness rather than breaking away from it. Imaginative painting was surrounded by, and supported by, flourishing crafts of portrait painting, illustration, and engraving. The public appetite for pictures seemed inexhaustible. The style of interior decoration (always a formidable influence) for a brief time called for pictures and more pictures, hanging them in row above row in the drawing rooms of the fashionable and the parlors of the comfortable. If means were not available for paintings, engravings took their place.

It was not the period of our greatest art: but it was the most fortunate period for the artist. Prosperity for a brief moment touched him with its golden wand: he could not only earn a living by the practice of his art; he might even become rich by it. Such a phenomenon, brief though it was, deserves our curiosity.

The interest in landscape had a strong influence upon all other branches of painting, for everywhere in the Western world painters were becoming more and more interested in light. Painting out-of-doors made them conscious of the higher luminosities of sunlight, far up the scales of tone and hue, beyond the sober palette that painters were then using. The movement toward luminism and toward a higher key began first among the romantic landscapists. It produced in Europe a break with accepted practice and a war of styles. American luminism presents a different history in the generation of 1850. Its struggle was against its own inner uncertainty. American painters, having not yet formed a strong, coherent national tradition of style, groped their way forward by individual experiments, not all great or even successful, yet tending toward a common goal: nature, and how she should be portrayed.

Nature is vast beyond the reach of human powers to observe or comprehend. Any period when men strive to assimilate into art new aspects of this all-embracing and elusive infinity is always a time of flux and variety. But in addition to the search of nature (as if this were not enough) three other violent sources of change came bursting into the artist's quiet workroom.

One was the influence of the newly risen science of chemistry, which, within little more than two generations, transformed the medium with which the artist works. In addition to the simple earth and vegetable pigments that had been on the artist's palette since painting began, a veritable rainbow of new chemical paints of a most attractive gaiety became available.

The year 1856 is a landmark in the history of the painter's medium. It is the year of the discovery of the first coal-tar color, mauve, by an English chemist named W. H. Perkin, later knighted in recognition of his work as founder of the gigantic, modern, coal-tar dye industry. Chemistry had begun the transformation of the artist's pigments even before this time. Prussian blue, discovered in 1704, was the first chemical color. The early nineteenth century brought in a series of powerful new greens, blues, and yellows: cobalt green and cobalt blue, zinc white (instead of lead white), chrome green and chrome yellow, all early in the century; emerald green in 1814; artificial ultramarine, in 1826, to replace the expensive pigment made of crushed lapis lazuli from China or Tibet; *éméraude* green in 1834; cadmium yellow about 1846 (thirty years after the discovery of cadmium in 1817).

After 1856 a series of sharp new reds and purples flared upon the artist's palette. Mauve, the first coal-tar color, was quickly followed by magenta and cobalt violet (1859) and cobalt yellow (about 1861). In the next few years most of the ancient mineral colors and practically all the organic colors gave way to new synthetic products. Some of these proved to be fugitive and quickly faded, others blackened in chemical combination with other pigments, but all were new, brilliant, and irresistibly tempting to the artist's eye.

In America, where a strong discipline of style had not yet been created, it was inevitable that painters should be not only betrayed by the chemical impermanence of these new colors, but confused by the novelty. The average picture of the sixties was more highly colored than that of the forties. But the harmony was lost. The problem of style was to find a new harmony, balance, economy, among so many novel and confusing possibilities.

The second great outside force was social change. In the United States, as in Europe, the middle of the nineteenth century saw the rise of a new middle class, enriched by the Industrial Revolution, and very powerful after 1850 in the patronage of the arts. This new class of patrons of art was wealthy but untraveled. It represented the simple outlook of an age before rapid travel and communication had begun to break down barriers and dissolve insularities. It was untouched by classical education. Its tastes were simple, pious, and domestic. It valued easily understood subject matter, sentiment and meticulous execution (qualities by no means bad for painting, provided imagination, style, and power are also present), and was prepared to pay lavishly for them. The artists so fortunate as to please it died rich.

A third external force was the growing influence of the camera. It was used at first by a few gifted men who made the early days of photography exceptionally interesting. If we find so much pleasure in the sober power of fact, the earnest severity of the photographs of David Octavus Hill, Brady, Nadar, and the other pioneer photographers, how must they have impressed the eyes of painters to whom all this was absolute novelty? The question answers itself: we know that painters of every shade of temperament were fascinated and deeply impressed.

If we add to these formidable circumstances the fact that the terrible tragedy of four years of civil war, 1861-1865, cut across the lives of this generation, one may understand why the story of American luminism and naturalism in the years after 1850 is confused and difficult to tell. It does not resolve itself into one or two familiar names or movements but was complex, experimental, diverse, and much of its work was left as unfinished business for the next generation, which forgot all about it.

In 1863 the irritable but highly intelligent James Jackson Jarves, writing on the condition and prospects of art in America, considered landscape to be the one real achievement of American painting.[1] Let us take his opinion as guide and begin with the landscape painters.

There were two main roads of the exploration of nature. One was luminism, an exploration of light; the other was naturalism, a passionate faith in nature as the key to art.

Luminism was an intuitive search by American painters for a style of light, growing out of the tonal painting of the thirties and forties. It is an entirely different phenomenon from American *Impressionism*, which begins twenty or thirty years later. American Impressionism was a struggle to adapt an already perfected style, worked out by the French Impressionists, to a different landscape and a different temperament. *Luminism* was a struggle to find a style, to express a growing but as yet uncrystallized intuitive vision. American painters (like their colleagues all over the Western world) felt a mysterious tide of interest in light that, in the fifties and sixties, dominated the direction of artistic development. Luminism grew up within romantic realism, gradually altering it more and more into a style of light. I group under this heading landscape painters like Kensett, Whittredge, Sanford Gifford, and a number of others less well remembered.

As an example of the rather delicate bouquet of American lumi-

---

[1] *Fine Arts Quarterly Review*, I (1863), p. 393 ff. The landscapists he mentioned were Cole, Church, Bierstadt, Kensett and Gifford, Colman and Inness, Hunt, Vedder, La Farge, Dana, and Babcock.

nism let us take John Frederick Kensett (1816-1872). Born in Connecticut, he was taught engraving by both his father and his uncle, Alfred Daggett, a bank-note engraver of New Haven. His style never lost the quality of clear, delicate line and precise spacing gained from this training. In New York City he met Durand, Casilear, and Thomas P. Rossiter and in 1840 went to Europe with these older men to study the European galleries. He worked for one winter in Paris as an engraver, then went to England, where he remained two years.

"My real life commenced there," he wrote to Henry Tuckerman, the historian of this period, "in the study of the stately woods of Windsor and the famous beeches of Burnham and the lovely and fascinating landscape that surrounds them."

Returning to Paris, he sketched in France for a short time; then with Benjamin Champney, another American painter, made a long sketching tour, on foot, up the Rhine, through Switzerland, to Italy. He took a studio in Rome with Thomas Hicks and lived there two years, making long sketching tours in the summers through southern Italy. Finally, he returned to America by way of Venice and a journey through Germany. When he returned to New York at the end of 1847, his paintings sent from Italy to the exhibits at the National Academy of Design had already made his reputation.

Kensett's European experience is worth recounting in detail because it is typical of a whole generation. The art student of the forties and fifties went abroad not to learn the style of one man, or one school (Düsseldorf was a temporary phenomenon and painters soon learned better), but to learn about art from travel, from pictures, from the life of many cities, and from the landscape itself. A generation later the increase in numbers was to produce great factories like Julian's in Paris for grinding out art students; but in Kensett's time the American art student abroad was on his own in the world of galleries and artists' studios.

Kensett's art required for each picture a fresh observation of nature. Each picture is based upon its own place, time, and point of view, carefully and exactly observed (Fig. 9-1). Therefore, although making his home in New York City, he traveled widely in search of new impressions: the Adirondacks and White Mountains; the rocky New England coast; the wide marshes of Long Island; the Catskills and the Hudson River; even the upper Mississippi and the Western mountains furnished his subject matter. Yet all his pictures strike a very consistent and personal note. In drawing they are small and precise, in arrangement clear and well ordered, as one might expect from one trained as an engraver. The bright new pigments did not interest him. His painter's eye for light found its tools in delicate aerial tone and transparent depths of space, modulated in simple gradations, rather than in gaiety of hue. Whatever the subject, his works are filled with a sense of solitude and space. The mood is pensive, often tinged with melancholy, but clear and tranquil. His is a quiet art, narrow in range, but sensitive and, to me, delightful.

Worthington Whittredge (1820-1910) represents another type of luminism. He was born on a pioneer farm in the forest of southern Ohio; but he was drawn by some mysterious attraction, like a bee

-1.   John Frederick Kensett: *River Scene* (1870).
Courtesy of The Metropolitan Museum of Art.)

9-2.   Worthington Whittredge: *The Trout Pool.*
(Courtesy of The Metropolitan Museum of Art.)

to honey, to Cincinnati, where there were artists. There he became an excellent landscapist, in style even then possessing an understanding of light as the great source of poetry. He spent ten years abroad, but he returned doubting the desirability of long foreign study for an American. On the first day after his return to America he went to the galleries of The New-York Historical Society to see Cole's *Voyage of Life* and *Course of Empire* and Durand's *Thanatopsis*. "I may have been a little nervous, I cannot say, but when I looked at Durand's truly American landscape, so delicate and refined, such a faithful if in some parts sombre delineation of our own hills and valleys, I confess the tears came to my eyes." One cannot understand the American romantic landscapists without knowing that they felt such an identification of themselves with their own land and sky.

Whittredge painted broadly and atmospherically, using luminosity and subtle range of tone as his medium; color he used soberly and sparingly. His art is remarkable for a limpid self-effacement; a sensitiveness to the life of nature; an understanding of the character of a place, a season, an hour of the day. In the details of his landscapes, one sees that things are studied and understood, as well as felt. A tree is a strong column that really grows out of the ground and spreads delicate, flexible branches in air as in *The Trout Pool* (Fig. 9-2). These are the virtues of the best romantic realism, and not small virtues; Whittredge created, in addition, his own quiet poetry of light, his distinctive note of silence and repose.

As a remarkable example of *naturalism*, we may take the painter F. E. Church (1826-1900). His landscapes, too, are filled with light, not only of the sun, but of an intellectual vision. In the early nineteenth century, the vast, unrolling, apocalyptic vision of nature opened by the pioneers of science seemed like one of Church's own early landscapes—the earth at dawn, seen from a mountain top from which one looks out over a sea of mist beyond which the sun is rising, tinging the dissolved wreaths of cloud, and rocks, and trees with rose. It was a heroic and inspiring vision, which Church tried heroically to translate into landscape painting.

From the first Church showed a better sense of light and tone than his teacher, Thomas Cole. He studied skies, and light, and atmosphere, painting wide views of hill and valley, or dawn or dusk seen from some lonely height in the Catskills. He was endowed with a phenomenal skill of hand and, in his earliest pictures, achieved an admirable unity of light and vigor of tone, in spite of an engraving-like sharpness of detail. His *Sunset* (1856) (Utica) and *Morning* (1856) (Albany) are remarkable examples of this phase.

In 1852 appeared the *Personal Narrative of Travels to the Equinoctial Regions of America* of the great German naturalist, Alexander von Humboldt. Humboldt's speculations, written in his study

9-3.   Frederick E. Church: *Housetop in Ecuador* (1857). (Courtesy of the Cooper Union Museum.)

9-4. Frederick E. Church: *Niagara* (1857).
(Courtesy of The Corcoran Gallery of Art.)

in Berlin as he mused upon Andean landscapes visited forty years before, became a challenge to the young American in Catskill, New York. They fired Church to test himself against that Andean landscape, and to make himself the great artist-explorer of his time. He made two trips to Ecuador, in 1853 and in 1857; in 1859 he went to Labrador to study icebergs;[2] in 1865 he visited Jamaica; and in 1868 he went to Europe and the Near East, not to study picture galleries, but the Bavarian Alps and the landscapes of Greece, Syria, and Palestine.

His traveling sketches (a profusion of which are preserved at Cooper Union), done in oil on paper, are little miracles of observation, tone and light—often anticipating by twenty years the qualities of Winslow Homer (Fig. 9-3). Inspired by a passionate quest for knowledge, he really learned his subjects until his mastery of the inner structure and life of each facet of nature—a tree, a rock, a dawn sky, a floating iceberg—is like the knowledge shown by the great Chinese landscape painters. His large compositions, built in the studio from these sketches, are less satisfactory. He aimed to

[2] His traveling companion, Louis Noble, described this trip in *After Icebergs with a Painter* (1861).

9-5. George Inness: *Peace and Plenty* (1865).
(Courtesy of The Metropolitan Museum of Art.)

create impressions of the grandeur and awe-inspiring power of nature in *Niagara* (1857) (Fig. 9-4), *Cayambe* (1858), *The Heart of the Andes* (1859), *Cotopaxi* (1862), *Aurora Borealis* (1865), *Jamaica* (1867), *The Parthenon* (1871). They are all, however, flawed by an overinsistence on detail and a smallness of touch (what might be called the defects of his virtues) and by a weakness of color: forgetting his early simplicity of tone, Church lost himself in a gaiety of color that he could not organize.

Another painter of this period sought a different solution of the problem of landscape. George Inness (1825-1894) belongs, for the first half of his career, to the period of naturalism and luminism. The other Inness—the painter of vaporous, dreamlike landscapes—is the artist after the age of fifty.

Inness' first aim was to give American romantic realism a painterly breadth of touch and richness of impasto. He wished to break away from the linear quality of Durand and Cole, to dissolve outline in atmosphere and color, to achieve the largeness of touch and richness of tint which he was one of the first Americans to admire in the Barbizon painters. The first mature statement of his new style, perhaps, is the *Delaware Water Gap* of 1861 (The Metropolitan Museum of Art); the grandest and most eloquent, the *Delaware Valley* of 1865 and the heroic-sized *Peace and Plenty* (1865) (Fig. 9-5), in whose mood of joy and calm one can feel the emotions of a sensitive mind at the close of the Civil War. Inness never surpassed these pictures in eloquence or harmony of style. Yet they are exceptions in his work.

In 1859 Inness went to live in Medfield, a little village about twenty miles southwest of Boston in the pleasant but somewhat monotonous rolling landscape of eastern Massachusetts. He found there a countryside of small scale and intimate feeling, more like the landscape around Barbizon than the spacious, deep, all-embracing views preferred by other American romantic landscape painters. Inness' aim was now to base the appeal of his pictures not on any special beauty of the scene depicted, but upon esthetic harmonies— breadth of touch, a simple massing of light and shade, and conscious harmonies of color. These are important qualities of style. Yet there was also something lost. The coolness of palette, the depth and freshness of air which breathes from a picture by Kensett, for example, is never found in Inness. The heavy, rather airless quality one finds in the Barbizon painters, like Diaz or Rousseau, whom he admired, marks Inness also.

Within the poles of luminism and objective naturalism, American landscape painting developed for twenty years and more. They were powerful inspirations. The period is a prolific one for landscape painting and variety is its keynote. Neither in technique nor point of view do its artists conform to a pattern.

A painter in whom both inspirations are joined was M. J. Heade (1819-1904). Born in Lumberville, Pennsylvania, he led the wandering life characteristic of these artists, living and traveling over most of the United States, Europe, and South and Central America. From 1866 to 1881 his headquarters were in New York city but in the latter year he settled in St. Augustine, Florida. At that moment the art of painting was becoming centralized in New York city and a painter outside New York was quickly forgotten. Heade disappeared totally, to be rediscovered only in the 1940's. An intense love of nature and of light were the mainsprings of his art; but his interest in light (which led him to paint brilliantly naturalistic sunsets) was combined with the delicate, precise drawing characteristic of this whole school. In American luminism the study of light was combined with and kept within the bounds of exact linear outline, instead of dissolving outline as it did in French painting. Heade's sense of the mystery and poetry of nature is best expressed, perhaps, in a series of paintings of tropical hummingbirds. In 1860 he met an amateur naturalist, the Reverend J. C. Fletcher, who had spent several years in Brazil. They projected a book on the hummingbirds of South America and went to Brazil together in 1863-1864. The

9-6.   Martin J. Heade: *Orchids and Humming Birds.*
(Courtesy of The Detroit Institute of Arts.)

9-7. Sanford R. Gifford: *In the Wilderness* (1861).
(Courtesy of The Toledo Museum of Art.)

book was never published but it led Heade to paint a remarkable
series of pictures (some of which may date from later journeys that
took him all over South America) of the vivid little birds in their
setting of bright strange flowers and tropical jungle (Fig. 9-6).

Sanford R. Gifford (1823-1880) was a luminist who is close to
Kensett in the delicacy of his observation of aerial tone and in the
pensive mood of his art. He, too, traveled widely in search of subject matter, visiting Europe in 1855-1857 and again in 1868-1869,
when he went as far as Athens and the Nile. Whittredge in his
Autobiography gives an engaging description of how casually Gifford would start off on these expeditions, simply slinging a knapsack
on his back, not even bothering to lock the door of his studio. But
he was not an artist of the picturesque. His subject was the ethereal
delicacy and the wonderful unity of light, shimmering in transparent
skies, reflected upon waters, enveloping all things in nature within
its radiance (Fig. 9-7).

The study of light did not lead the American luminists to the same rich, coloristic style that was developing in France. There the study of light led painters to direct painting, piling on a thick impasto and dissolving outline in vibrations of color and atmosphere, especially after Daubigny introduced the practice of painting out of doors, and after water color became popular. But the Americans of this group continued to make studies from nature either in small pencil drawings, as delicately precise as a steel engraving, or in very small color sketches. The large oils were executed in the studio; and his poetic use of light was held within the control of clean, exact outlines and a thin, carefully applied film of paint. After 1875, when the main effort of a new generation of American painters was to learn the European use of impasto and mastery of the broad, full-loaded brush, the small, exact stroke of the older generation was held to be a sin against art. It is only today, when the stylistic wars of the seventies have faded from memory, that we can again see the painters of 1850 for what they are, interesting and sensitive artists using a style of their own age.

A rich new vein of the strange, the fantastic, and the wonderful in nature was discovered by this generation, in the far western United States. In the forties began the migration by wagon train across the plains and mountains to Oregon, followed by the Gold Rush to California. These settlements had leaped over, without occupying, nearly two thousand miles of wilderness; until the coming of transcontinental railroads, Oregon and California were isolated. The task of linking East and West by exploring expeditions and railroads was one of the great national undertakings of the mid-century; and a succession of expeditions aroused intense popular interest as they brought to light the spectacular natural wonders of the West.

Albert Bierstadt (1830-1902), was the child of German immigrants from Düsseldorf. He went back to his parents' home city to study painting, in 1853-1856, and spent a winter in Rome with Whittredge, 1856-1857, before returning to the United States. In the spring of 1858 he joined an expedition under General Frederick W. Lander, sent by the Federal government to map an overland wagon route to the Pacific. They crossed the high plains along the North Platte and advanced into what is now Wyoming; there Bierstadt left the expedition, spent the summer sketching among the Wind River and Shoshone mountains, and returned to New York.

The pictures done from these sketches, 1859-1863, brought him immediate and sensational popularity. Indeed he deserved it, for these paintings introduced both a fresh talent and a novel and dramatic subject. Bierstadt had learned in Europe a simple, tonal style that is at its best in these early works. The *Thunderstorm in the Rocky Mountains* (1859) (Fig. 9-8), for example, is a delightful canvas: simple, luminous, well observed, and full of the poetry of the untouched wilderness.

In the next twenty years Bierstadt enjoyed a popularity and financial reward such as no other American artist has received. His pictures commanded higher prices than had ever previously been paid to an American painter and were extravagantly praised both here and in England; Congress purchased his *Discovery of the North River by Hendrik Hudson* (1875) and *Entrance into Monterey* (1878); he built a thirty-five room stone and marble studio home overlooking the Hudson at Irvington, that was one of the

9-8.   Albert Bierstadt: *Thunderstorm in the Rocky Mountains* (1859).
(Courtesy of the Museum of Fine Arts, Boston.)

sights of America, visited by traveling celebrities; he grew wealthy, a national hero, decorated by foreign governments. Then the tide turned. His house burned in 1882; new fashions in art appeared; in 1889 the committee of New York artists selecting American paintings for the Paris Exposition refused to hang his *Last of the Buffalo* as out of keeping with the new French ideals of American painting; and the old artist found himself in financial difficulties. The close of his life was a sad anticlimax.

It is hard for us to see Bierstadt's pictures dispassionately: their romantic melodrama has received too much praise and too much blame. It is my opinion that both praise and blame have been excessive. One misses in Bierstadt's works the deep passion of Church's vision of nature. They are exaggerated in feeling and often marred (in his later years) by his inability to control the hot, bright colors he adopted. Yet there is also something original in Bierstadt which it is snobbish to deny: he is a first-rate second-rate talent.

The generation of 1850 was as prolific in genre painting as it was in landscape. The new generation began with a most promising talent. Richard Caton Woodville (1825-1856) grew up in Baltimore, where he had the advantage of studying good Dutch genre paintings in the collection of Robert Gilmor, an influence which was stronger and healthier than his studies in Düsseldorf after 1845. Woodville drew more expressively than Mount; his color was not only fresh and clear but as solid as that of a Dutch little master. He died, unfortunately, at thirty-one, an age when an artist begins, if he can, to turn youthful brilliance into mature art. Woodville had everything except time. He left a small number of very able pictures, of which *Politics in an Oyster House* (Fig. 9-9) is perhaps the most completely satisfying.

Eastman Johnson (1824-1906) had, on the contrary, a long lifetime in which to mature his gifts. Born in rural Maine of good family, he had a year or two of training with a lithographer in Boston and at eighteen became a successful portrait draughtsman in crayon. After several years' study in Düsseldorf and The Hague, he returned to America where he finally settled in New York City.

The afterglow of romantic humor and sentiment plays upon Johnson's work. Life is pleasant; people are interesting to watch, whether they are the well-to-do inhabitants of brownstone houses of New York, or the Negroes in the South, or farm folk of New England.

9-9.   Richard Caton Woodville: *Politics in an Oyster House* (1848).
(Courtesy of The Walters Art Gallery, Baltimore.)

An early work, *Old Kentucky Home, Life in the South* (1859) (New-York Historical Society), is charming, sentimental anecdote; though it contains too much, and floats on the surface of things, it has always been popular. *Shucking Corn* (1864) (Toledo) shows that he quickly learned to simplify, to let the inner life of his figures speak more quietly, through more natural movements, to work with light and shadow. The *Boyhood of Lincoln* (1868) (University of Michigan) and the *Family Group* (1871) (The Metropolitan Museum of Art) show his mature powers: acute observation; easy and expressive drawing; a warm affection for simple human life.

In a series of paintings done in the 1870's, during summers spent on Nantucket Island, he brought his luminism to its culminating point. In a picture of cranberry pickers, called *In the Fields* (Fig. 9-10), it is not the human warmth that strikes us; the feeling is

9-10.   Eastman Johnson: *In the Fields.*
(Courtesy of The Detroit Institute of Arts.)

purely objective—people, place, hour, seen together in the unity of a flood of light. There is no amusing anecdote, only a fine unity of tone and mood. In such a picture Johnson steps out of his period and moves, for a moment, across the threshold of the next period of art, into objective realism.

In New York City especially but to some extent in other centers flourished, in the third quarter of the century, a large school of genre, anecdote, and historical painters. Easy, skillful, charming, sentimental, they were overrated in their own lifetime and forgotten today when "story telling" is wholly out of fashion.

George Templeton Strong, the New York diarist, was a thoroughly conventional person. When he tells us, therefore, after visiting the National Academy of Design on April 17, 1846,[3] that he disliked Mount's *Eel Spearing at Setauket* (which had been painted for the diarist's father) and praises instead the works of Daniel Huntington and Emanuel Leutze, he is recording not only a preference but a widespread change of taste. The grave mood of meditation upon the past, the slow savoring of the flavor of things gone which romanticism had introduced, had slowly declined into sentimentalism and historical anecdote. The third quarter of the century was the great age of the sentimental historical subject, such as Leutze produced, and the sweet, vague, fancy works for which Huntington was famous.

In certain old families and clubs that dislike change, one still sees the dark, stiffly posed, rather dry portraits of Daniel Huntington (1816-1906). He was a very prominent and well-liked artist at one time in New York, president of the National Academy of Design, and successful in the very literal kind of portrait we associate with the impact of the daguerreotype upon American taste. One would assume, from these portraits, that he was a man wholly without the qualities of imagination or invention. Yet his large, vague pictures based on Bunyan's *Pilgrim's Progress*—such as *Mercy's Dream* (in several versions, the earliest, 1842, in the Corcoran Gallery of Art) and *Christiana and Her Family Passing Through the Valley of the Shadow of Death* (Pennsylvania Academy of the Fine Arts)—and numerous other literary subjects were immensely admired. To our

[3] *The Diary of George Templeton Strong*, ed. by Allan Nevins and Milton Halsey Thomas, New York, The Macmillan Company, 1952, Vol. I, p. 276.

eyes, they seem typical sugar-and-water confections of nineteenth-century sentiment. One of Huntington's famous historical subjects was *The Republican Court* (1861), a costume illustration representing a presidential reception in Washington's time, which found its way via engraving into the national mythology.

The most prolific painter in this historical vein was Emanuel Leutze (1816-1868), who belongs as much to Düsseldorf as he does to America. Born in Württemberg, he was brought as a child by his family to the United States. In 1841 he returned to Germany to study at Düsseldorf. He remained nearly twenty years, marrying there and making Germany his home.

Düsseldorf has been mentioned frequently in this record: it is time to say something about the qualities of this school, which was once so famous. Its style was formed by the Düsseldorf theater, devoted to German romantic-historical plays, which were, both in subject matter and the style of acting, melodramatic in the extreme. The painters of Düsseldorf specialized in historical and literary illustrations, drawn in laborious detail, colored rather than painted, and conceived in the melodramatic and sentimental style of the romantic theater.

Leutze painted in Düsseldorf a long series of American historical subjects, of which *Washington Crossing the Delaware* is the most famous. The best and the worst thing one can say of these pictures is that they were perfectly adapted to the popular taste of their day. A generation of American school children learned to visualize history in terms of some of his historical compositions. If history were a matter of heroic poses, this might have done no harm.

The popularity of genre was reinforced by the increasing popularity of the illustrated book, the illustrated magazine, the steel engraving, and the lithograph. A new type of magazine appeared in which the illustration was the keynote. The *Illustrated American News* (1851) was the first, followed by other short-lived journals; then two papers which became national institutions, *Frank Leslie's Illustrated Newspaper* in 1855 and *Harper's Weekly* in 1857. A host of genre painters and illustrators supplied their illustrations.

The illustrated weeklies created a new type of journalist-illustrator, who traveled about the country making quick drawings of landscapes, city scenes, or news events. Both the illustrator and the wood engraver were, however, pressed for time and developed a method of collaboration which, though efficient, gave rather disappointing results. A typical artist of this type was A. R. Waud (1828-1891), a quick, skillful observer and a principal war artist for *Harper's Weekly* during the Civil War. Waud took time to draw only the principal figures and details, roughly indicating how subsidiary parts were to be done, and adding pencil memoranda to guide the "re-drawers" who, like the rewrite men on the modern newspaper, put the thing into shape. Such a method did not produce sharp and original observation.

But in magazine and book illustration the standard improved rapidly. It was helped, as in previous decades, by the immigration of skilled engravers from abroad. W. J. Linton (1812-1897), who came to the United States in 1867, was an extremely well-trained engraver. His excellent *History of Wood Engraving in America* (1882) is a valuable source book and critique of the period.[4] His influence was certainly effective in raising the standards of black-and-white engraving on wood. The skill of the engravers, the address of the artists, the growth of publishers, the rise of a vigorous national literature creating an eager reading public—all these factors combined to stimulate a beautiful and interesting period of illustration. Engraving became more delicate and clear in line, richer in tone; illustrated volumes grew more elaborate; gift books, *éditions de luxe,* richly illustrated volumes of travel became more common.

F. O. C. Darley (1822-1888) was the most productive and best known illustrator of his generation. The sheer bulk of his production is impressive. He worked in all media: making outline drawings to be reproduced in lithograph; book and magazine illustrations to be cut in wood; wash drawings to be reproduced in large steel engravings; pencil drawings for bank note engravings on steel. His subjects covered a wide sweep of American life and although his facility sometimes betrayed him into conventionality, he had the qualities of easy composition, variety, and sense of character that are the mark of the true illustrator. His drawings for the novels of Cooper and Dickens, done in the sixties and engraved on steel, are, in the opinion of Weitenkampf, the height of his mature powers.

An influential illustrator was Harry Fenn (1845-1911), who came

[4] Linton, W. J., *The History of Wood-Engraving in America*, Boston, Estes and Lauriat, 1882.

9-11. Harry Fenn: *The Battery and Castle Garden.*
(From *Picturesque America*, 1872.)

to this country at the age of nineteen, like Linton, as an engraver;
but he soon became a prolific and active illustrator. He was one of
the founders of the American Watercolor Society in 1866 and also
one of the chief figures in Appleton's great project of illustrating the
beauties of the American landscape that resulted in the two massive
volumes of *Picturesque America* (1872-1874), edited by William
Cullen Bryant (Fig. 9-11). Its artists included Harry Fenn, Thomas
Moran, J. Douglas Woodward, Homer Martin, R. Swain Gifford,
A. R. Waud, Casilear, Bellows, and Kensett. The harmony between
the rich, warm blacks of the wood engravings, the silvery steel engravings, and the type face make it an example of nineteenth-century graphic style at its best.

There were still many portrait painters at work in the third quarter
of the century. Nearly every town of any size supported one or more.
It would be impossible to mention all their names; and, in most
cases, they do not deserve it, for they represent a headlong decline
of style.

Formal portraiture as a major branch of painting could not sur-
vive the rising popularity of photography. The camera is one of the

inventions of nineteenth-century technology that brought the hand-craft period to an end. The craft it destroyed was the craft of por-trait painting.

Daguerre's invention of 1837 spread with the speed of Mercury across the Atlantic. Even before Morse returned with the process from Paris in 1839, other Americans were experimenting with it from the printed descriptions. The new invention brought im-mediate death to the craft of the miniature painter; and within a generation the steady production of portraits in oil, which for two hundred and fifty years had been the staple and mainstay of the profession of painting in America, came abruptly to an end. After the seventies portraits, and often very good ones, continued to be painted, of course. But they were a luxury product only required when, for reasons of prestige, a photograph was not good enough.

Perhaps, from a purely esthetic point of view, the loss will not seem very great, since portraiture on the best level was not wholly extinguished. It is also true that the portrait, as a staple of painting, was neither so exacting nor so inspiring as the religious subjects which were the staple of Italian painting through so many centuries. Yet from the social point of view the change was calami-tous. With the disappearance of the demand for portraits, painting ceased to be one of the skills for which society had a need, and a pursuit by which a man could earn a steady if modest living in any city of the land. As the portrait painter vanished, there appeared the impoverished bohemian artist, insecure, embittered, earning his living by teaching instead of by the practice of his art, and depend-ent for the sale of his work upon the whims of fashion. The effect upon the artist and upon the art of painting was hideously de-structive.

The climate of those decades was not, one would say, favorable to idealism. Yet there were artists who drew their inspiration from the world of thoughts and dreams.

William Morris Hunt (1824-1879) came of a well-to-do family in Brattleboro, Vermont. His brother, Richard Morris Hunt, be-came a very successful eclectic architect, famous for transplanting French chateaux to Fifth Avenue, New York, and Newport. Hunt went to study at Düsseldorf, which was then at the height of its fame; but after nine months left for Paris where he studied under

9-12. William Morris Hunt: *The Flight of Night* (1878). (Courtesy of The Pennsylvania Academy of the Fine Arts, Philadelphia.)

Couture (1847), then with Millet. From these men who were the *avant garde* of painting in the forties Hunt learned a new ideal of poetic figure painting. The means employed by Millet in his transformation of French figure painting were a heavily loaded, broad brush, a warm, shadowy palette, and a vaporous modeling of the figure in rich, glowing color and tone. Hunt, on his return to the United States in 1855, set himself to work out a vision of American art in those terms. He settled first at Newport, then at Boston; there he exerted a profound influence upon New England taste.

Intelligent, enthusiastic, ardent when his interest was aroused, yet impatient of discipline, Hunt had qualities that made him an excellent teacher; but somehow he was never able to carve out a solid block of life to master in his imagination and to make his own, nor to carry his fine studies to a solid, big conclusion. Perhaps this was why, when his great opportunity came, he produced his greatest

work but broke down under the strain: his first personal achievement as a painter was also his last.

In 1875 he was commissioned to paint two murals in the new State
Capitol of New York at Albany. He chose an allegoric subject that
had interested him all his life, *The Flight of Night* (Fig. 9-12), from
a Persian poem about Anahita, the goddess of Night. It was for him
a symbol of the darkness of ignorance fleeing before the light of
civilization. Because of bad planning on the part of the builders, the
murals had to be executed under great pressure and difficulty in
the autumn of 1878; the physical strain, however, was less severe
than the fear of failure which tortured him as he worked. The murals
were well received but Hunt collapsed, was never able to resume
work, and in the next summer died under circumstances that have
always been explained as suicide. Within a short space of time the
murals themselves were ruined by damp. All that is left is a series
of studies, of which *The Flight of Night* in the Pennsylvania Academy of the Fine Arts is the most nearly complete. It is a composition
of light and movement, large in scale, grave and impressive in its
imaginative poetry, the one effective ideal composition by an American painter of Hunt's generation. Beside it the ideal compositions
of Daniel Huntington, Leutze, or T. Buchanan Read seem trivial
period pieces.

As a center of enthusiasm for French painting in America, Hunt
was perhaps of even greater significance than as an artist. It was
Hunt who, as an ardent interpreter of French art, created an enthusiasm for the Barbizon painters, for Millet, Corot, Rousseau, Daubigny, in America even before they were fully accepted in France;
it was Hunt who turned the eyes of American students to Paris
rather than to Italy and thus began the long period of French influence upon American painters. In the circle closest to him, John
La Farge, William and Henry James were among the young people
touched by Hunt's teaching.

A still more complicated case of imaginative power, skill, and
amateurism was William Rimmer (1816-1879), physician, anatomist,
sculptor, painter; and self-taught in all things. (Not the least curious
aspect of this complex man was his belief that he was the son of the
lost French Dauphin.) His natural talents were extremely great;
but misfortune and tragedy followed his steps, and little is now left
of his work.

Rimmer's imagination was haunted by the nude human figure and by wild images of struggle, violence, and exhaustion—"Equestrian battles, wild charges, the rush of banners, armies sweeping up dizzy parapets, the fall of angels, the thunder of demon wings."[5] He was so careless of his pigment that many of his pictures have disintegrated or been destroyed. Yet a picture like *Flight and Pursuit* (Fig. 9-13) (1872) is one of the most passionately convincing and disturbing visions of nightmare painted in this century.

Realistic anatomy, violent movement, imagination, and eccentricity mark all his surviving works in oil or pencil. Rimmer had talent but was never able to channel it into any conventional category nor to fit himself as a craftsman into society. He had few orders for sculpture during a lifetime of effort; he showed his pictures so rarely that, during his life, this side of his activity remained unknown. The only use society could find for his talents was as teacher of artistic anatomy. He began lecturing on this subject in Boston in 1861, with great success: John La Farge, William Morris Hunt, Daniel Chester French, Frederick Vinton, Frank Benson all testify to his imaginative ability as a teacher. For four years, 1866-1870, he was director of the art school of Cooper Union in New York City. But he was too independent and far-seeing for its trustees and was allowed to return to Boston. There his life continued, harassed, miserably poor, and intensely creative in its own strange fashion, to the end. There is no other ideal artist of the age whose creations are more personal, more difficult to see, or more uneven and impossible to generalize upon: at their best, his hallucinatory visions stare at us from the past like the eyes of the basilisk.

The Civil War had an effect familiar to us from the wars we have ourselves experienced, of throwing people back upon themselves and their own inner resources, forcing a reappraisal of life and its goals. The war also brought in the North a great growth of industry and manufacture, producing greater concentrations of population and wealth than had ever existed before in our cities. A new period of urban life began and brought, among other things, new civic institutions, new ideals and amenities, as well as grave new problems. The public gallery of art, toward which American artists and art-

[5] Lincoln Kirstein, *William Rimmer*, Whitney Museum of American Art and Museum of Fine Arts, Boston, Exhibition Catalogue, 1946-1947.

loving citizens had been making a variety of efforts for three quarters of a century, at last emerged as an institution apart from the academy, the athenaeum, or the art school.

The Metropolitan Museum of Art was organized in New York at a meeting in 1869 called by the art committee of the Union League and presided over by William Cullen Bryant. In 1870 Boston took a similar step. A board of trustees was organized to build a public museum of fine arts, to replace the exhibition activities of the Athenaeum, and the semiprivate Boston Art Club. In Washington, the Corcoran Gallery of Art was founded by the private benefaction of the banker W. W. Corcoran. The Pennsylvania Academy of the Fine Arts in Philadelphia was rehoused in a monumental structure in Ruskinian Gothic style built 1871-1876 and opened as part of the Centennial Celebrations of 1876.

Another museum and school of art grew out of the Centennial year

9-13. William Rimmer: *Flight and Pursuit* (1872).
(Courtesy of the Museum of Fine Arts, Boston.)

in Philadelphia. The state of Pennsylvania and the city of Philadelphia erected for the Exposition of 1876 an art building, Memorial Hall in Fairmount Park, intended as a permanent building to serve afterwards as a Museum of Art and Industry. The inspiration was the South Kensington Museum in London which had grown out of the profits from the Crystal Palace Exhibition of 1851. Memorial Hall became, in 1877, the museum portion of a new organization, The Pennsylvania Museum and School of Industrial Art, chartered as a state "museum of art in all its branches and technical applications, and with a special view to the development of the art industries of the State, and to provide instruction in drawing, painting, modelling, designing, etc."[6]

From 1850 to 1875 painting was, as I said at the beginning of this chapter, in every sense a popular art. Luminism, naturalism, sentimentalism were movements that grew out of or were in touch with main currents in American culture. American painting in this generation was like a native apple tree on a New York hillside at the height of its growth, bearing sweet, small, old-fashioned apples. The machine age was cutting at its roots and the next generation of painters had no liking at all for its fruit. They had studied abroad and seen, growing in the rich soil of Europe, a variety of rich, spectacular, and exotic fruits. Returning to this country, they looked with contempt on the poor thing they found here; hacked off its top branches; and endeavored to graft upon it shoots gathered from all the European schools. Some of the grafts flourished; others, less expertly done, died; the tree itself, cut both in root and branch, received a severe shock.

[6] *Handbook* of the Pennsylvania Museum, 1907.

Ten

THE ATTRACTION OF EUROPE:
AMERICAN IMPRESSIONISM
AND OTHER MOVEMENTS

THE QUARTER CENTURY after the Philadelphia centennial of 1876 was so complex that, for purposes of clarity, I have divided it into three chapters. The cosmopolitan strain in American painting became dominant in the seventies. Painting in Europe was extraordinarily rich, profuse, and brilliant. It was natural that it should make its influence felt; moreover, Americans played a part in it. That is the subject of the present chapter. Yet there were also great figures who doggedly hewed their art out of native experience: they were so important for our culture that they require a chapter to themselves. Finally, the strain of idealism produced some remarkably interesting figures who demand study in a third chapter.

Before we come to the tidal wave of expatriates in the seventies, there is a solitary, striking figure, earlier and greater than any, who typifies, because in some measure he created, the mood and temper of the last quarter of the century. Many of its most distinctive traits— its cosmopolitan inspirations, its exoticism, its cult of bohemianism and of art for art's sake—were established for English-speaking peoples by James A. McNeill Whistler (1834-1903).

American romantic painters had shown many admirable qualities:

10-1. James Abbott McNeill Whistler: *The Last of Old Westminster* (1862). (Courtesy of the Museum of Fine Arts, Boston.)

delicacy of feeling, warmth, modesty, subtlety. But toward the end, when a pedestrian naturalism became common and sat in the seats of authority, it grew drab and wearisome. Late nineteenth-century naturalism lacked the exotic; it did not satisfy the need for lovely and arbitrary invention, for the capricious and the exquisite. There came a great craving for the exotically beautiful. Whistler, an artist of decorative genius, was born to feel and satisfy that hunger.

Whistler was born in America, the son of an army officer who had resigned from the service to practice civil engineering. He grew up abroad, chiefly in St. Petersburg, where his father's profession took him from 1842 to 1849. He had some instruction in drawing at the Academy of Fine Arts in St. Petersburg and at the United States Military Academy at West Point. At the age of twenty-one he returned to Europe, never again to visit his native land. His first two years abroad (1855-1857) were spent as a student in the studio of Gleyre in Paris. His life thereafter was passed in Paris, London, and Venice. During his London years he became such a celebrity and made such an impression upon English society that the English have treated him as one of their own painters. Actually he was a type of the new cosmopolitan age, American in his quick receptivity to new ideas, and in his cleverness at improvising upon them; but belonging to no country except the new cosmopolitan world of art that he helped to create.

When Whistler arrived in Paris in 1855, the great flowering of the genius of French painting was just in preparation. The chief figures, at that moment, were still the aged Ingres and Delacroix, great neoclassicist and great romantic. But Whistler admired a controversial young painter named Courbet, whose objective realism then seemed to hold great possibilities for the future. He thus ranged himself at once on the side of the objective realists of his own generation, who believed art was something to be made of direct observations of nature, not woven from dreams, or memories, or ideal images.[1] Whistler's early oils use the thick, pasty impasto and deep, warm tones derived from his study of Courbet—like *The Last of Old Westminster* (Fig. 10-1) (1862), *The Coast of Brittany* (1861) in Hartford, or *The Music Room* (1860) (Freer Gallery, Washington). The first *Thames* series of his etchings (1860) also shows him as an objective realist, acute in observation, forceful in statement.

But a characteristic of the restless minds of the new age of which Whistler was typical was the variety of their inspirations. From the Parisian painters he had learned a creamy softness and fluency in

[1] I use the term *objective realism* for this period in contrast to *romantic realism* for the preceding period. The problem of creation, for the generation of 1870, was to become what Cézanne called Monet, "He is an eye," and added reflectively, "but what an eye!" The romantic realists, however transparent and self-effacing in style, were moved by sentiment. Theirs was an age of great dreams—of freedom, liberty, philosophical idealism, religious faith, which cast a veil of feeling over all. In the realism of the new age the bouquet of tenderness is gone. The objective realists devoted themselves with passion and excitement to exploring the world by the organ of sight alone. They were anti-idealistic; facts were exciting enough.

handling oil paint. From Velásquez he learned the value of the long line, the cool, empty background, the refined black and silver-gray tonality. From Japanese prints he absorbed the quality of two-dimensional pattern that was then so surprising to Western eyes: the exact, unexpected placing of detail within the rectangle of the picture; the clean harmonies of cool, flat tones. Transforming all these into something Whistler's own was an exquisite sense of decoration and a very personal interest in light. His contemporaries, the Impressionists of Paris, were lovers of the sun. Whistler was unique in his passion for twilight and night.

With his exquisite sense of decoration he refashioned the familiar portrait into a highly personal new form. One of his earliest full-length portraits and a masterpiece of his first period was *The Woman in White* (1862) (Washington, National Gallery of Art), which was one of the sensations of the Salon des Refusés in 1863, where the new movements in French painting first revealed their strength. It is a brilliant demonstration of a new idiom in painting—light in key, the colors forming broad areas (whose mere breadth was shocking then), without reflections from one to the other, but with long, clean edges, presenting bold contrasts of warm against cool, light against dark, hue against hue.

To emphasize the quality of formal, decorative harmony he was pursuing, Whistler began to call his works "symphonies" or "arrangements." The *Woman in White* is gravely impressive but static. Whistler went on to add a slight but expressive gesture of the whole figure that creates character and mood with surprising force. What melancholy and self-pity, for example, are implicit in the slouching pose of *Thomas Carlyle* (Fig. 10-2) (1872) in contrast to the control and silent force of character of the *Portrait of My Mother* (1871) (Louvre), a picture with a quality of inevitability which its popular fame cannot extinguish.

Landscape he likewise transformed into a formal harmony of tone which he called the "Nocturne," and made a lyric upon the beauty of twilight or darkness. One of the most famous, a study of fireworks at night in an amusement park on the Thames, has the instantaneous quality, the quick accent of a moment of life caught in passing and fixed forever. Whistler was not alone in seeking this quality—his friends in Paris, Degas and the Impressionists were also masters of it; and so were Winslow Homer and Thomas Eakins—it

10-2. James Abbott McNeill Whistler: *Thomas Carlyle* (1872).
(Courtesy of The Glasgow Corporation Art Gallery, Scotland.)

is one of the special charms of painting in this last quarter of the nineteenth century. The poetry of glowing spots of light drifting downward in the night sky has never been better observed nor more elusively stated. Whistler called it *Nocturne in Black and Gold— The Falling Rocket* (ca. 1874) (Plate IV) (The Detroit Institute of Arts).

He was very active and productive in the eighteen-seventies. In 1877 he exhibited a group of nine pictures at the Grosvenor Gallery in London which included the *Carlyle*, two other important portraits, and four of his most famous and successful Nocturnes. A number of pictures in the group represent the climax of his powers. Unfortunately the exhibition was attacked with insane violence by Ruskin, who wrote of the *Nocturne in Black and Gold—The Falling Rocket:*

> For Mr. Whistler's sake, no less than for the protection of the purchaser, Sir Coutts Lindsay [founder of the Gallery] ought not to have admitted works into the gallery in which the ill-educated conceit of the artist so nearly approached the aspect of wilful imposture. I have seen, and heard, much of Cockney impudence before now; but never expected to hear a coxcomb ask two hundred guineas for flinging a pot of paint in the public's face.

Whistler sued for libel. The trial proved a field day for a conservative public's feelings of scorn and hilarity toward an artist of challenging novelty. Although Whistler won the suit (he was awarded a farthing damages), the public sided with Ruskin, and Whistler was forced into bankruptcy (May, 1879).

The Ruskin suit was a tragedy, for it brought out in Whistler the dark side of his nature. He became a man at war with the public. Using all his wit and brilliance as a propagandist, he set himself to prove that the artist was a superior being of finer qualities than ordinary mortals, whose gross minds and dull perceptions were incapable of understanding either the artist or his work. In so doing, he transferred to England and America the war of words between the bohemian and the bourgeois then raging in Paris: a war in which insults and scorn took the place of interest and curiosity as the normal relation between the artist and his fellow men.

Whistler's arguments have been repeated by smaller figures until they have almost become the basic philosophy of our world: for still today the artist looks on the layman as a fellow of no perception; and the most generally held layman's belief about art is that if one can understand an artist he can't be a very good one. It is a far cry from this to the concept of the inevitability and universality of great art. Yet Whistler's achievements—his decorative Impressionism, his elegance of style, his sharp grasp of character, his sense of the poetry of night—were real and notable. He was a great, or if not a great, a consummate, artist, who achieved perfection within his chosen range. His aloofness from all that is commonplace and local, his concentration upon style, his preciousness were characteristics of a major artist.

We come now to the esthetic revolution of the seventies. Unlike Whistler's highly personal innovations and discoveries, the series of stylistic changes that now set in was an affair of movements and schools.

The Philadelphia Centennial Exposition of 1876 may serve as a convenient symbol of the end of romanticism. The Exposition marked one hundred years of American independence; but its chief effect on the popular imagination was not to solidify an established tradition of the past but to dissolve it. The romantic movement had endured a long time. A reaction was inevitable and, when it came, it was impatient and drastic. The young artists of the seventies could see no good in their elders; they were convinced, without a doubt, that merit in American painting began with them.

In the hundred years before the Centennial the United States had produced a national culture. Its value was not perhaps so much in the greatness of individual talents as in its spontaneous and instinctive character. This intuitive harmony between art and life, this oneness of the artist with the society around him was broken in the next period. The last quarter of the century was a period of growth and new knowledge, but also a time of disintegration and destruction. What disintegrated was precisely the unconscious whole. What was lost was the unity of a culture that had been, within its limitations, large and creative. No subsequent generation has been able to rebuild that unity.

Yet a change was necessary and inevitable. The romantic painters had not achieved the highest levels of style (and style, if not everything in art, is a necessity), while in Europe, especially in France, painting was rising to one of its great points. It was natural that American painters should respond to the technical changes abroad and should strive to learn what they could from their gifted contemporaries. More than this—with the development of railroads and steamships, it had become suddenly easy to go abroad. The romantic artist had dreamed of Italy and the Rhine, but he saw these usually as a mature man who had found himself artistically and knew what he needed. The new generation went abroad as young and plastic students who knew little or nothing of themselves before arriving in Munich or Paris, and who returned home with the idea that the aim of painting was to paint like the teacher they discovered there. The habit of study abroad was no new thing, but a change in its scale and atmosphere became striking in the seventies and continued through the eighties and nineties with ever increasing momentum. Rome, Paris, Venice, Florence, London, Munich, Antwerp, The Hague were simultaneously or successively the training grounds of American painters. In the eighties Paris became the predominant center; but, a little earlier, Munich enjoyed a great vogue.

The best known of the Munich-trained Americans was Frank Duveneck (1848-1919), the son of German immigrants, who was born in Covington, Kentucky. When he went to Munich in 1870 the teaching at the Royal Academy was still in the hands of painters of romantic-historical subject pictures; but a new star was rising in the figure of Wilhelm Leibl, one of the greatest of German objective realists, who had learned a broad, brilliant, painterly style from his study of the pictures by Frans Hals and Rubens in the Pinakothek. From Leibl and from the Pinakothek, Duveneck learned what came to be called in America the "Munich style"—a manner of painting that was realistic and atmospheric in vision, dark and warm in tonality, and dashing in its bravura displays of brushstroke, of broad lights brushed fluently into a dark, red-brown, shadowy ground.

Duveneck returned to America in 1873 and at first his work was little seen. In 1875, however, he showed five of his canvases at the Boston Art Club, where his novel palette, his unheard-of breadth and facility of brushstroke, created a sensation. William Morris Hunt was enthusiastic; orders for portraits showered upon him; he became overnight a national figure.

Samuel Isham had already observed in 1905 that "The canvases

10-3.   Frank Duveneck: *The Turkish Page* (1876). (Courtesy of
The Pennsylvania Academy of the Fine Arts, Philadelphia.)

that so electrified Boston seem today typical of a school rather than
of a distinctly original artist."[2] Duveneck had got hold of a way of
painting which looked at once modern and like the time-darkened
old masters. As his life unrolled, it became evident that although he
had a new palette and brushstroke and a new way of painting the
posed model, he had nothing very much to say beyond his technique. *The Turkish Page* (Fig. 10-3) (1876) is perhaps a canvas
that gives the best measure of his powers: large in scale, brilliant in
its slapdash bravura, painted with real delight in the medium and
in the artist's own fluency, it still is a flashy and arresting canvas.
But back at home in Cincinnati, without picturesque Bavarian mod-

2 *The History of American Painting*, New York, The Macmillan Company,
1927, p. 381.

els to paint, and without the surrounding activity of European artists to sustain him, his later life became a long anticlimax to his early fame.

It is worth while to spend this much time upon Duveneck, who is a pleasing and graceful, but on the whole not an important painter, because his story is one that has been repeated over and over again and neither the artists nor the public have yet learned its lesson. The past three quarters of a century have been filled with a succession of such overnight successes. They sweep across the country, each a national sensation (we love sensations and novelties), setting up a shock wave that swings a whole school of imitators, minnow-like, into its train as it rolls across the continent; then fade, like Duveneck. In retrospect, they prove to have been only clever pupils, who caught something of the manner of an able new painter abroad and, on their return home, are mistaken for masters. A new way of painting is always interesting both to painters and lovers of painting: but we have still to learn that readiness to imitate an attractive new style is not the same thing as originality.

A great many other Americans studied in Munich, but as the brilliant blond palette of Paris made itself felt, the Munich school faded away. The stronger figures, like W. M. Chase, developed away from its mahogany-dark palette; or, if they did not, they failed to develop at all. The Munich manner did not transplant well to America. It did not seem to lend itself either to the American face and style of dress or to the landscape here; and the Bavarian peasant subjects these men brought home have long since lost their novelty and disappeared from the walls of our museums and homes.

By far the larger contingent of American students went to Paris. From the seventies on, every French painter who gained prominence, every French movement which appeared collected a number of American pupils and followers: Gérôme, Fortuny, Bouguereau, Millet, Bonnat, Constant, Bastien-Lepage, Carolus-Duran, each had his followers. Finally, in 1888, Theodore Robinson discovered Monet at Giverny and was the first American to follow the Impressionists, abandoning the French tradition of drawing entirely for the new technique of light, air, and broken color, which later so many Americans were to adopt.

But most American students attended the Académie Julian. The influx of foreign students into Paris in the last decades of the century (Russian, Polish, English, Irish, American) was so great that it overwhelmed the existing official schools and produced its own institutions, of which this was chief. The Académie Julian was started as a business proposition by Julian, who provided a hall and models, hired painters to criticize the students' work, and collected the fees. The room was always filled to capacity, so that the students had scarcely elbow room. Instruction in Julian's thus reverted to what it had been in the eighteenth century—drawing the human figure; painting was something the student did on his own at home.

It was not a bad training, so far as it went. Saturated with hard work and sense of *métier*, it gave foreign students a glimpse of the French painter's pride of profession; an opportunity to absorb the atmosphere of a great, active center of their art; and a sense of belonging to a tradition bigger and older than themselves. The products of this training became, by the nineties, the predominant group in America, as the Munich group was in the seventies. One has only to leaf through the pages of Sheldon's *Recent Ideals of American Art* (1888), which celebrated the triumph of this European-trained generation, to see how firmly people believed that a new and greater era of painting had now begun in America. There is hardly one of the painters described by Sheldon who was not soundly trained; probably none who did not paint at least one good picture. Yet out of the 185 painters Sheldon describes perhaps five are of any interest to us today. (And of these five, three are so treated as to show that their work was quite misunderstood at that time.)

One asks one's self: Why has time taken such a terrible toll of this generation? What was lacking? Not talent, not training, nor opportunity.

What was lacking was a personal point of view. The young students from America, with their native receptivity and openness to new impressions, were able to learn what was teachable in the style of the French painter who was admired at the moment; and did so, often, with surprising rapidity and cleverness. The problem was, upon their return to America, to find something of their own to say with this style.

The landscape painters found that the light was different in America; the trees grew differently; the white farmhouses of New England did not fall into compositions as did the old stone villages of

10-4.   Mary Cassatt: *Young Women Picking Fruit* (1891).
(Courtesy of the Carnegie Institute, Pittsburgh.)

Normandy or Brittany. The figure painters found no picturesque peasants in smocks and wooden shoes driving oxcarts. Instead, they found American farmers in ordinary clothes using the new McCormick reaper and John Deere steel plow. And to many, after their gay student years abroad, America itself seemed dull and insipid. Some of them solved the problem by staying abroad; not because, like Copley and West, they could find a career there that was denied them in the United States, but because they liked the atmosphere of Munich or Paris better than Chicago or New York.

The expatriate element in American art assumed a prominence, in the quarter century after 1875, that it had never had before. Those who returned tended to congregate in New York, where they felt themselves nearest to Europe. New York was the great port of entry for European products, natural and artistic, and the city nearest to Europe in atmosphere. The already predominant position of the city was steadily reinforced, as the European-trained painters congregated there: by the end of the century, the centralization of our artistic life had gone so far that it was almost impossible for an artist to gain a reputation or to secure an audience if he did not live in New York City.

The two major figures of the Paris-trained generation of the seventies were John Singer Sargent and Mary Cassatt.

Mary Cassatt (1845-1926) is one of the few American painters known to European critics and mentioned in European histories of art. As a consequence she has been given, I suspect, a somewhat disproportionate place in the story of our art. Her family lived much abroad, and although she grew up in Philadelphia and studied at the Pennsylvania Academy of the Fine Arts, from 1866 onward her life was spent in Europe. Settling finally in Paris in 1873, she became an admirer and friend of Degas and, through his influence, joined the Impressionist group, of which she became a distinguished minor member. She was a figure painter who learned much from Degas, Manet, and Japanese prints, and developed an admirable manner, large in drawing, broad and luminous in color. What robs her, in my opinion, of the place to which her powerful style would otherwise entitle her, is her excessively unadventurous mind—for the paintings of her mature period are nearly all variations of a single picture, a mother and child. It is hard to see greatness in such monotony of subject. Had her mind been as free and vigorous as her method, she would have been a notable figure in the history of American art.

Her most original work was done in the nineties. Inspired by an exhibition of Japanese prints in Paris in 1890, she put a vigor of outline and color pattern into works like the color print series of 1891, or oils like *Young Women Picking Fruit* (Fig. 10-4) (1891) or *The Bath* (ca.1892) (Art Institute of Chicago) that make them personal and interesting experiments in style. At about the same time also, following the lead of Degas, she turned enthusiastically to pastel. The dry luminosity of the medium suited her and in it she achieved some of her most brilliant effects. Yet if she achieved style—which is something—it was nonetheless always within territories of art already discovered and cultivated by others greater than she; so that she seems, in retrospect, to be no more than a good painter of the second rank. Perhaps her greatest influence upon American taste was exerted by her success in inducing American friends and relatives to buy the paintings of her friends, the Impressionist painters—an influence of which the Havemeyer collection in The Metropolitan Museum of Art is a notable example.

John Singer Sargent (1856-1925) was born in Florence, Italy, the son of American parents living abroad. He had his first artistic training in Florence; but the family wandered foot-loose about Europe until, in 1874, they settled in Paris. There, at eighteen, he entered the studio of Carolus-Duran, who was not only a brilliant draughtsman but a painter with a very exact control of mass, tone, and line. Sargent, a precocious pupil, emerged from his schooling with perhaps the most thoroughly trained and controlled talent an American painter has ever had. An immense natural facility combined with his exact and lucid vision and dispassionate temperament made him seem to his contemporaries the culmination of American objective realism.

Like Whistler, he settled for a time in Paris. In 1879-1880 he visited Spain and Morocco; *El Jaleo*, in the Gardner Museum, Boston, is a result of this visit. Sargent removed in 1885 to London, which was thereafter to be his headquarters for life. In 1887, however, he came to the United States to paint several portraits. An exhibition at the St. Botolph Club, Boston, was the foundation of a great enthusiasm for his work in America; and this was the first of many visits to Boston. The trustees of the Boston Public Library in 1890 gave him one of the large decorative commissions in their new building of which Boston was so proud. Many friendships also helped attach him to Boston, which became his American *pied à terre*, rather than his family home, Philadelphia.

In his own time, Sargent's instantaneous, photographic vision, which catches the casual movement of life so vividly, seemed startling, even disturbing. One of his most satisfying works, to our taste, is his portrait of *Robert Louis Stevenson* (1885) (Fig. 10-5). But Stevenson himself, writing to their mutual friend W. H. Low (letter of October 22, 1885), found the picture somewhat disconcerting.

10-5. John Singer Sargent: *Robert Louis Stevenson* (1885).
(Courtesy of Mr. and Mrs. John Hay Whitney, New York; photograph courtesy of The Metropolitan Museum of Art.)

Sargent was down again and painted a portrait of me walking about in my own dining-room, in my own velveteen jacket, and twisting as I go my own moustache; at one corner a glimpse of my wife, in an Indian dress, and seated in a chair that was once my grandfather's; but since some months goes by the name of Henry James's, for it was there the novelist loved to sit—adds a touch of poetry and comicality. It is I think excellent, but is too eccentric to be exhibited. I am at one extreme corner; my wife, in this wild dress, and looking like a ghost, is at the extreme other end; between us an open door exhibits my palatial entrance hall and a part of my respected staircase. All this is touched in lovely, with that witty touch of Sargent's; but, of course, it looks dam queer as a whole.[3]

Sargent was at his best in this type of composition (which the French call the *portrait d'apparat,* the portrait of a person in his natural setting): he was, I think, a genre painter by natural gifts, and a painter of fashionable portraits only because his conventional habit of mind did not allow him to refuse to do the kind of thing people wanted of him.

His best period was in the first years after the Spanish visit of 1880, when, under the influence of Velasquez, he worked in a dark, rich palette, using strong contrasts of tone. All his gifts are at their best in the picture of the *Four Daughters of Edward Darley Boit* (1882) (Museum of Fine Arts, Boston). The four little girls in a vast, dim interior have the informal ease of children at home, as if caught by a snapshot; yet the picture has also the comprehensive grasp of a whole phase of life that only an artist's mind can convey. This picture and others of the same type show Sargent's rich, sure sense of tone. When he shifted later to the blond Impressionist palette his sense of hue was neither so sure nor so pleasing.

In later life Sargent found refuge from his own success as a fashionable portrait painter in painting landscapes in water colors, creating a peculiarly positive yet liquid style, of which the *Piazzetta* (The Brooklyn Museum) is a good example. In his water colors everything flows and swims in the vibration of dazzling summer light. His manner is so personal that one either likes or dislikes it; no middle ground is possible.

[3] *The Letters of Robert Louis Stevenson,* edited by Sidney Colvin, New York, Charles Scribner's Sons, 1911, vol. II, p. 289.

The American painters who remained in Europe—with the exception of Whistler, Sargent, and Cassatt—do not seem to have
made a strong or lasting contribution to American imaginative life.
At least, they are not remembered.[4] Whether or not one enjoys
Whistler's fastidious decorative elegance or Sargent's brilliance and
cool detachment, they were very substantial and powerful talents,
who took a front rank in the artistic life of their own day. But the
cosmopolitan movement, on the whole, as we look back upon it,
dwindles in the perspective of time.

A good place to study its character is in those ground floor rooms
of the Gardner Museum in Boston that everyone hurries through on
the way to the great things upstairs, but which are nonetheless worth
lingering in if one likes to savor the erratic wanderings and strange
revolutions of taste. One sees there a collection formed in the
eighties and nineties, preserved unaltered: the major and the minor,
the enduring and the transient, left hanging together without any of
time's ruthless editing. It is a curious experience to find one's self
transported back into the intellectual atmosphere of that day, which
was so confident of its own superiority to the old, provincial, romantic America. As a whole there seems a general thinness and lack of
blood. This painting, one feels, had become an exercise in taste
and talent rather than a vehicle for creative passion and power.

The painters who brought their new techniques back to their own
country seem to have chosen the more difficult yet the better part,
if one may judge by the fact that more of their names have survived.
Yet their return to this hemisphere was not easy. To the young
students who began returning in the seventies, their eyes filled with
the facile charm of Munich brushwork or the elaborate theatrical
brilliance of the Salon, the exhibitions of the National Academy of
Design seemed niggling in handling, woolly and insipid in color.
The older American art, they felt, was stuffy and out of date. A war

---

[4] Those who will read Sheldon's *Recent Ideals of American Art,* or the wiser
views of the period in Sadakichi Hartmann's *A History of American Art* (1902),
and Samuel Isham's *History of American Painting* (1905) will find the names
of the expatriate painters of the last quarter of the nineteenth century, both the
few who are remembered today and many who are forgotten. I am not sure that
all these deserve their present oblivion. The foreign flavor which was once the
key to their success now works as strongly against them.

of generations broke out. The new men founded the Society of American Artists in 1877 in competition with the National Academy of Design. The New York Etching Club (1877) and the American Watercolor Society also gave them space to exhibit and the *American Art Review*, founded in Boston in 1880, a journal to support them. In the first exhibitions of the Society of American Artists, the Munich-trained men were predominant, but in the eighties and nineties the Parisian technique and palette came to the front.

The most influential figure among those who returned to this side of the Atlantic was W. M. Chase (1849-1916) and his story is instructive. Born in Indiana, he studied with local portrait painters in Indianapolis and in New York at the National Academy of Design; then went to St. Louis, where his family had moved. In 1872 some businessmen of that city, impressed by his talent, raised money

10-6.   William Merritt Chase: *In the Studio* (1880-1883).
(Courtesy of The Brooklyn Museum.)

10-7. Theodore Robinson: *Girl at the Piano.*
(Courtesy of The Toledo Museum of Art.)

10-8.   Childe Hassam: *Southwest Wind* (1905).
(Courtesy of the Worcester Art Museum.)

to send him abroad. When asked if he would like to go he replied,
"My God, I'd rather go to Europe than go to heaven." Chase's pictures in his Munich period are less flamboyant than Duveneck's
and are painted in a luminous gray and brown tonality that is pleasing. In 1877 he spent nine months with Duveneck in Venice. Then,
in 1878, the newly organized Art Students League invited him to
New York as teacher of its painting class. He returned with a halo of
European success and a large collection of pictures and curios, which
he installed in a spacious studio at 51 West 10th Street that became

a noted meeting place for the artists and students of New York. His paintings that show its interior, like *In the Studio* (Fig. 10-6) (1880-1883) in the Brooklyn Museum, or one in Pittsburgh, are revealing documents of the taste for artistic "atmosphere," by which was meant a picturesque ensemble, exotic bits and pieces, and decorative souvenirs of travel.

During the eighties he abandoned the grays and browns of Munich for the blond palette of Paris and the facile brushstroke of Sargent. He worked with great rapidity, so that he was able to keep up a large production of portraits, still lifes, and landscapes and at the same time to teach great numbers of students. As a painter, Chase was a man of talent rather than power and conviction; but as a teacher he was a man of extraordinary effect. Through his influence, before the end of the century a composite technique of the bright Impressionist palette and the dashing brushstroke of Sargent had become the vernacular of American painting.

The broken color of Monet, which Theodore Robinson (1852-1896) brought home, had a much lesser influence, perhaps because Robinson had not the health to be a vigorous leader. By nature he was a realist. His early works, like the *Girl at the Piano* (Fig. 10-7) are in a dark, warm, tonal style and attractive in their direct, modest observation. In Baur's sympathetic monograph one can read the story of his vain struggle to adjust the Impressionist technique to the different light and larger scale of the American landscape before ill health brought his sensitive but slender talent to an end.

Childe Hassam (1859-1935), trained in Boston, was an interesting luminist even before he went to France. His early tonal style, shown in a picture like *Columbus Avenue, Boston, Rainy Day* (1885) (Worcester Art Museum), owes something to Whistler, perhaps, in its soft grays, but nothing yet to Paris. In 1886, at the age of twenty-seven, he went abroad and joined the army of students at Julian's; but it was the touch and palette of the late Monet that he brought home. Almost alone among the American Impressionists, Hassam has the quality of uncomplicated happiness that makes his French contemporaries so delightful. His *Southwest Wind* (Fig. 10-8) (1905) is an admirable example of his later style. It is simply a row of poplar trees with the wind ruffling their leaves and turning up the silver undersides, and behind them glimpses of some white buildings and the sea. Flooded with a clear white noonday light, it

10-9. George Inness: *Grey Day, Goochland* (1884).
(Courtesy of the Phillips Collection, Washington, D.C.)

is a piece of summer wind and sun and freshness translated into art. His later years, unfortunately, showed a sad deterioration from this fresh and easy style.

The most conspicuous reaction of American painters to Impressionism was, however, something quite different. They turned the new color harmonies and the atmospheric touch of French painting into a muted, decorative, luminist style. The subdued color harmonies and muted quiet of Whistler's portraits and Nocturnes are a highly individual but, in this context, not an isolated phenomenon. They form part of the mood of quietism (not unlike that of Allston

10-10.   Thomas Wilmer Dewing: *A Lady in Yellow* (1888).
(Courtesy of The Isabella Stewart Gardner Museum, Boston.)

in the eighteen-twenties) to which American taste now returned. One can see it in artists as original and diverse as Whistler, Inness, and Twachtman.

Inness spent most of the years 1870-1875 in Italy and found, in the landscape around Rome, not only popular success but the beginning of a new development. After his return he became increasingly a painter of mood; his subjects dissolved into soft, muted, shimmering color. His later pictures, with their mystical mood and soft veils of color, belong essentially to American decorative Impressionism,

10-11.   John Henry Twachtman: *Sailing in the Mist*. (Courtesy of The Pennsylvania Academy of the Fine Arts, Philadelphia.)

although Inness arrived there by his own quite original path. The extravagant popularity of these pictures at the close of the nineteenth century reveals, in fact, a striking change in taste. After 1875 a revulsion against naturalism took place and many artists, together with a large segment of their public, turned toward a Tennysonian, trance-like idealism, in which the note of reality, like the echo calling, grew ever fainter (Fig. 10-9).

Inness was not the only painter who began in the older landscape school but developed into this kind of Impressionism of mood. Alexander H. Wyant (1836-1892) and Homer Martin (1836-1897) followed similar paths—and, on a lower level, so did Thomas Moran (1837-1926), whose dramatizations of grandiose Western scenery were very popular.

In 1895 a group of New York and Boston painters exhibited together, under the name of the Ten American Painters. The Ten were: Thomas W. Dewing (1851-1938); Edmund C. Tarbell (1862-1938); Frank W. Benson (1862-1951); Joseph De Camp (1855-1923); J. Alden Weir (1852-1919); John H. Twachtman (1852-1902); Willard L. Metcalf (1858-1925); E. E. Simmons (1852-1931); Childe Hassam (1859-1935); and Robert Reid (1862-1929). After Twachtman's death in 1902, Chase took his place. As a group The Ten formed a kind of academy of American Impressionism. But some of them were more than this.

Dewing was one of the most original. His small pictures of women seated in cool dim interiors, very precisely and delicately drawn and sensitive in tone, are good examples of the quiet, dreamlike poetry for which the painters of the nineties were seeking (Fig. 10-10).

Twachtman preferred slight, intimate little glimpses of nature and, eliminating depth almost entirely, transposed his subjects into a vague shimmer of color so soft it seems to float on the surface of the canvas. *Sailing in the Mist* (Fig. 10-11) is one of the most attractive examples of this gentle, evanescent style—a delicate soap bubble of blues and whites like a Debussy étude in paint.

The achievements of this quarter-century are just far enough away to be difficult to estimate fairly. They are not close enough to art today to be felt as vital, nor distant enough to be interesting as history. Yet one can perhaps draw certain conclusions from facts that are not likely to be distorted by our admittedly imperfect perspective.

Judged by the development of the institutions of art, painting grew increasingly popular. The art museum, born in the seventies, developed rapidly in the atmosphere of the new age. Boston, New York, Philadelphia, and Washington having led the way, after the Centennial other cities followed. By the close of the century, an art museum was an accepted part of civic life in our major cities; in many others there were art associations, art clubs, and exhibition societies that were to develop into art museums later. The Pennsylvania Academy of the Fine Arts, The Corcoran Gallery in Washington, the Art Institute of Chicago, and the National Academy of Design in New York held national exhibitions of painting and the Carnegie Institute had launched an ambitious program of international exhibitions.

The art schools of the country were also put on a better basis. Thomas Eakins, returning from Paris in the seventies, reorganized the old school of the Pennsylvania Academy of the Fine Arts in Philadelphia. In 1875 the National Academy of Design in New York city closed its art school for lack of funds. L. E. Wilmarth, its instructor, and the student body organized the Art Students League as a drawing and sketch class. The National Academy reopened its school in 1877 and Wilmarth returned to take charge. But in October, 1877, the Art Students League also reopened with Walter Shirlaw teaching painting, Jonathan Hartley sculpture, and F. S. Church composition. In 1878 W. M. Chase began his famous painting class; Shirlaw took composition; and Hartley sculpture. The new movement thus had an art school of its own with an aggressive leadership, and in the Society of American Artists (1877) an organization for its exhibitions.

But, alas, the same wind of change that gave the American Impressionists their sense of superiority encased in their experience of European travel also deprived them of their livelihood. What had been a secure and established profession in the third quarter of the nineteenth century became, in the era of Ward McAllister and The Four Hundred, a poverty-stricken and insecure pursuit—as it has remained since.

There were many reasons for this disastrous change, chief among which was that the artists' more wealthy patrons had also been affected by the taste for foreign travel. They too had seen the Salon and had learned to admire the fashionable painters of Paris—Meissonier or Bouguereau or Cabanel—and the Paris-trained Americans did not seem so glamorous or desirable as the originals. The patrons of conservative tastes remained faithful to the older men of the National Academy of Design, while the patrons of advanced tastes preferred to buy European paintings rather than American. Yet although it became impossible for artists to sell their pictures, the demands to study painting multiplied. Art schools and painting classes were springing up; everywhere there were students eager to attend painting classes; and teaching, rather than the practice of his art, became the economic support of the painter.

The rise of the art dealer as an intermediary between the artist and the public had begun with the midcentury and developed steadily. By the nineties New York had a large group of dealers' galleries, some of which sold the best European art, some the best American. Others sold the fashionable pseudomasters of the day. It would be idle to generalize as if these galleries were all alike.

But if collecting by vogue appeared, there were also collectors of the true mettle, who find in works of art an answer to the inner needs of one's imagination and temperament. It is enough to mention a few names, such as Quincy Adams Shaw, Isabella Stewart Gardner, Henry G. Marquand, Benjamin Altman, J. P. Morgan, Henry Walters, W. L. Elkins, John H. McFadden, George Gunsaulus, John G. Johnson, James E. Scripps, all of whom began, in the last quarter of the century, to bring to America some share in the great artistic heritage of our civilization; and to whose discrimination and devotion we owe a lasting debt of gratitude.

Yet for most American artists it was a time of great difficulty. They were the beggars at the feast, picking up the crumbs that fell from the tables where the European painters of fashionable reputation were feasting.

There were other destructive aspects of the period. The handcraft skills and traditions lost ground steadily before the machine; the factory, rather than the craftsman's workshop, became the source of more and more of the things with which the American people lived and furnished their homes. This was not in itself bad. Machine production can be beautiful as well as economical and useful. Many years had to pass, however, before the problem of machine design was to be grasped or mastered.

As the camera had destroyed the crafts of miniature painting and portraiture, the photoengraving process in the nineties destroyed the craft of wood engraving, which had made the two preceding decades the golden period of American illustration. A new type of magazine also appeared, cheaper than the famous monthlies, addressed to a less sophisticated public, and with them the art of the illustrator began to decline.

Worst of all, the American intelligentsia lost its self-reliance. The great lesson which Emerson had taught the romantic period was that poverty and rude setting were not obstacles to the inner life: it was possible to be a thinker and an artist in an unknown American village. At the end of the century, European experience had become the prop of everything; the cosmopolitan generation had become ashamed, not only of the provincialism of their parents, but of themselves. The mark of culture became a nervous, apologetic attitude about America; self-reliance gave way to the kind of groveling colonialism represented by Charles Eliot Norton's remark to his class at Harvard in the nineties, quoted by Ferris Greenslet, "There are handsome landscapes in our country but in America even the shadows are vulgar."

Thus, the period of eclectic cosmopolitanism was marked both by growth and decay. It created a greater knowledge of the world of art, a wider experience, some brilliant individual achievements. But it lost ground in respect to the harmony between the artists and society, in self-knowledge, in the disintegration of the handcrafts, and in self-reliance.

Eleven

OBJECTIVE REALISM:

THE INDEPENDENTS

ONE OF THE REVEALING SIGNS of weakness in this generation is that it ignored many of its own best painters because they were too independent, too original, too far removed from cosmopolitan taste and the fashionable modes of painting. In this chapter I shall try to tell the story of the independent painters, for whom the first task was to see life from their own point of view in space and time, and whose technique grew out of their personal vision.

Underlying the closing decades of the nineteenth century—whether we are dealing with solitary individualists in America or gregarious students in Paris and Munich—was the mental climate of objective realism, the climate of the age of science. The simple life of an earlier, agricultural America gave way before the rise of giant industry and finance capitalism, the growth of great cities and of social classes, all the gathering phenomena of modern mass civilization. Not Jefferson, or Emerson, but Darwin now offered the great challenge to the mind; as once Gibbon and the first archaeologists had conjured, from beneath the soil of Italy, a pageant of classical antiquity to astonish and fascinate mankind, so now a still more vast vision of life arose. In these later decades of the nineteenth century it was paleontologists like O. C. Marsh and Cope, picking up stones in the cuttings made by the transcontinental railroads across the vast, empty plains of Nebraska, who conjured from the old bones of the earth the story of ancient life that Darwin had inferred in the

Origin of Species—dinosaurs; saw-toothed, reptilian birds; the fossil sequence of the horse, developed with such beautiful logic and coherence from its five-toed ancestor. Biology, geology, physics, chemistry, and economics guided the thought of the age. Life seemed no longer a problem for reason, as the men of the eighteenth century saw it; or for feeling, as the romanticists believed: in place of the Enlightenment, or Transcendentalism, came an overmastering appetite for cool observation of fact.

In the creative imagination, objective realism was the main stream of the arts. But true art, even when devoured by a passion to observe and record, is still poetry. Now it was the poetry of light and of nature studied with passionate intensity that haunted the imagination of the Western world, both among the Impressionists and the independent or isolated painters.

11-1. Winslow Homer: *Prisoners from the Front* (1866).
(Courtesy of The Metropolitan Museum of Art.)

So strong is the kinship of these independents in some instances to American romanticism, in the grave and brooding note of their work and in the dark, warm tones of their palette, that it is tempting to consider them as a continuation of romanticism. The afterglow of romantic feeling lingers upon them; but the greatest and most typical figures, like Winslow Homer and Thomas Eakins, belong nonetheless to objective realism.

Their independence did not mean that they turned their eyes away from what was going on in their art elsewhere. Each of them studied or traveled abroad. Both Homer and Eakins show in the luminosity and monumental simplicity of their work that they were working their own way toward the coloristic style that was flowering at that moment in France. But their point of departure was from American experience, rather than European, and they arrived in consequence at their own independent results.

Winslow Homer (1836-1910) was the only one of the great independents to achieve recognition in his lifetime. In spite of severe criticism caused by his lack of "finish," his early works made their originality felt; and his late paintings of the sea became almost a national epic. Yet as late as 1908 a writer in the *International Studio* expressed angry resentment of his lack of suavity: "There is none who, from the technical standpoint, commonly paints more hatefully than he, and yet at the same time none who, as a rule, produces greater pictures."[1]

At nineteen Homer was apprenticed to the leading Boston lithographer of the day, John H. Bufford, but after completing his two-year apprenticeship he left the shop. "From the time I took my nose off that lithographic stone," he said later, "I have had no master; and never shall have any." In 1859 he moved to New York City and became for the next seventeen years a free-lance illustrator, chiefly for *Harper's Weekly.*

Although the black-and-white woodcuts of the pictorial weeklies in Homer's time remained crude and harsh, he learned to work with clear-cut outlines and broad planes that made the most of his medium. As one turns over the pages of *Harper's Weekly* for the sixties and seventies, Homer's illustrations stand out, not only by their freshness of observation, but by their sweeping energy of line and effective massing of lights and darks. During the Civil War he went

[1] Leila Mechlin, *International Studio*, XXXIV (1908), cxxv.

south with the Union armies and made many drawings for *Harper's Weekly*; during the war, in 1862, he did his first painting in oil.

His early oils, inspired by wartime scenes, are sober in color, but show the discipline of his work as an illustrator in their grasp of character, their simple expressive drawing, and their breadth of tone. The masterpiece of this phase is *Prisoners from the Front* (Fig. 11-1) (1866). It shows a Union officer examining a group of Confederate prisoners in the midst of a devastated Virginia landscape. In its contrast between the pale, earnest civilian-in-uniform on the one side, and on the other the haughty, graceful cavalier-officer, elegant even in his rags, it tells us all one needs to know about the two temperaments which were at war in that conflict. It was exhibited at the National Academy of Design in 1866 and created a sensation—for it was the most powerful and convincing painting that had come out of that terrible national experience—and made its author famous. It was one of the pictures sent to represent American painting in the Paris Exposition of 1867, where its fidelity and power were recognized by both French and English critics. Although Homer could be criticized and attacked after this, he could not be ignored.

From his very first essay in oils, Homer was launched upon the study of light. In 1867-1868 he went to France for a few months, looked at the Louvre, painted a little in the country, enjoyed Paris, and returned home. He went his own way, not in ignorance but in complete independence of other men's work. Homer's exploration of light took him in a different direction from French Impressionism. His long discipline in black-and-white made itself felt: instead of dissolving outline and form into a vibration of light and color, he developed luminosity within a construction of clear, firm outlines and broad planes of light and dark (Fig. 11-2).

Until 1874 Homer continued to work for *Harper's Weekly* while slowly perfecting his painting. One can watch his eye grow gradually keener and more sensitive to nuances of light, his sense of movement more expressive, his grasp of character deeper. His interest was in human life, out-of-doors under the sky and in sunlight; he liked the simple and unaffected flavors of humanity and showed almost a Dutch genius for the beauty of the ordinary and the everyday. He painted these flavors—the Negroes in the South (Fig. 11-3), soldiers in camp, children on farms, woodsmen in the Adirondack

11-2. Winslow Homer: *Long Branch, New Jersey* (1869).
(Courtesy of the Museum of Fine Arts, Boston.)

forests—with keen perception and an utter lack of sentimentality.
Many of his early pictures of children and young girls show great
delicacy of sentiment, without any of the oversweetness that spoils
so many nineteenth-century genre paintings; others, like the *Camp
Fire* (1881) (The Metropolitan Museum of Art), noteworthy originality in their treatment of the masculine world of outdoor life that
Homer was to make peculiarly his own.

Homer did some of his greatest works in the seventies; yet, although his ability was recognized, his works did not sell. In 1881,
at the age of forty-five, he made a clean break and went to the bleak
North Sea coast of England at Tynemouth where he lived and
painted for two years in solitude. On his return to America, he
abandoned New York and settled at Prout's Neck, a lonely spot on
the granite coast of Maine. The scale of his work changed: he painted

11-3. Winslow Homer: *Springtime in Virginia* (water color).
(Private collection, Detroit.)

larger pictures; his subjects became the sea and the contest between
man and the forces of nature. At first his marines were consciously
heroic in theme: *The Herring Net* (1885) (Art Institute of Chicago);
Undertow (1886), *The Life Line* (1884) (Philadelphia Museum of
Art); *The Fog Warning* (1885) (Boston) and *Eight Bells* (1886)
(Addison Gallery, Andover). These subjects of men at work, and in
danger, are monumental in scale, painted with rather liquid color
and a broad atmospheric touch, yet with solidity and great plastic
strength. In the nineties he began a series of pictures in which the
theme is the power and loneliness of the sea itself. Famous examples
are *The Northeaster* (1895) and *Cannon Rock* (1895) (both in The
Metropolitan Museum of Art) and *Eastern Point, Prout's Neck*
(1900).

Throughout these years it was his habit, also, to get away from Prout's Neck on a long trip each year. He visited the Caribbean and explored the Adirondacks and the Canadian forest. The water colors, done out of doors on these journeys, are among his finest works, painted with the force and authority of oils (Fig. 11-4). He never was confused by the fluidity of water color into treating it as a sketchy, accidental medium; on the contrary, he gave it great solidity and strength. Some large oils also came out of these later experiences in the forest. His *Huntsman and Dogs* (1891) (Fig. 11-5), in which excited dogs and sullen, silent hunter seem completely part of the vast solitude of mountain and forest, is one of the great imaginative treatments of the wilderness in American art.

Homer's achievement was to create his own vision of the world and a style to express it. It was an imaginative vision of nature, and of man's life as part of nature, that is one of the original creations of the age. It is also one which embodies deep, national memories

11-4. Winslow Homer: *Saguenay River, Lower Rapids* (water color, 1899). (Courtesy of the Worcester Art Museum.)

of the wilderness and the pioneer, so that, for Americans his work and his pictures have the eloquent overtones of a national heritage.

Thomas Eakins (1844-1916) was born in Philadelphia and spent his life there. He was trained at the Pennsylvania Academy of the Fine Arts and in 1866 went to Paris, enrolling in the Ecole des Beaux-Arts under three teachers, Gérôme, Bonnat, and the sculptor, A. A. Dumont. He worked so hard under Gérôme that he fell ill and went for seven months to Spain, to seek a change of climate. There he painted few pictures but learned much from the great Spanish realists, Velásquez and Ribera. When he returned to Philadelphia he had absorbed the disciplined French understanding of the human figure and Gérôme's love of precise, factual statement; but instead of devoting his knowledge to factitious reconstructions of history in the manner of his teacher, he turned a trained objec-

11·5. Winslow Homer: *Huntsman and Dogs* (1891).
(Courtesy of The Philadelphia Museum of Art.)

tive eye upon his native city of Philadelphia, studying its people, its life, its sports and recreations, its home life, its scientific interests —but especially the character of its men and women. Not since Copley had an American portrait painter shown so searching a penetration into character as Eakins in his Philadelphia portraits.

Eakins was interested in light; but his studies of the old masters, especially Rembrandt and Ribera, had turned him away from the upper end of the color scale where the Impressionists were at work, toward a Rembrandtesque warmth and depth of tone which, at their best, seem completely appropriate to the silent intensity of his portraits. His habits of thought were very like those of the scientists and university professors among whom he found his best portrait subjects.

His scientific interests culminated in *The Gross Clinic* (Fig. 11-6) (1875), which represents one of the outstanding surgeons of the day, and a dominating figure in the Jefferson Medical College, Philadelphia, where Eakins himself had studied anatomy. The tall, magnetic figure of the doctor dominates the complicated group; he pauses during the performance of an operation to speak to an amphitheater of students. A single figure, the patient's mother who covers her eyes in horror, brings out by contrast the objective atmosphere of calm scientific skill and intelligence. It was Eakins' vision of the heroic world of science: the figures are life-size, painted with somber richness of tone and dramatic lighting. Eakins himself was never to surpass this work of his young strength, nor was another artist to make such an effort to bring the world of science or technology into art in the United States until Rivera painted his frescoes of mass production in Detroit in 1932, fifty-seven years later. But Eakins was too bold for his times. The picture was refused admission to the American section of the Centennial Exhibition (although the jury accepted five other works by him) and he was able only with difficulty to have it hung in the medical section. The public rejection of this masterpiece of his early manhood, his failure to win recognition and support for work of such power, were a defeat from which Eakins' art never recovered. He continued to paint admirably—indeed some of his best smaller pictures were painted in the eighties and nineties—and he did one other big medical group, *The Agnew Clinic*, in 1889. But his art was never again quite so powerful or so ambitious.

11-6. Thomas Eakins: *The Gross Clinic* (1875).
(Courtesy of the Jefferson Medical College and the
Philadelphia Museum of Art, Philadelphia.)

In 1879 Eakins took over the professorship of drawing and painting at the Pennsylvania Academy of the Fine Arts. The change was a revolution in the teaching of painting. Eakins subordinated drawing from casts to the study of the nude human figure in the "life class." The most searching and severe teacher in America, he made his pupils concentrate on mastery of the living figure, lecturing to them on anatomy and teaching them also to model in clay as a discipline in plastic feeling. He taught his students to *draw with the brush* in light and tone, and founded a teaching tradition so solid that it survived his own dismissal and, through his assistant and successor Thomas Anshutz, nourished a surprising number of the best American painters of the early twentieth century. But again Eakins was too drastic and too tactless; his career as a teacher at the Academy came to an end in 1886 in a quarrel over his insistence on the nude male model in classes for women students.

The sober severity of his work may be seen in his dusky, luminous

11-7.   Thomas Eakins: *Sailing* (ca. 1874).
(Courtesy of The Philadelphia Museum of Art.)

11-8. Thomas Eakins: *The Pathetic Song* (1881).
(Courtesy of The Corcoran Gallery of Art.)

landscapes, such as *Sailing* (Fig. 11-7) (ca.1874); the Rembrandtesque gravity and intensity of his portraits, in *The Writing Master*, a portrait of his father (1881) (The Metropolitan Museum of Art); the psychological depth and dignity of his genre, in *The Pathetic Song* (Fig. 11-8) (1881). Yet as he grew older the rebuffs and disappointments of his career drove his sensibility back upon itself: his art did not grow richer with age, as one would hope, but narrower and drier. His objective imagination had to feed upon the outer world, but the outer world rejected him. Gradually the sap and vigor went out of his work and his later life was passed in obscurity.

Yet it is a mistake to think of Eakins as an isolated figure in Philadelphia: he was isolated, it is true, by matters of tact and in degree of ability; yet at the same time he is typical of something basic and enduring in the atmosphere of that city of Franklin and Bartram and the Peales. A passion for the actual, a Dutch sense of the poetry of fact, seemed native there. This is more often realized, perhaps, in the history of American science, where Philadelphia is written large throughout the century, than it is in the arts; for its artistic talents in the later nineteenth century showed a tendency to leave home for greener pastures elsewhere. But I think it is not wholly fanciful to find something forthright and ruthless in Sargent's powers of observation, something downright, too, in Mary Cassatt's way of seeing, that are close to Eakins and to the predominantly scientific-artistic character of the city.

A different development of this ruthlessly factual imagination was a Philadelphia school of still life, led by William M. Harnett (1848-1892), whose rediscovery has been one of the adventures of modern art criticism. Harnett supported himself by engraving silver in Philadelphia and New York until the age of twenty-seven. He also studied drawing in night classes, first at the Pennsylvania Academy of the Fine Arts, later in New York City at the National Academy of Design and Cooper Union. He turned to oil paint only in 1875 and when, in the following year, a depression in the silver engraver's trade threw him out of work, he went back to Philadelphia and took up painting still life as a career.

The still lifes of his first period (Philadelphia, 1876-1880) derive in style from the pictures done by James and Raphaelle Peale fifty years before, but are harder and more illusionistic in approach. They are tight, dry little compositions of objects piled at the edge of a table, like the Peale still lifes in composition, but notable for a personal choice of subjects: the smoking scene still life (built around a pipe, beer mug, and newspaper); the writing table still life (books, papers, and quill pen the principal elements); and *trompe l'œil* paintings of paper money (old, worn bills of American paper money of the Civil War period, whose worthlessness is indicated by the name "shinplaster" popularly applied to them). These pictures sold well enough to enable him, after four years, to make the trip abroad that was then the goal of every American art student. Harnett lived in Europe six years (1880-1886), chiefly in Munich, and supported himself by his painting. The interests of contemporary European painting affected him little, but he learned a richer, more painterly use of his medium by studying the seventeenth-century Dutch.

When he returned to America, he settled in New York City. In this last period (1886-1892) he returned again to his own themes of simple, humble, everyday things: but with a difference. Now he was a master of luminosities and textures, which he could sustain with remarkable intensity throughout compositions of great size, up to nearly six feet by four in dimension (Fig. 11-9).

Sometimes the major works of his last period are compositions in depth; *The Magic Flute* (1887) (collection John S. Newberry, Jr., Detroit) is an example. More often, they were *trompe l'œil* compositions of objects hanging on a painted, wooden door: *The Old Violin* (1886) (collection Mrs. Charles F. Williams, Cincinnati); *The Faithful Colt* (1890) (Hartford, Wadsworth Atheneum); or, *Old Models* (1892) (Boston, Museum of Fine Arts) are characteristic and famous. These pictures are painted with such love for the objects represented and such delight in the process of painting that the exhilaration in the painter's heart gives them not only a convincing life but a haunting mood of mystery and joy.[2]

John F. Peto (1854-1907), Harnett's friend and disciple, made still life a gentle poem on the "fantasticality of the commonplace and the pathos of the discarded," to use Frankenstein's happy phrase.

[2] The essential study of Harnett and his school is Alfred Frankenstein, *After the Hunt, William Harnett and Other American Still-Life Painters, 1870-1900,* Berkeley, University of California Press, 1953.

11-9.   William M. Harnett: *After the Hunt* (1885).
(Courtesy of Mildred Anna Williams Collection,
California Palace of the Legion of Honor.)

11-10.   John Frederick Peto: *The Poor Man's Store* (1885).
(Courtesy of the M. and M. Karolik Collection, Museum of
Fine Arts, Boston.)

Peto took over many of Harnett's motifs; but his temperament was very different. His style matured in the eighties and nineties. It is based upon harmonies of softly muted luminosities; but his work is neither so lustrous nor so forceful as Harnett's, gentler, more atmospheric, and more relaxed. Peto is uneven in quality yet his best works, like *The Poor Man's Store* (Fig. 11-10) (1885) or *After Night's Study* (The Detroit Institute of Arts), have a touching and appealing quality that is indescribable, since it is a purely visual sentiment. If Harnett is a master of textures, Peto is a poet of soft, dusky luminosities.

One has to turn to the magazine illustrations of the eighties and nineties to find a flourishing and popular art of observation of American life. Indeed, the story of objective realism would be incomplete without some account of the development of illustration, for the painter-illustrator was one of its distinctive features, and magazine illustration formed one of its most important points of contact with the public. Some of the painters already discussed were illustrators. Others, like Edwin A. Abbey, Howard Pyle, A. B. Frost, C. S. Reinhart, and Frederic Remington, applying the atmospheric technique of objective realism to magazine illustration, made the last quarter of the nineteenth century the golden age of this branch of American art.

The man who seems to have been born for this period and medium was Thomas Nast (1840-1902), a child of German liberal refugees from Germany, who went to work at fifteen as an illustrator for *Frank Leslie's Illustrated Newspaper*. Nast learned his trade at work and by looking at the great English illustrators, Leech, Keene, and Tenniel. He found his true role during the Civil War and his true medium in *Harper's Weekly*, whose staff he joined in 1862. After the war, following his own inclinations and those of the editors, Fletcher Harper and George William Curtis, he made the magazine a strong liberal and reform influence. He found his mature graphic style in 1869, when he began to draw with a pencil instead of a brush. Pencil gave a hard, incisive line, easy for the wood engraver to reproduce, and perfect for the harsh, urgent eloquence of his ideas. His fierce attacks upon the corrupt "Tweed Ring" in New York City politics were perhaps the most effective editorial cartoons ever known in America; certainly they were the first to impress the

whole nation and have never been surpassed in vitriolic intensity
(Fig. 11-11). Between 1862 and 1886, when he left *Harper's Weekly*,
Nast lifted his branch of American graphic art, the political cartoon,
to a new level of influence and importance.

Only a few illustrators can be mentioned out of the crowd of able
men at work in the period. In the seventies C. S. Reinhart (1844-

11-11.   Thomas Nast: *Can the Law Reach Him?—
The Dwarf and the Giant Thief.*
(From *Harper's Weekly*, January 6, 1872.)

11-12.   A. B. Frost: *I Am Here for a Purpose.*
(From "The Squirrel Inn," *Century Magazine,* June, 1891.)

1896) was chief of the school. Trained in Munich, he returned to New York in 1870, just at the beginning of the great period; later he lived for a long time in Paris.

Arthur B. Frost (1851-1928) was a pupil of Eakins, who went to work for *Harper's.* His special gift was for drawing American rural life, showing a fidelity and freshness that retain their flavor instead of fading with the passage of time as so many clever illustrations do (Fig. 11-12). His best known illustrations are for stories by Mark Twain, Frank R. Stockton, and Joel Chandler Harris.

In the eighties the great names were Edwin Austin Abbey and Howard Pyle. Both, however, were masters of the historical imagination and will be discussed in the next chapter.

Then there was Frederic Remington (1861-1909) who made himself the recorder of the old West, of the open range, the cowboys, and the Plains Indians. He was an admirable illustrator, especially in black-and-white and in bronze. The self-taught cowboy artist, Charles M. Russell (1864-1926), less skilled than Remington, is enjoyable for his understanding and sympathy for the life of the Indian and the cowboy: it was a life he was part of and in his small sketches made most convincing.

The independents all used light as a medium; yet they are not Impressionists. Unlike the painters of Paris (and those who followed them), they never sacrificed resonance of tone to brilliance of hue: their palettes kept the broad scale of light and dark that the old masters had shown (and, indeed, all Western painting down to 1860). Their pictures, hung among the French or American Impressionists, seem almost as warm and deep-toned as those of the seventeenth century. To their own time, which identified modernity with bright, blond color, their depth of tone was a grievous fault; so was their lack of the clever, sweeping brush stroke, so much admired in Sargent, Boldini, and Zorn. Compared to the suavity and sweetness of the American Impressionists, their style seemed rugged, harsh, displeasing. They might have said, in the words of Edward Hopper, that what they were interested in was *an art of intense reality*. But intense reality was disagreeable. Only in magazine illustration was an intense interest in subject matter allowable: there it did not seem to conflict with the fashionable avoidance of anything but the esthetic in life. Even today the independents' works are too dark, too sober, too rough; above all, too real for conventional tastes, and their fame has never spread beyond the United States. But with time the force of their achievement has made itself felt. Winslow Homer and Thomas Eakins are now accepted as two of the greatest names in our art.

Twelve

THE WORLD OF HISTORY,
MEMORY, AND DREAM

IDEALISM, the appeal of the universal in thought and the generalized in feeling, did not altogether disappear during the decades of objective realism. It is striking, in fact, to see what tremendous effort was put forward in the last three decades of the nineteenth century by thinkers, artists, scholars, religious leaders in every country of the West, to find a new form of ideal thought or rekindle an old one. In every country there were painters who strove to create a monumental and ideal art on the model of the great mural cycles of the fourteenth and fifteenth centuries; there were other brooding, meditative artists, in whom we can find the origins of the subjective and expressionist tendencies which burst into life early in the twentieth century. In America there are three important figures of this later idealism: La Farge, who made the old imagery of classical and Christian culture live again and founded a new enthusiasm for mural decoration; Ryder, who created an ideal world out of his dreams; and Vedder, who created a strange kind of ancient mythology all his own.

Although the second half of the nineteenth century saw spectacular advances made by the physical sciences, the same period saw a striking growth of the more mystical and liturgical Christian churches, notably the Roman Catholic and Episcopal. If someone may object that the first was largely fed by immigration, this was not true of the second which, from a disorganized and unpopular group after the Revolution, rose to a strong, wealthy denomination in the late nineteenth century, actively building churches and cathedrals and offering the best American artists a new opportunity for monumental art. Also, a whole series of new Federal, state, county and city buildings were erected. The desire for monumental decoration, which began with the churches, widened to include these governmental structures and other new architectural expressions of the community such as the public library, the art gallery, the university. If this decoration degenerated at the end into insipid sentimentality in men like Blashfield and Kenyon Cox and is today largely ignored or discounted, it seemed at the time one of the serious and hopeful movements of American art; and I believe it was.

The great figure of this movement was John La Farge. La Farge was an artist with a mind: his art is the expression of a wide-ranging, acute, and subtle intelligence. He is one of the remarkable group of the friends of Henry Adams which included, besides La Farge: H. H. Richardson, the architect; Augustus Saint-Gaudens, the sculptor; John Hay, the statesman. Adams, the philosopher of the group, has given in his writings (*The Education of Henry Adams*, 1907, and *Mont-Saint-Michel and Chartres*, 1904) an acute analysis of the dilemma of minds born to deal with life in terms of ideas and ethics, who found themselves living in the United States of the reconstruction period. The tide was setting strongly against them: it was the age of the mechanistic philosophy of Herbert Spencer and the materialistic determinism of Marx; of the cynical power-worship of Bismarck; the corruption of American civic and national life. Adams' *Education* offers a picture of a philosophic mind finding eighteenth-century rational humanism ineffective to explain such a world, in search of a new philosophy. He speculated with two hypotheses—that the development of life was governed by the mechanical principles of science or by the power of emotion. But what ground was there to stand on to relate these two?

Adams himself saw only the decadence of all he believed in and failed to find another positive philosophy to take its place. Yet when one looks at the artists of his circle, it is evident that they were anything but frustrated or decadent. Never have American artists of major talent had greater influence or occupied a greater national position than did they.

John La Farge (1835-1910) was one of the old New York French colony: his father, an officer in Napoleon's army, was a refugee from

Santo Domingo; his mother was the daughter of Binsse de Saint-Victor, a refugee from the Terror. Though passionately American, he was also proud of his French heritage; growing up as the child of two traditions prepared him later to have a sense of kinship with all culture. His family sent him to Europe in 1856 where he saw something of French painting: he met Chassériau and spent a few weeks drawing in Couture's studio, more with the idea of enriching his education than of studying professionally. It was after his return to America that, under the influence of William Morris Hunt, he turned to painting as a profession.

His first efforts show the strong vein of naturalism that ran through his life's work. Of *Paradise Valley, Newport* (ca.1866-1868) (Miss Mary B. Lothrop), the most important of these early studies, he said, "I wished my studies from nature . . . to be free from *recipes*, and to indicate very carefully in every part, the exact time of day and circumstance of light." This faithfulness to an exact moment and place gives the picture its character: it is a portrait of the unity of light flooding a little featureless hollow among the moor-like fields near Newport. He painted other landscapes; did book illustrations; made studies of flowers, curiously real and curiously poetic at the same time; and still lifes, like the *Greek Love Token* (Fig. 12-1) (1866), which have the factual mystery of a *trompe l'œil*.

It was H. H. Richardson, the great pioneer architect, who plunged him headlong into mural painting. With acute discernment, Richardson turned to John La Farge to decorate the great somber inner space of his Trinity Church, Boston. The problem was to create an atmosphere of solemnity, which would wipe away the everyday mood from those entering and prepare the mind for meditation and worship. La Farge rose to the challenge. With little time or preparation, he and a group of young assistants produced the first artistically successful treatment of a great interior by an American painter.[1] The completion of these decorations on January 13, 1876, marks the beginning of the second great wave of mural painting in America.

The walls of Trinity seem, however, but a beginning compared with some of his later work: the *Athens* (Fig. 12-2) in the Walker Art Gallery, Bowdoin College (1898); the *Ascension* in the Church

---

[1] Francis Lathrop was La Farge's chief helper. Lathrop, Millet, Maynard, and Kenyon Cox, among other helpers, later became mural painters themselves.

12-1. John La Farge: *Greek Love Token* (1866).
(Courtesy of the National Collection of Fine Arts,
Smithsonian Institution, Washington, D.C.)

12-2. John La Farge: *Athens* (1898). (Courtesy of
The Bowdoin College Museum of Fine Arts.)

of the Ascension, New York City; the *Four Aspects of the Law* in
the Supreme Court Chamber of the Minnesota State Capitol; or the
lunettes of the *Law Givers* in the Baltimore Court House. La Farge
was a colorist. Instead of following the example of Puvis de Chavannes, who toned down the richness of oil colors with white in
order to emulate the flat, cool effect of medieval frescoes, La Farge
worked his way to the conclusion that mural painting should be
fully realized in form and in luminous, atmospheric color. American
painting thus returned once more to the example of the Venetians.

Mural decoration is a *public* art: that is, its measure of success is
that it embodies a subject of general interest and an emotion that
has meaning for all. The late nineteenth century lacked the common
faith that had given the medieval artists their themes; it lacked the
education in classical literature that furnished the imagery of the
Baroque. La Farge was nevertheless remarkably successful in choosing out of the growing sense of world culture in his age vivid images

from the poetry of Greece and Rome, from the Bible, from the history of Europe and of Asia, and making these seem both effective and convincing.

His weakness was a naturalism, in harmony with his time, that made him approach these themes with a factual technique: there is often a certain fussy insistence on small detail, in draperies and accessories, that is disturbing. He thus reveals in his own way the conflicting ideal and factual tendencies of his age, with which Henry Adams was struggling. He is an uneven artist; sometimes greatly successful, sometimes failing lamentably. But in the best of his murals La Farge achieved a noble solemnity and great richness of feeling.

He was unique, moreover, in his sense of ensemble. At Trinity Church, Boston, he did a whole interior. Next he did the chancel of St. Thomas' Church in New York City, an ensemble of stained glass, painting, carving, and inlay; the reredos was a high relief by Saint-Gaudens, on either side of which were two large paintings by La Farge. He consciously revived the workshop tradition of the arts, employing many young artists as well as artisans; he was both able and prepared to execute anything from a large altarpiece for a church to the decoration of a music room for Mr. Whitelaw Reid (with two large paintings by the head of the workshop) or of an interior for Mrs. Cornelius Vanderbilt without paintings.

Yet it is perhaps not in these works on a great scale—portentous though they were—but in his small studies and drawings that one comes closest to the complex, subtle, and reflective mind that fascinated Henry Adams (Fig. 12-3).

About the time of the completion of Trinity Church, he began experimenting also with stained glass, which became in his hands a second, more specialized form of mural painting. Noticing the iridescence on a commercial soap dish, he thought that there must be qualities of reflected and shimmering color in glass that had not yet been realized. From this suggestion sprang his own experiments. As he succeeded, and his colored glass became more and more a splendid and diffused richness, he eliminated the leads as far as possible, so that the whole window becomes a composition in the glow of light. His glass was a personal achievement. No one else could handle it with artistic success; and he left no successors, unless one can call Tiffany glass such.

La Farge was also an articulate artist and set a high standard both as writer and lecturer. He was a man of great culture, experience, and sympathy; no one, perhaps, represents the breadth of interest and of inspiration of the period with greater dignity.

Albert Pinkham Ryder (1847-1917) lived in a world as private and enclosed as that of LaFarge was spacious. Born in New Bedford, Massachusetts, he had the sea in his background; but when he was twenty-one, his family moved to New York. He studied with a romantic painter, William E. Marshall, and in 1871 at the National Academy of Design; but he was essentially a self-taught artist, developing his own style from his experience as a painter of decorative screens and lacquers; and his own imaginative world out of his walks at night about New York, his memories of the sea, his love of music. In the midst of New York City he lived the life of a solitary,

12-3.   John La Farge: *The Strange Thing Little Kiosai Saw in the River* (1897). (Courtesy of The Metropolitan Museum of Art.)

his studio a picturesque confusion of dusty piles of newspapers and magazines, empty cereal boxes, dishes, and an accumulation of rubbish that left only a path from the door to his easel and chair— a studio that has become a legend. His art matured slowly. He exhibited at the National Academy of Design first in 1873, and from 1878 to 1887 in the Society of American Artists also, but without attracting much attention. Ryder did not enjoy travel; of the Euro-

12-4.   Albert P. Ryder: *Siegfried and the Rhine Maidens.* (Courtesy of the National Gallery of Art, Mellon Collection, Washington, D.C.)

12-5. Elihu Vedder: *The Lair of the Sea Serpent* (1864).
(Courtesy of the Museum of Fine Arts, Boston.)

pean galleries he said only, "We all like our own songs the best."
He preferred to walk by the sea on Cape Cod or in Central Park at
night; it is said that he made several voyages to London and back
with a sea captain friend, only to stay on deck all night long to
watch the moonlight and moving water. His most productive years
were from about 1880 to 1900. After this he tended to work over his
old pictures, repainting and altering, not always for the better. His
production was small, approximately one hundred and fifty works
(there came later to be ten times as many forgeries as originals)
and of these only a small number can be said to represent him at
his best.

Yet Ryder has come to have a great position in American art. The
brooding, dreaming element which runs through our imaginative
life—in Allston and Hawthorne, Whistler and Poe, Page and Emerson
—found exceptional expression in his few, small eloquent pictures
with their pigment like warm enamel in which a soft light seems to
linger.

12-6.   Elihu Vedder: *Ideal Head* (1872).
(Private collection, Winterthur, Delaware.)

In a famous letter to a friend he described his own art:

Have you ever seen an inch worm crawl up a leaf or twig, and then clinging to the very end, revolve in the air, feeling for something to reach something? That's like me. I am trying to find something out there beyond the place on which I have a footing.

This sense of eloquent mystery fills even his pictures which are based most directly on nature, like *The Dead Bird* (Phillips Memorial Gallery, Washington) or his *Self Portrait* (collection Mr. and

Mrs. Lawrence A. Fleischman, Detroit); it is embodied also in the dramatic visionary pictures drawn from Shakespeare or Wagner, *The Tempest* (The Detroit Institute of Arts), *Macbeth and the Witches* (Phillips Memorial Gallery, Washington), *Siegfried and the Rhine Maidens* (Fig. 12-4); it haunts his images of a boat flying over the moonlit waves of the sea. These pictures form a silent commentary upon the torrent of ambition and pleasure, power and material wealth, that roared about his studio on Fifteenth Street in New York; for him, it had only this meaning.

Elihu Vedder (1836-1923) was a descendant of the early Dutch settlers of the Hudson Valley, although the artist was born in New York City. He studied painting with Tompkins H. Matteson, the genre painter, in Sherbourne, New York, and with Picot in Paris. It is impossible to find any relation between either of these teachers and his later development. After living abroad in Paris, 1856-1861, he returned to New York City. The Civil War occupied all minds. He found it impossible to sell serious work and existed by doing hack work—comic valentines, sketches for *Vanity Fair*, diagrams of dumb-bell exercises for a teacher of calisthenics. It was while doing this potboiling that he conceived the strange, haunting ideas which he embodied in *The Questioner of the Sphinx* (1863) (Boston, Museum of Fine Arts), *The Lair of the Sea Serpent* (Fig. 12-5) (1864), *The Lost Mind* (1864-1865) (The Metropolitan Museum of Art). These are all storytelling pictures; and storytelling is out of fashion today. But they reveal a strange mind at work, a power of imagination capable of conceiving most unexpected and haunting images.

In 1866 he was able to return to Europe and settled in Rome, which became his home from 1867 until his death in 1923. He liked to roam about in the remote villages of the Campagna and the mountains. Some of his best works are small landscape sketches done on these expeditions, warm, dusky little pictures, painted in tone and simple, luminous colors, like an early Corot. He continued to paint imaginative fantasies, like the *Ideal Head* (Fig. 12-6) (1872), the *Cumaean Sibyl* (1876) (Wellesley College Art Museum), or *The Pleiades* (1885) (The Metropolitan Museum of Art), of an eloquent strangeness, although his style gradually changed. His later paintings are notable for their intricate and very interesting movement of line; but his color becomes chalky, pale, and ultimately very bleak. The masterpiece of his later style is, in fact, not a painting at all, but a series of more than fifty black-and-white illustrations for the *Rubáiyát of Omar Khayyám* (1884). During the enthusiasm in the nineties for mural painting he turned to that field, doing a large lunette, *Rome* (1894), in the Walker Art Gallery, Bowdoin College; and five wall paintings and a mosaic (1896 and 1897), for the Library of Congress, Washington. By this time, however, his style had become a cold, repellent mannerism; and these late works created a distaste for his work that has injured his reputation and concealed his real significance.

Vedder was a literary artist. His mind was intellectual rather than sensuous. The ancient mysteries and terrors which he imagined, or the melancholy hedonism and exotic splendor of the *Rubáiyát,* which were so congenial to his temperament, presented themselves to him in clear, intellectual images; they are unlike either the neurotic expressionism of our time or the world of shadows one finds in Ryder. He fits into no category and has therefore been ignored; but he is a master of subject matter, in a vein entirely his own.

The two famous illustrators who emerge in the eighties, Edwin Austin Abbey and Howard Pyle, also show the same hunger for the past.

Abbey (1852-1911) was born in Philadelphia and studied at the Pennsylvania Academy, though his real teachers were the illustrations in English books by artists like Millais, Rossetti, Houghton, Keene, which he saw in Philadelphia bookstores and antique shops. Abbey was born with a natural antiquarian taste and with an instinctive sympathy for the English seventeenth and eighteenth centuries. His illustrations for Herrick's poems, for Goldsmith, for *Old Songs,* and many of his illustrations for Shakespeare are little jewels of impressionist pen drawing and of happy sympathy for his subjects.

Howard Pyle (1853-1911) had the same instinctive love of the past, the same passion for antiquarian accuracy. He illustrated many books on American history which re-create with great vividness the people and scenes of the early days of America. But his reputation rests most firmly on his books for children. He wrote and illustrated a long series of children's books beginning with *The Merry Adventures of Robin Hood* in 1883 (Fig. 12-7). Pyle combined the suppleness and ease of a gifted observer, in the spirit of objective realism, with a passion for historical research. His figures are alive and convincing; every detail of costume and setting is based upon careful research. In his power to make the past come alive and in his charm of style, Pyle was extraordinary.

The Boston Public Library decorations are perhaps the best example of what the mural movement of the nineties means. Puvis de Chavannes' decoration in the stairhall, a work of the great Frenchman's old age and done without seeing the building, does not fit very

12-7.   Howard Pyle: *Merry Robin Stops a Stranger in Scarlet*. (From *The Merry Adventures of Robin Hood*, Charles Scribner's Sons, 1883.)

Merry·Robin·ſtops·a· Stranger·

in· Scarlet :·

happily in its place. E. A. Abbey gave his room of Arthurian legends at least a rich, decorative continuity and an atmosphere. But for an interior space, conceived as a decorative unity and given a powerful, dramatic atmosphere by means of wall paintings, I find to my surprise that Sargent's much criticized and highly unpopular room must be given honors that our period may be reluctant to grant.

This is not a universal opinion, by any means. Sargent's decorations were much criticized at the time, for not staying flat on the wall plane, as Puvis de Chavannes had said a mural should do— but the history of art is full of great wall paintings that contradict Puvis' dogma. They also seem, to some tastes, overdramatic; and this, one must allow, they are.

But the requirements of the mural are, that it must be:

1] monumental enough to be an enrichment of the building rather than an insertion, or patch, upon its fabric;

2] harmonious enough to be seen as a unit;

3] dramatic enough to give the room a life and atmosphere of its own; and,

4] complex enough to be seen again and again (for the room must be used and lived in), yet still reveal new details or suggest new thoughts. If these points are valid, Sargent's work, although executed in an outmoded manner and open to criticism in detail, succeeds in one respect, at least, better than any others of the decade—it creates a unified and effective whole.

Although after La Farge and Sargent the life went out of the revival of mural painting, the influence of the World's Columbian Exposition of 1893 marched on. For decades after, wherever there was a neoclassic public building, someone was likely to paint a mural. The men who produced these decorations were apparently convinced that the secret of mural painting was to represent a vaguely pretty woman in a long white robe. Standing with the Duomo and the Ponte Vecchio behind her, she represented Florence; seated or standing with appropriate emblems, she was Law, Fate, the Pursuit of Learning, the Telephone, or the Spirit of Ceramic Art; walking with Bible clasped in her hands, eyes upturned, the Pioneers crossing the Plains. (Needless to say, all these were actually painted, with many more of equal ingenuousness.) To us today, the Genius of Silliness seems to have been the muse most often consulted by these painters. What a waste of opportunity!

Thirteen

THE TWENTIETH CENTURY:

THE FIRST GENERATION

As WE REACH our own crowded and confusing century, let us look once again at the tendencies we have thus far considered permanent traits of painting in America that have served as it were as the warp threads of our story. Under the impact of novel influences and new problems in the twentieth century, these traits will seem to change greatly on the surface without, I believe, altering fundamentally underneath. These are:

1] The double perspective of our civilization: so gifted in observing and exploring the outer world of nature; so rich in memories and subtle in introspection; giving us the two categories of the imagination for which I use the terms, the real and the ideal; the work of art carved out of the experience of nature, and the work of art spun out of memories, traditions, literatures, dreams. As the direction of attention changes, the weight of emphasis swings from one to the other, but no generation is without artists of great talent to express each of these Janus-faces of our minds.

2] The double nature of the arts: art, and craft; unpredictable creativity, and disciplined skill; imaginative discovery, and practical livelihood; the ever fresh eye, and the traditional technical problems and traditional means of solving them.

3] The two poles of attraction: the life of our own country, so varied and interesting, yet so new, diffused, and raw; the tradition of our civilization, represented by Europe, so profuse in talents, concentrated and dense in flavor as a rich old wine; giving us the two tendencies—the cosmopolitan artist, drawn toward Europe and the traditional centers of art; the independent or nativist who wants above all to find the meaning of America and of the spot where he was born.

4] The effect upon the craft of painting of the wilderness continent and the advancing frontier of settlement, stretching the population so thin that many born to be artists grew up far from the skilled practice of art, thus giving us the phenomenon of the *untrained professional.*

The nineteenth century closed with the cosmopolitan tendency in the ascendant. The conspicuous effort from 1875 to 1900 had been to link our painting with that of Europe, and to make American talents part of the international life of art.

There were notable artists at work in the year 1900—Whistler, Sargent, Homer, Eakins, La Farge, Ryder were all still active. But they were old now. The tone of painting was set by the younger generation. The century closed on the pale, quiet note of the Ten American Painters and their contemporaries, who, in search of refinement, had excluded all but the purely esthetic from their attention. In style a watered-down combination of Sargent's brushwork and French Impressionism prevailed. This gentle, overrefined art was rudely challenged shortly after the turn of the century by a new generation of native talents from within, and from without by the furious explosions of Fauvism and Cubism in Paris, Expressionism in Germany, and Futurism in Italy, whose reverberations quickly reached our shores.

In the third quarter of the nineteenth century painting had been a popular and flourishing craft, practiced in every corner of the land and surrounded by its related and supporting crafts of illustration and engraving. By the end of the century, as Isham observed sadly, a man could no longer expect to earn a living by painting, no matter how hard-working or talented he might be. Portrait painting, the useful, bread-and-butter craft that had supported painters for two hundred years, was gone. Photoengraving had killed the beautiful craft of wood engraving that had flourished in the monthly magazines in the eighties and the decline of illustration had begun. Painting, without a staple product that society wanted, had become an insecure, impoverished pursuit whose rewards were at the mercy of fashion and the shifting breezes of reputation.

The rise of nineteenth-century technology and machine production had also worked devastation in the handcrafts. The men and women born to be craftsmen, displaced from their proper fields of skill and applied design, now came crowding into painting; though not suited to their gifts, it was the only outlet left to them. Painting thus became diluted with talents that did not belong to it; while the important task of the designer and craftsman—shaping and giving order and harmony to the whole setting of life—was abandoned to unguided machine production. Even if the result had been an enormous increase in the number of good painters, the vulgarization of all the objects that form the setting of our daily lives would have been a heavy price to pay.

Not only the poverty but, I believe, some of the restlessness of painters and painting in our time is connected with this change. Something of the regular rhythm of modern painting from revolt to rapidly hardening convention to renewed revolt is connected, in my opinion, with the want of balance in the arts caused by the destruction of the handcrafts. Nothing could be more overcrowded, insecure, and underpaid than the craft of painting in our times. All the more remarkable the daring, the invention, the stubborn devotion that have marked it as an art.

The revolt against the pale estheticism of second-generation Impressionism was touched off, first, by an exhibition of Eight American Painters, who showed together at the Macbeth Gallery, New York, in 1908. The Eight were united only by their friendship, for there was no common point of view of style; and they exhibited together only this once.[1] Yet the impact of the exhibition was such as to make it a landmark. Its significance lay in the fact that these artists were warm, courageous human beings who restored self-confidence and joy of life to American painting.

The leader of the Eight was Robert Henri (1865-1929), born in

[1] The exhibition was held at the Macbeth Gallery in February, 1908. The Pennsylvania Academy asked for the exhibition and afterward circulated it to eight other museums over a period of more than a year. Seven paintings were sold from the exhibit—four to Gertrude Vanderbilt Whitney, who was to play a notable part as friend and patron of independent artists in the next two decades. The best descriptions of the group and the exhibit are to be found in the catalogs of two retrospective exhibitions, *The Eight*, by John I. H. Baur, The Brooklyn Museum, 1943-1944, and *John Sloan*, by Lloyd Goodrich, The Whitney Museum of American Art, 1952.

13-1. William J. Glackens: *Chez Mouquin* (1905). (Courtesy of
The Art Institute of Chicago, Friends of American Art.)

Cincinnati, trained first under Anshutz at the Pennsylvania Academy, then at Julian's and the Ecole des Beaux-Arts in Paris. After further travels and independent work abroad in 1895-1897 and 1899, Henri settled in New York in 1900 to begin a long career, primarily as a teacher. His fundamental principle as a teacher, as John Sloan said later, was "the importance of *Life* as the primary motive of art." By this, rather than his style of painting, Henri challenged the whole prevailing mood of imitative estheticism. His inspiring, magnetic warmth as a teacher (enshrined in his book, *The Art Spirit*), his reawakening of the love of life and self-confidence in American painters, were his great contribution. His own paintings are direct, rather sketchy portraits, done in a style that reflected his admiration for Hals, Velásquez, and Manet, but marred by hasty and careless handling.

In 1907, the jury of the National Academy of Design, intolerant toward the younger generation, rejected the work of Henri's friends, George Luks, John Sloan, and William Glackens. Henri, in disgust, withdrew his own pictures from the exhibition. Arthur B. Davies had been exhibiting at the Macbeth Gallery, founded in 1892 as the first New York picture dealer's gallery devoted to contemporary American art. In 1908 this gallery asked Davies to arrange an exhibition of some of the younger painters that interested him. Davies selected eight painters: Henri, Glackens, Luks, Sloan, Shinn, Davies, Prendergast, and Lawson. The humorous street scenes of New York's crowded slums contributed by John Sloan seemed to have shocked the reviewers most: at least he was, of the group, the one who for years after met the most difficulty in selling his work. It is hard to believe now that the swift, sure brushstroke and gaiety of color of William Glackens' *Chez Mouquin* (1905) (Fig. 13-1), which was in this exhibit, can have seemed disagreeable at that time: yet even Ernest Lawson, a pleasant but far from exciting decorative Impressionist landscape painter, was accused of emphasizing the ugly in his landscapes.

The revolt of the Eight was not one of style or of the brush but of the heart: it was a reassertion of self-reliance, in the tradition of Emerson and Whitman, against an atmosphere of imitativeness and timid estheticism. It had its parallel in literature in the appearance of Dreiser, Frank Norris, and later of Sinclair Lewis to assert the importance of American life and daily experience as themes of art.

Of all the Eight, John Sloan (1871-1951) left the largest and most consistent achievement. Before coming under Henri's influence, in his newspaper period he was a successful black-and-white artist working in a clever, somewhat bookish *art nouveau* style. Henri turned his interest outward to the vivid actualities of life about him. His removal to New York from Philadelphia in 1904 gave him his great subject. He loved New York. He loved to walk its streets and watch the movement of the city; he loved the warm, rich flavors of human life in its great masses of people, on the streets, in their places of enjoyment, at home. His paintings were direct, spontaneous reports of what struck his keen and humorous eye (Fig. 13-2). As Lloyd Goodrich said, "His art had that quality of being a direct product of the common life, absolutely authentic and unsweetened, that has marked the finest genre of all times."[2] Sloan always drew with vitality and pungency. His color sense was not so sure as his sense of tone, so that his best work is to be found either in his drawings and etchings or in his early oils, painted in low-keyed, dusky tonal harmonies which he used with skill and richness.

William Glackens (1870-1938) also studied at the Pennsylvania Academy and worked for the *Philadelphia Press.* In 1895 he went to Paris for a year of independent work and, on his return, settled in New York, working as an illustrator for newspapers and monthly magazines and doing humorous drawings for *Life* and *Judge.* Other painters greatly admired his skill as a draughtsman: Guy Pène du Bois, the painter, who served for a time as art critic for the magazine *Arts and Decoration,* called him (September, 1914): "The best eyes in American art." Glackens first painted in the warm tonality that all these painter-illustrators adopted, partly out of admiration for Manet, partly in revolt against the sugar-and-cream palette of the American Impressionists. Later, under the influence of Renoir, he adopted a bright, sharp color that does not please the eye as much as his early, darker but more harmonious work. As an observer, Glackens showed a cooler temperament than Sloan; his pictures are those of a gay but rather detached observer (Fig. 13-1).

George Luks (1867-1933), on the contrary, was one of those roaring, gusty painters who become legends in their lifetimes, but of whom very little is left when their vital personality is gone. He had great love of life and fantastic humor and, as his friend Shinn said,

[2] *John Sloan,* Whitney Museum of American Art, 1952.

he was "a great actor and a fascinating liar. . . . Only George Luks's great ability as a painter could excuse his weaknesses." After the Pennsylvania Academy, Munich, and the *Philadelphia Press* he moved to New York in 1896, where he drew a comic strip for the *New York World*—how far from the code of genteel estheticism!— and about 1902 turned to painting in a style inspired by his love of Frans Hals.

Everett Shinn (1876-1953), the youngest of the group, was a clever illustrator whose best work has grown out of his love of the theater and his love of Paris, both of which he has painted with gaiety and charm.

13-2.   John Sloan: *The Wake of the Ferry* (1907).
(Courtesy of the Phillips Collection, Washington, D.C.)

The other members of the Eight show the diversity of inspiration that was to be an outstanding characteristic of twentieth-century painting.

Ernest Lawson (1873-1939), a pupil of Twachtman, was a decorative Impressionist; but from love of the massive richness of oil paint he developed his own style in which the image of the thing painted seems sunk, still visible but partially obliterated, in the spongy depths of the paint.

Maurice Prendergast (1859-1924) was the only member of the Eight from outside New York. He grew up in Boston, traveled and painted abroad a good deal, and moved to New York only in 1914. He was a pioneer of the impulse (apparently latent in all Impressionism) to turn its medley of small brushstrokes into a pattern and thus to stylize nature into a two-dimensional color mosaic. Nature interested Prendergast only as a point of departure: his goal was a

13-3.   Maurice Prendergast: *The East River* (1901). (Collection of The Museum of Modern Art, New York, gift of Mrs. John D. Rockefeller, Jr.)

13-4.   Arthur B. Davies: *Along the Erie Canal.*
(Courtesy of the Phillips Collection, Washington, D.C.)

tapestry-like composition of fresh, luminous, happy colors. Older than the others, he had already developed in highly personal water colors, in the nineties, his art of cheerful, multicolored pattern (Fig. 13-3). It is a question in my mind whether his later oils, delightful in color but monotonous in subject and composition, represent any actual advance over the early water colors.

Arthur B. Davies (1862-1928) was, on the other hand, a painter of idyllic visions and reveries, in the tradition of Allston and Ryder. Unlike Ryder, Davies was not a recluse; he was, on the contrary, a man of culture and wide knowledge, whose paintings were fed by memories of poetry and of the past. The frieze-like designs of nude figures and rhythmic colors which form his mature style (Fig. 13-4) might have made better mural paintings than most of those being done by the mural specialists of that time but Davies, with rare exceptions, preferred the idyllic and intimate to the monumental. At the end of his life, however, he turned to tapestry design for which his art was most suitable, and had his designs woven at the Gobelins factory in France.

As one looks back at the period 1900-1914, however, it is obvious that the painter-illustrators of the Eight were by no means an isolated phenomenon. The first decade of the century was filled with efforts to break away from the decorative direction that Impressionism had taken, and to adapt its luminous colors and strongly emphasized brushstrokes to a new realism and zest for life.

Some of the artists who took part in this new movement of realism worked in New York. George Bellows (1882-1925) was an artist who preferred the strong, hearty, pungent flavors of life—prize fights, religious revivals, New York's swarming streets, or the drama of the

13-5.   George Wesley Bellows: *Introducing John L. Sullivan.* (Courtesy of Mr. and Mrs. John Hay Whitney, New York.)

13-6. Rockwell Kent: *Horn Island*. (From *Voyaging Southward from the Strait of Magellan*, G. P. Putnam's Sons, 1924.)

great rivers that surround Manhattan. Time has not sustained Bellows' contemporary fame, which was based in part on big, violent pictures of boxing matches that seemed at the time very bold and exciting (Fig. 13-5). He was a rapid and slashing rather than a fine draughtsman, and his color was often bad, so that he was at his best, probably, in his lithographs. Perhaps his energy and gusto might have matured artistically had he not died prematurely at forty-three; but his surviving work, marred by careless handling and coarse color, seems now faded and, worse still, mediocre.

Rockwell Kent (born 1882) also began as a painter of landscapes and marines, working in a dark palette close to that of the Eight. Later he turned to book illustration in black-and-white. He was a wanderer by temperament, who lived in Maine, Newfoundland, and Alaska; explored Tierra del Fuego and the Straits of Magellan in a small boat; and wrote of his travels in books illustrated by himself. His *Wilderness* (1920) and *Voyaging Southward* (1924) (Fig. 13-6) are visually about the best American books of their period in their balanced harmony of text and illustrations. His admiration for William Blake helped shape his dramatic black-and-white style: ideal rather than realistic; marked by tall, slender, generalized figures, whose flowing sweep of line and contrasts of tone often give eloquent expression to moods of loneliness and tension.

Jerome Myers (1867-1940) was, like Sloan or Bellows, a painter of New York's streets and slums; but he created out of this subject matter an art with neither Sloan's warmth nor Bellows' violence. Instead, his pictures are tender and darkly luminous little canvases, idyllic or sometimes gently fantastic in feeling (Fig. 13-7). His is a personal art, handsome in color, and too generally overlooked today in the silence that always falls after a generation's passing.

13-7. Jerome Myers: *The Children's Theatre.* (Courtesy of The Detroit Institute of Arts.)

Guy Pène du Bois (1884-1958), another painter-illustrator, made the night life of New York his theme. He was a witty, intelligent man and a good critic; but like Forain, his contemporary in Paris, he fell into a painting formula that quickly grew wearisome.

By 1900, New York City had reached the peak of its dominance as the center of American painting. There also took place then the first attempts to break away from it, not by the process of other cities reasserting their vitality and attraction, but by the creation of artists' colonies. Chief among those founded in the early 1900's were at Taos, Provincetown, New Hope, and Carmel. The aim of an artists' colony, presumably, is to create a congenial, stimulating atmosphere for artistic production—which is not always what is achieved. It was originally also an impulse of realism, a desire to paint something of great character and interest in the American land. The fact that the famous artists' colonies, too, rose out of the new realism of the beginning of the century is not often remembered.

These colonies grew out of the desire to break away from New York, or Europe, and to find a new inspiration in the American scene. The Taos colony was in existence by 1900. Joseph Sharp (1859-1953), who had studied in Europe with Duveneck, discovered Taos Pueblo and persuaded some of his friends and fellow pupils to settle there. Oscar Berninghaus, Ernest Blumenschein, Irving Couse, Walter Ufer, and Victor Higgins were the pioneers at Taos, finding their subjects in the people of the Indian town as The Eight found theirs in New York City. Charles W. Hawthorne (1872-1930), founder of the artists' colony at Provincetown, found his subjects, too, among the fishermen and townspeople of the little fishing port; but he was also an important stylist. He combined the inspiration of the deep tonal palette of Venetian painters, like Tintoretto, with the urge rising everywhere at that time in twentieth-century painting— the urge to simplify the language of painting into planes of color, laid one against another like the tesserae of a mosaic. He achieved this in his own personal way, but his sense of style made him one of the most influential painter-teachers of the early twentieth century.

In general, the American realists of the early twentieth century continued the tradition of warm, tonal luminism which the independent painters of Eakins' time had maintained, in opposition to the world-wide popularity of the Impressionist palette of cool, bright, variegated hues. Artists such as Sloan or Glackens were at their best in their early deep-toned works and found it hard to master the blond French palette. The other urge—to simplify painting into flat, rhythmic patterns of color—seems to have been felt more strongly by the subjective artists who turned away from nature toward intuitive and ideal inspiration. Maurice Prendergast and Arthur B. Davies, Charles W. Hawthorne and the mural painter Augustus Vincent Tack (1870-1949) all show this impulse in their various ways.

What is the source of this urge to stylize and conventionalize, to simplify nature into flat, glowing areas of color and bold patterns of line, that sprang up everywhere in the first decade of this century? The popular impression is that it represents the influence of the Armory Show, which introduced "modernism" (as the influence of French Post-Impressionist painting is called) into America. This is, however, far too easy an answer. All the original American artists who seem now to deserve remembrance were already moving toward an ideal, stylized art before the Armory Show; the painters whose modernism dates from it are the derivative figures who have been forgotten.

The reaction from objective realism to the unrealistic styles of twentieth-century art—in which drawing and color are released from any necessity to represent what the eye sees in nature, expressing instead formal harmonies of the mind's invention—was in part one of those alternating tides in the direction of attention that are normal in our history. We are the heirs not only of Greek rationalism and centuries of disciplined observation of the outer world of nature but of the inwardness of the Orient, whose great representative is Christianity, to which the wisdom of this world is foolishness. Our intellectual and artistic history is a succession of alternating tides of these impulses, realistic and idealistic, objective and subjective.

After the scientific rationalism of the late nineteenth century came a reaction to the emotions, to intuition and dream. Not merely a reaction: an active cultivation of the unreal, the irrational, the primitive. For into this alternation of reason and instinct, logic and intuition, came an influx of ideas from outside the Western tradition. From 1850 onward Western artists, especially in Paris, experimented with and adopted a succession of forms from the non-European arts. With the twentieth century, the stream of influence from outside the Western tradition became a roaring flood. An artist like Picasso is typical of our times: he has roamed through the history of art, borrowing suggestions from Negro sculpture, from late Greek vase painting, from Visigothic sculpture in Spain, from the arts of New Guinea, and, it may be, from the newspaper comic strip, and with demonic energy and eclecticism has invented one new style after another of extraordinary brilliance. The major part of the twentieth-century artists' revolt against the nineteenth century has been shot through with inspirations from ancient, primitive and, almost always, non-European forms of art.

Thus, as artists turned again toward an ideal art, a great wave of influence from exotic, mystic, and irrational arts outside our civilization fell heavily against the swinging pendulum. If one were to read only esthetic theory it would seem that Western art had now completed a circle and returned to the position of Winckelmann and neoclassicism—that beauty was to be found not in the face of nature, but only in the inner world of the mind. In practice, however, nothing now seemed more boring to artists than the classical Greek or Roman art admired by Winckelmann's contemporaries. Japanese prints, Persian pottery, medieval stained glass, Negro masks and fetishes, South Sea idols, Egyptian sculpture were to this generation what the Roman marbles of the Vatican Gallery and the Louvre had been to the neoclassicists.[3]

[3] This movement first found expression in the most highly self-conscious centers of painting, Paris, Berlin, and Vienna. The French created the clear, logical styles of Fauvism and Cubism, the Germans and Austrians an emotional expressionism. Knowledge of these movements was brought to the United States by a generation of Americans who studied in Paris in the decade 1900-1910. Lloyd Goodrich called their roll in an interesting, retrospective exhibition at the Whitney Museum of American Art, called *Pioneers of Modern Art in America* (1946). The men who went to Paris from 1900 on and felt the impact of Fauvism and Cubism were Alfred Maurer (who went to Paris in 1897); Bernard Karfiol (1901); Samuel Halpert (1902); Maurice Sterne (1904); Max Weber (1905); Abraham Walkowitz (1906); and after these, Walter Pach, Charles Demuth, Morgan Russell, Stanton Macdonald-Wright, Thomas Benton, Arthur Dove, Andrew Dasburg, Morton Schamberg, Charles Sheeler, Marguerite and William Zorach, Joseph Stella, Arthur Carles, Marsden Hartley.

The years from 1905 to 1908 in Paris saw the great retrospective exhibitions of Cézanne and Gauguin as well as the birth of Fauvism and Cubism. Most of the American students came to know the Parisian leaders of painting, Matisse, Derain, Braque, Picasso, and plunged ardently into their new movement—the liberation of color from natural appearance and the construction of ideal rhythmic harmonies instead of the depiction of the outer world. Gertrude Stein's Saturday night receptions formed a meeting place for some of the Americans in Paris and became a center of propaganda for the new movement.

If the public and juries were hostile to John Sloan, it may be imagined how difficult it was for the disciples of the newest movements to show their work when they returned home. The first gallery open to them was the Photo-Secession gallery, owned by Alfred Stieglitz, which became famous as "291," its street number on Fifth Avenue. Stieglitz was a formidable personality and controversialist, a passionate defender of the artists he believed in, and an autocrat in his own circle. He exerted a strong influence on public opinion.

But the public at large was introduced to the new movements by the Armory Show of 1913. The exhibition was the project of a group of liberal-minded artists. All but one of the Eight were involved in it, as well as Bellows, Du Bois, Myers, Walt Kuhn, Allen Tucker, and a dozen more. Arthur B. Davies was president of the group, and with the aid of Walt Kuhn and the assistance of Walter Pach in Paris, organized the international section of the exhibition. Its purpose was twofold.

The first and main aim of the Armory Show was to carry on the revolt of the Eight against the intolerance of their own profession. There was need of a place where the younger artists could show their work, and the catalogue of the Armory Show lists 1,112 works by 307 American artists (although others were added until the total is said to have been 1,600 pictures).

But the part of the exhibition that attracted most attention was the international section, which offered the first full representation in America of Cézanne, Gauguin, Van Gogh, and the living artists of Paris. The "shock" of the exhibition was Marcel Duchamp's *Nude Descending a Staircase*. Although called international, this section consisted almost exclusively of the school of Paris. For a long time after this American artistic opinion remained unaware of the vigorous experimental movements in Germany, Italy, and England.

The uproar over the Armory Show was prodigious. The eye is a conservative organ. Most people do not use their eyes intensively, and the thought patterns connected with the sense of sight are few and rudimentary. Americans, as a matter of fact, had then little opportunity to see contemporary painting. New York had drained away the best contemporary talent from the rest of the country, and the few strong artists outside New York lived largely in isolated colonies. Without a vigorous artistic life in most parts of the country it is no wonder that public taste was sluggish. But if there was small public for good painting—or painting of any kind—there was a huge and clamorous newspaper press that filled the country with the noise of this distant war and popularized the Cubist joke. After the exhibition closed in New York its international section was shown in Chicago where the students at the Art Institute school burnt a Matisse in effigy. However, the time was soon to come when, if an American painter did not choose to follow the lead of Paris, he had better learn to eat grass.

For a cultural change as great and abrupt as this a price must be paid, as Toynbee would say. Among the American converts to Fauvism and Cubism were many who exhausted their energies in breaking away from their background and had no vitality to create something of their own. Cubism in its strict form—the keen, logical analysis and re-creation of form, as practiced by Picasso, Braque, and Gris in the heroic days of the movement—was never followed or even understood in America. The wave of imitations of Cézanne or the Fauves (also ill-digested enough) also soon passed. What took root in America was a love of more rigorous and stylized ways of painting than had been practiced before, an interest in rhythmic pattern, and a use of free simplifications of the image of nature to emphasize either the construction of the picture or the artist's mood.

The most consistently strong and productive original artist in America was John Marin (1872-1953), the dominant figure of the twenties, who lived long enough to become the patriarch of American painters and to produce some of his finest work in his fifth decade of painting.

13-8. John Marin: *Maine Islands* (1922). (Courtesy of
the Phillips Collection, Washington, D.C.)

Marin was an architect for four or five years before he began to
study painting at the Pennsylvania Academy under Anshutz (it is
remarkable how many of the best of the early twentieth-century
Americans came out of Anshutz's classes) and later at the Art Students League. In 1905 he went abroad and stayed until 1910. He
etched many European city views, inspired by Whistler: subtle studies of shimmering light and atmosphere upon the face of Venice, or
Paris, or Amsterdam. The water colors done in Europe before his
return to New York show his first, tentative attack upon the central
problem of his art: how to translate the light and movement of
nature into an architectonic construction of shimmering, fresh, radiant colors.

New York's skyscrapers and the American landscape, particularly on the coast of Maine, seemed very exciting to him when he returned to America. "These [my] works," he wrote in 1928, "are meant as constructed expressions of the inner senses, responding to things seen and felt." Color became an explosive, graphic language for the heroic poetry of rocks, and sun, and sea, for the drama of skyscrapers and elevated, for mountains and clouds. The phrase "pertaining to," in the title, was often his way of expressing this oblique relation to things: *Pertaining to Deer Isle; Pertaining to Stonington Harbor.* However abstractly expressed, his paintings aimed to express the poetry of the actual things of nature: but nature was transposed to a new plane of excitement, and described in a coloristic shorthand.

His major medium, for the quarter-century after his return to America, was water color. He used it in a staccato, dynamic style

13-9. John Marin: *Sea Piece* (1951). (Courtesy of Mr. and Mrs. Lawrence A. Fleischman, Detroit.)

13-10. Charles Demuth: *Acrobats* (1919). (Collection of The
Museum of Modern Art, New York, gift of Mrs. John D. Rockefeller, Jr.)

that was new, yet with the same finality and authority one sees in Winslow Homer's use of the medium. Several of his technical devices—the self-enframing image; the breaking of the vista into several separate but related compartments; the emphasis on both depth and the flatness of the picture plane at the same time (so different from Matisse's way of doing it) were very original graphic inventions (Fig. 13-8). In the twenties he again turned back to oils, which he used much like water color—emphasizing transparency of color and the dry, dragged stroke of the brush.

In pictorial language Marin has been one of the inventive painters of his age. It is a pictorial language, not of formal harmonies, but of lyrical expression; and a lyrical expression, not of the studio world of objects on a table or a model posing on a stand, but of the expansive, joyful poetry of earth, and sun, and sea (Fig. 13-9).

Marin was always an independent, in the modern movement but apart from it. Charles Demuth (1883-1939) loved the life of the art centers—Paris, Greenwich Village, Provincetown, then at the height of their bohemian effervescence—and was in temperament very much part of the world of *avant-garde* estheticism. But his cool, watchful, aloof personality and his jewel-like style, precise and elegant as a print by Utamaro, were highly original.

Like Marin, Demuth used water color with great distinction. His style was a combination of clear, sharp, pencil outline with wet, free, color washes of eggshell translucence; the effect is a combination of delicacy and strength (Fig. 13-10). In the years 1915-1919 he did many illustrations, not for actual publication, but to re-create for himself in his own pictorial terms the writing that interested him—Henry James's horror stories, Zola, Wedekind, Poe. He showed a special fondness, also, for vaudeville and café and bar life. Andrew Ritchie calls these latter the "distillations of that period of esthetic bohemianism that flowered during the first two decades of this century and whose roots were in Paris, London and Berlin. . . . No other American has given us by implication so sensitive and so subtle an account of the cynicism and disillusionment that marked the years before and during World War I."[4] But if these scenes of *vie de bohème* are part of a general mood at this time, they are treated with a cool, formal detachment, as if seen through a window

[4] Andrew C. Ritchie, *Charles Demuth*, New York, Museum of Modern Art, 1950.

of quartz through which no warmth could penetrate, that is entirely personal with Demuth.

One of his entertaining inventions was what he called the poster portrait. These were in oil and were characteristically oblique, symbolic portraits of a few of his intimates like Georgia O'Keeffe, Arthur Dove, Marsden Hartley, and John Marin. The portrait of the poet, William Carlos Williams, *I Saw the Figure Five in Gold* (1921) (The Metropolitan Museum of Art), is outstanding, a bold, strong, interesting picture which could be the product only of a highly individual mind and eye. It illustrates also Demuth's tendency to draw inspiration from the geometric shapes of architecture and modern technology. It seems odd, yet characteristic, that this elegant esthete should have been one of the first to discover the cold beauty of the machine.

The touch of Cubism seems to have stimulated many Americans. In France the first enthusiasm for intellectual analysis of form gave way, about 1915, to a second phase in which the medium of oil paint —its colors, textures, and brushstrokes, spots, stripes, stripplings, its scrapings and grainings, its effects of mass and thinness—became both the medium and the subject of pictures. In France, this second phase was to produce a new period of decorative invention. In the United States, on the contrary, the effect of Cubism was to produce a heightened awareness of form, a love of clean lines and architectonic shapes; and these were turned outward into a new approach to nature. Demuth illustrates this development very clearly; and so does Charles Sheeler (born 1883). Like so many other good painters of this generation, Sheeler was born in Philadelphia and studied at the Pennsylvania Academy; but after a visit to Europe in 1909, which brought him in touch with the school of Paris, he settled in New York. In 1912 he took up photography for a living, a fact which was to have an influence on his painting. After a period of experiment with Cubist analysis of form, he turned in the twenties toward an objective art based on careful observation. With a deep feeling for American traditions and sources, he discovered qualities of clean, strong form in Shaker buildings and craftsmanship; in the stone barns of Pennsylvania; in New York skyscrapers; in the gigantic new concrete and steel industrial architecture. By translating this discovery into painting, he was able to reinterpret eloquently to Americans their own native setting. Sheeler's series of paintings and photographs, made in 1927 and 1930, of the River Rouge plant of the Ford Motor Company, probably more than any other work opened the eyes of his generation to the severe beauty of functional engineering design (Fig. 13-11).

Preston Dickinson (1891-1930), another significant figure of the twenties, found in the bridges and industry of the Harlem River or the ramparts and stone houses of Quebec subjects for paintings of an austere, intricate beauty of plane and line in oil or pastel.

Lyonel Feininger (1871-1956) had gone to Europe in 1887 at the age of sixteen, and lived in Germany until the rise of the Nazis drove him back across the Atlantic in 1937, fifty years later. His art thus belongs to the story of painting in Germany, rather than in America. But it is curious to find him developing, in Berlin, along lines parallel to those we have been tracing—adapting the Cubist language of line and plane to the poetry of light and nature.

13-11.   Charles Sheeler: *Classic Landscape* (1931).
(Courtesy of Mrs. Edsel B. Ford, Detroit.)

13-12. Joseph Stella: *The Bridge* (1920-1922).
(Collection of The Newark Museum.)

Joseph Stella (1879-1946) was born in Italy and came to New York at the age of twenty-three. After working for some years as a magazine illustrator, he returned to Italy for study in 1909. There he came in touch with the Futurist movement and in 1911 with French Cubism. Returning to New York, he too turned to the bridges and lights of New York for large, dramatic, and highly personal pictures of the beauty of technology (Fig. 13-12).

For some reason the impact of Fauvism on American colorists was not so immediately helpful as Cubism had been to the American sense of form. Marsden Hartley (1877-1943) was a born colorist who, after studying with Chase in New York between 1900 and 1910, had worked his own way toward the liberation of color and the stylization of nature. In Berlin, where he spent much of the time from 1912 to 1915, he found himself for the first time in huge, abstract still lifes. His *Portrait of a German Officer* (1914) (Metropolitan Museum of Art) in glowing, clangorous, primary-color-notes, red, white, yellow, green, and black, on a black ground, has all the color-eloquence of a great Fauve painting. He was not to do anything so personal and strong again for twenty-five years.

It was not until the end of his life, when he had returned to his native state of Maine, that he found himself again. Then, in a style of glowing color and massive paint, filled with a peculiar sense of leaden weight, he painted the beautiful still lifes of rocks and ropes, shells and dead sea-birds, the landscapes, and the figure subjects (which are also still lifes) on which his final reputation as a painter rests (Fig. 13-13).

There were other gifted colorists in this generation: Walt Kuhn (1880-1949); Max Weber (1881-1961); Arthur Dove (1880-1946); Arthur B. Carles (1882-1952); Clayton S. Price (1874-1950); yet not one can be said to show a steady, sustained, self-confident activity. A restless series of experiments with new manners, or an esthetic thinness, a meagerness of production haunts them all. Who can say what Max Weber really is, for example, out of all the manners he has tried? To me he is an admirable still-life painter; and a good figure painter when interested in his subject, as when for a time he turned to themes of Jewish traditional life that meant much to him as a human being: but he has been so much else!

The exhibition of the Eight at the Macbeth Gallery in 1908 is the accepted symbol of the first artistic movement of the twentieth century, the revolt of the realists against the estheticism of the nineties. It was a momentary grouping within a much larger movement. In the work of all the early twentieth-century realists is an underlying note of what in the nineteen-thirties would have been called regionalism. They were men in love with their subjects—the crowded life of New York, the Portuguese fishermen of Provincetown, the Indians and fierce sunlight of New Mexico, or the landscape of the Delaware Valley. By 1914, one may say, the point of view of the realists had won its place and been absorbed into the stream; by 1920 its stimulus was gone.

But the vital movement of the times was not realistic. The direction of attention was surging away from nature toward the lyrical and subjective imagination, toward a formal and stylized art. The various forms of idealism took shape at the same time, between 1900 and 1914; but the important American painters of this movement had to wait another decade for recognition. In the years between the close of the 1914 war and the great depression, reinforced by some able recruits from a still younger generation, they won recognition and gave a new shape to the imaginative life in the United States. That period, however, is partly the story of the next chapter, for two brilliant generations met in the art of the twenties.

Gradually collectors appeared to support the new taste: John Quinn, advised by Walt Kuhn; Miss Lillie Bliss, advised by Arthur B. Davies; Albert C. Barnes, introduced to the new taste by Glackens; Frederic Clay Bartlett, the painter, whose collection in the Art Institute of Chicago exerted an early and very potent influence; and most personal of all, Duncan Phillips, who in 1918 founded in Washington the Phillips Memorial Gallery, the first public institution devoted to twentieth century taste. Finally, the Museum of Modern Art was founded in 1929 in New York City, with the primary support of Mrs. John D. Rockefeller, Miss Lillie Bliss, Mrs. Cornelius Sullivan, and A. Conger Goodyear. Its first series of exhibitions: *Cézanne, Van Gogh, Gauguin, Seurat; Painting in Paris;* and *Modern German Painting and Sculpture,* selected and interpreted with superb taste and eloquence by Alfred Barr, presented European Post-Impressionism and twentieth-century developments with an éclat that roused immense popular support the nation over.

The first three decades of this century also brought great changes in the opportunities to see the range and height of the art of painting. The art museums of the chief American cities, though founded twenty-five years before, were, in 1900, still in their infancy. Their collections were small. The perspective offered by them upon the range and greatness of the arts was spotty and of indifferent quality. The twentieth century was to change all this. A period of tremendous collecting set in, more ambitious and more discerning than had ever existed before in this country.

It is characteristic of the change in atmosphere that collecting now turned to the mystical ages of art. Admirable collections were formed of the glorious ranges of medieval art: in Boston, Cambridge, New York, Cleveland, in the John G. Johnson Collection in Philadelphia and the Walters Collection in Baltimore. The unequalled collections of Asiatic art were formed in Boston, in the

13-13.   Marsden Hartley: *Log Jam, Penobscot Bay.*
(Courtesy of The Detroit Institute of Arts.)

University Museum, Philadelphia, and the Freer Collection, Washington. The wonderful Egyptian and Greek collections of Boston and New York took shape. Rich collections of primitive arts and pre-Columbian archaeology were formed in the University Museum, Philadelphia, the American Museum of Natural History and the Museum of the American Indian, New York, and in the Peabody Museum in Cambridge. Great panoramas of European painting were the aim of all ambitious museums. In forming these, a notable emphasis was put on the medieval centuries of painting, which had been weakly represented in American collections before 1900. The new directions of attention among artists were thus paralleled by new interests among historians and scholars.

New York City became an important depot of the international art market. And, as it became an art dealing center, news magazines of New York exhibitions appeared: *The Art News* (founded 1902) and *The Art Digest* (founded 1926). *The American Magazine of Art* (1908) was founded by the American Federation of Arts as a journal of popular education, a function which *Art and Archaeology* (1908), published by the Archaeological Institute of America, undertook for the ancient, medieval, and primitive arts.

Thus a world horizon was created for the arts in America; and for the first time the great inheritance of the human race was brought together here for study and reflection.

Fourteen

THE TWENTIETH CENTURY:

THE SECOND GENERATION

In 1920, as the American people sank back wearily from their surge into international politics, it did not seem that American painting was about to enter a brilliant period. Other arts were flourishing. Architects were piling up skyscrapers which boldly expressed American business' awakened pride and self-consciousness. An outburst of talented writers in the early twenties gave us a vigorous, imaginative, national literature and theater. The motion picture had won a world-wide audience.

But the 1914 war had, in fact, given a fresh impetus to the lack of self-confidence in the arts and in social attitudes that the Eight had fought against. It seemed, in 1920, that the revolt of the realists had failed and that the feeble eclectic temper of 1900 had returned with renewed force. It seemed as if the fashionable and well to do of America felt the need more than ever to clothe themselves in the borrowed splendors of Europe's past, or in something that might pass for them. Among the intelligentsia, the urge to escape from the world of George F. Babbitt took another form. It was the great expatriate period when, for hosts of writers and painters, Paris seemed the only possible place to live.[1] A few little spots where artists gathered, in Greenwich Village or another colony, might try

[1] "The trouble with the United States," said Gertrude Stein in the thirties, explaining to someone why there was no landscape painting in America, "is that it has no sky."

to reproduce a bit of transplanted Left Bank atmosphere here and there. But on the whole, in the opinion of the intelligentsia, America was hopeless.

In the midst of these fogs of self-doubt, the best of the painters who had appeared before 1914 were still struggling for a hearing. They were gradually to win recognition when a vigorous second generation began to come forward and reinforce their ranks.

In the nineteen-twenties two groups of artists stood out in New York City. One was the circle around Alfred Stieglitz—John Marin, Marsden Hartley, Arthur Dove, and a new recruit whose first exhibition of drawing was arranged by Stieglitz in 1917, Georgia O'Keeffe —and other painters, like Demuth, who were intimates of that circle. The other group was younger on the whole and mostly products of the Art Students League; they found a haven in the Whitney Studio Club, sponsored by Gertrude Vanderbilt Whitney.

The Club was a place for informal gatherings and exhibitions of unknown or struggling artists; gradually these exhibits grew more important until, in 1931, they evolved into an institution, the Whitney Museum of American Art. The policy of this institution, in all stages of its evolution, was to encourage artists and especially, of course, the New York artists on its own doorstep. John Sloan, Alexander Brook, Peggy Bacon, Yasuo Kuniyoshi, Eugene Speicher, Edward Hopper, and many others benefited by this haven in the nineteen-twenties.

This leads us to speak of a new phenomenon, the rising influence of the art dealer in contemporary art. In the nineteenth century the American artist had looked to annual exhibitions, modeled upon the Salon in Paris and the Royal Academy in London, as the gateway to recognition and professional success. The large, rather miscellaneous national surveys continued, but beginning with the exhibit of the Eight at the Macbeth Gallery in 1908, the small group or one-man exhibition at the New York gallery of an astute art dealer became more and more the means by which reputations were made and paintings were sold. Macbeth, Stieglitz, Daniel, Rehn, Kraushaar, Edith Halpert were pioneers of a new relation between artists and public in the story of American painting.

Another new factor was a higher level of the journalism of art. *The Dial*, transferred in 1916 from Chicago to New York, was a highly articulate and intelligent force acting upon taste in America. In 1920, Hamilton Easter Field, with the financial help of Mrs. Whitney, founded *The Arts*. Field was a critic of broad culture, quick sensibility, and the independent mind of his Quaker heritage, who made *The Arts* the best periodical of the kind that we have yet produced. American art was well served by Field until his untimely death in 1922, after which Forbes Watson, assisted by Lloyd Goodrich, continued *The Arts* in the same tradition of broad interests and intellectual independence until it died in 1931.

In the 1920's the Stieglitz circle received a distinguished addition in Georgia O'Keeffe (born 1887); for a time, indeed, the honor of American painting was felt to rest upon the triumvirate of Marin, Demuth, and O'Keeffe. Her paintings of American architecture (her *American Radiator Building* is one of the best things ever done with the vastness and mystery of New York City) (Fig. 14-1) and of landscape, her giant-sized flowers, her austere paintings of bones and skulls helped to create in us the love of disciplined line and clean proportion that has since permeated (and how much for the better!) the arts of applied design and architecture. In her art, loneliness, silence, the inner world of contemplation became a new form of poetry of unmistakable eloquence and personal accent.

Stieglitz was a passionate believer in his artists and a masterful propagandist for them. Much of his early energy went also into interpreting the stylized and emotional forms of expression developing in Europe. But this group, if very influential, was small. Many good painters working along similar lines were not a part of it.

Stuart Davis (b. 1894) was the son of the art director of the *Philadelphia Press* who had employed Sloan, Luks, Glackens, and Shinn, and been a friend of Henri back in the nineties. Though a pupil of Henri in 1910, Davis was schooled on modern French painting which he saw in the Armory Show and in New York Galleries: the decisive influence upon his development was the late, color-rich phase of Cubism, out of which he created his own poster-like style of composition. He uses highly simplified but still recognizable objects in flat brilliant colors with much amusing use of lettering, to form compositions of great decorative warmth and gaiety. Davis's work has freshness, a personal accent, and wit (a quality very rare in our painting) (Fig. 14-2).

14-1. Georgia O'Keeffe: *American Radiator Building*. (Courtesy of the Stieglitz Collection, Fisk University, Nashville, Tennessee.)

Karl Knaths (born 1891), like Stuart Davis, was one of the first of the new generation to accept Cubism as a new basis for painting. Unlike the earlier colorists influenced by Cubism, whose work was changeable and uncertain, Knaths has evolved a consistent, personal style, a balanced harmony of geometry and soft, radiant color. He has worked by himself (since 1919 his home has been in Province-town) and stands alone (Fig. 14-3).

The influence of the school of Paris was a discipline through which a great many other painters passed, between 1910 and 1930, who later developed in quite other directions. It brought also a new discovery, or perhaps one should say a new sympathy. The creators of the stylized, emotional art of the twentieth century, the most advanced and self-conscious artists of Europe, discovered an un-

14-2.   Stuart Davis: *Garage Lights* (1931). (Courtesy of The Rochester Memorial Art Gallery.)

14-3.   Karl Knaths: *Pine Tree.* (Courtesy of
the Phillips Collection, Washington, D.C.)

conscious echo of their own interests at the other pole of artistic consciousness in the naïveté of children, artisans, and peasants. Fauvism and expressionism made the discovery of folk art and popular art, the art of untutored levels in our own society.

When a Pittsburgh carpenter and housepainter named John Kane (1860-1932) in 1927 submitted a picture to the jury of the Carnegie Exhibition, it was accepted for exhibition and hung among the works of the skilled, self-conscious professionals. From that time Kane's landscapes of Pittsburgh—memory pictures painted in low quiet tones, of a simple, childlike affection for the city in which he had spent his life—were widely exhibited and much enjoyed.

The naïve memory-landscapes of Joseph Pickett (1848-1918), a carpenter-shipbuilder of New Hope, Pennsylvania, who painted as a hobby, suddenly began to please more than did the famous professionals of the New Hope artists' colony.

Horace Pippin (1888-1946), an unschooled Negro of West Chester, Pennsylvania, unfitted for labor by a war wound, turned to painting. "Pictures just come to my mind," he explained, "and I tell my heart to go ahead," an explanation of his innocent art which needs no further comment. His discovery and exploitation as a painter in 1937 did not change his art, although it was too much for him as a human being.

The same was happily not true of the delightful old lady of Eagle Bridge, New York, who became known as Grandma Moses (1860-1961). Her success as a painter, which made her a beloved national character, did not alter in the least either her gaiety or her attractive, simple humanity.

A large proportion of the artists who made their names in the twenties first exhibited their work at the Whitney Studio Club. John Sloan had his first one-man show there; so did Edward Hopper, Reginald Marsh, Guy Pène du Bois, Henry Schnakenburg, Andrew Dasburg, Molly Luce. The early group exhibitions at the Club, before 1920, showed all of the Eight, as well as Bellows, Kent, Winthrop Chanler, Eugene Speicher, Maurice Sterne, Samuel Halpert, Henry McFee, Stuart Davis, Paul Berlin, and Louis Bouché; later Ernest Fiene, John Carroll, Arnold and Lucile Blanch, David Burliuk, Glenn Coleman, Georgina Klitgaard, Henry Mattson, Kenneth Hayes Miller, Pop Hart, John Steuart Curry, and many others who were significant in the artist-life of New York. Three painters only must serve to represent here this large and influential group.

One of the first of the younger generation to get a hearing was Alexander Brook (born 1898), at one time assistant director of the Studio Club. In the nineteen-twenties and -thirties Brook was a leader in the protest against too slavish a following of Paris; and his warm human sensibility and subtle style were, and remain, sensitive and refreshing. The lyrical charm and rich color of a still life like *A Number of Things* (1935) (Boston, Museum of Fine Arts), or the Tanagra-like grace of the figure called *Ann* (1935) (The Metropolitan Museum of Art) are admirable, although in the kaleidoscopic changes of taste they have now come to be considered old-fashioned because based upon nature.

Peggy Bacon is a satirist whose shrewd and caustic observation expresses itself both in words and graphic images. If I had to select one typical example of her shafted wit, I think it would be the drawing of Childe Hassam in her volume of portraits in words and black-and-white, called aptly *Off with Their Heads* (1934).

Yasuo Kuniyoshi (1893-1953), born in Japan but receiving his artistic education in America, accepted the stylized drawing and color of the twenties. He created first a somewhat drab and edgy style, but interesting in its quality of outline and amusing amalgam of Japanese and Western conventions. After a visit to France in the late twenties, he became aware of the beauty of Western oil paint and developed a subtle coloristic style that made him one of the leading painters of the thirties and forties in New York.

These New York painters of the twenties did not form into tight little groups and evolve programs of esthetic dogma as the painters of Paris did. They developed as individuals, trusting in their own intuitions, forming their own style out of the influences and ideas boiling in the teeming atmosphere of New York studios and exhibitions. Their subjects were not novel or unusual. They used traditional themes—posed figures, still lifes, and landscapes—but brought to them an expert and disciplined grace of style. They continued the American tradition of independence, experiment, and intuitive rather than theoretical approach to painting and to life.

There was one field, however, where the emphasis upon expression and the freedom of drawing of the twentieth century was quickly accepted and became a popular art in the best sense of the words. That field was humor. Many of the painter-illustrators of the first generation made drawings for *Life* and *Judge*. Glackens, Sloan, Luks, and Shinn all had a vein of pleasant humor. But the illustrative technique of the Charles Dana Gibson era, around 1900, was pen-and-ink drawing which was not particularly suited to the freer pictorial vision developed by the new century. During the 1914 war Sloan, Bellows, Glackens, and Art Young all made drawings for *The Masses* and they substituted for pen-and-ink the freer, more atmospheric line and tone of pencil or crayon. Rollin Kirby (1875-1952) introduced the use of crayon and pencil into the newspaper cartoon. He first spent a decade (1901-1910) in New York as a magazine illustrator before turning to newspaper work. In 1914 he became political cartoonist for the brilliant, liberal *New York World*.

The magazine *Vanity Fair*, in the twenties, under the editorship of Frank Crowninshield, also was important graphically. Chiefly it popularized modern French art and a new standard of photography. It found in the Mexican artist Miguel Covarrubias, and the man-about-town dandy and wit, Ralph Barton (1891-1931), two draughtsmen who were able to express the lighthearted mockery of the times; Gluyas Williams (born 1888) became there another voice of the period.

The foundation of *The New Yorker* in 1925 gave the new school of graphic humor its greatest medium. The irreverence of the twenties, gradually mellowing into an urbane sense of life's absurdities, and the new, freer, expressive, economical, graphic style produced a whole garden full of notable graphic humorists: James Thurber (1894-1961) (Fig. 14-4); Constantin Alajálov (born 1900); Alan Dunn (born 1900); Helen Hokinson (1893-1949); Peter Arno (born 1902); Richard Taylor (born 1902); and more recently Robert Day (born 1900); Richard Decker; Whitney Darrow, Jr.; and Charles Addams form a remarkable school of expressive draughtsmanship. Their popularity is so great that no description or comment is necessary, except to emphasize that their work is art as well as humor.

The same can be said of the transplanted Austrian, Ludwig Bemelmans (1898-1962), whose work as both writer and artist has added a new note to the charm of life.

To Norman Rockwell (born 1894) we must be grateful for rescuing the magazine cover from the endless repetition of insipid

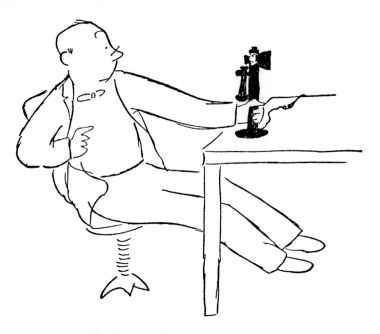

14-4.   James Thurber: *Psychiatrist about to Phone his Wife.*
(From *Let Your Mind Alone!* Harper & Row, Publishers, Inc., 1937.)

girls' faces and making it a medium for the humors of everyday life.

The comic strip had been a feature of American newspapers since the nineties, supplying an unpretentious form of broad, low comedy. It was a true twentieth-century popular art, too familiar to be noticed, until George Herriman (1881?-1944) in 1911 developed the figure of Krazy Kat. Herriman made the comic strip the expression of a curious, highly personal drollery.

The graphic humor of the twentieth century has been extremely individual, varied in style, pungent in flavor—a popular art of the first caliber.

On the serious and self-conscious levels of American culture, however, in spite of the vitality of many artists who seem to us now in retrospect to have made the twenties a remarkably interesting period, it would be hard to describe, to those who did not themselves experience it, the subservience of American polite taste in that decade to foreign leadership. Calvin Coolidge spoke for a majority opinion when, on receiving an official invitation to send an American representation to the *Exposition des arts décoratifs*, held in Paris in 1925, he replied that America had no art to send.

A reaction against extremes of cultural subservience and expatriate temper was inevitable. At its best, the reaction came quietly. Certain artists appeared who had something of their own to say, which, being deeply original, gave voice to the thoughts and emotions of their own land and people.

In general it can be said that a nation's art is greatest when it most reflects the character of its people. . . . The domination of France in the plastic arts has been almost complete for the past thirty years or more in this country. If an apprenticeship to a master has been necessary, I think we have served it.

These words, spoken by Edward Hopper (born 1882 at Nyack on the Hudson River, of mingled Dutch and English ancestry) might be taken as a keynote of the thirties. Hopper was no flag-waving nationalist. His first exhibition at the Whitney Studio Club in 1920 was of paintings done in Paris. But during his long, slow development he had matured a point of view in diametric opposition to the rising tide of the "international modern." Hopper's personal vision contradicted the strongest trends of the day: "Instead of subjectivity, a new objectivity; instead of abstraction, a reaffirmation of representation and specific subject matter; instead of internationalism, an art based on the American scene."[2] He felt the need which Eakins had felt fifty years before, to create an art of intense reality out of his own world. He found himself first in etching, more slowly in water color and oils: he was fifty before he found both his style and his audience. His subject matter was the face of the American city and countryside. People are only an incident in his works: light is the theme and the means by which his art is built. To achieve his personal vision, he lived in a self-enforced isolation in the midst of New York City almost as complete as Ryder's was. A brooding spirit of loneliness and the light-bathed, objective poetry of architecture, which man has built and in which his life is embodied, fills his work (Fig. 14-5).

2 Quoted from Lloyd Goodrich's admirable essay, *Edward Hopper Retrospective Exhibition*, Whitney Museum of American Art, 1950.

With Hopper the independent, native trend of Winslow Homer reasserted itself in the midst of the clamorous studio world of New York City. And, as if the time had come in the thirties to reassert the life and the diversity of this vast country, other independent voices were heard. They were not a group, nor a school; they had individual points of view and developed individual manners. But they showed that the long period of assimilation was over and a nationwide development beginning again.

Something of the urbane spirit of Franklin still lingers in Philadelphia: it is an old city, yet unself-conscious; very native and yet at home in the world. Franklin Watkins (born 1894) created an art in that same easy, urbane, yet individual spirit. His art springs from a broad culture and knowledge of the whole tradition of painting, from the Middle Ages to Post-Impressionism; his sensitive, handsome, coloristic style is both very knowledgeable and very personal.

14-5. Edward Hopper: *Early Sunday Morning* (1930).
(Courtesy of the Whitney Museum of American Art, New York.)

14-6. Franklin C. Watkins: *Thomas Raeburn White* (1940). (Courtesy of Mr. and Mrs. Thomas Raeburn White, Penllyn, Pennsylvania.)

He is interested in human personality and is one of the great portrait painters of our time (Fig. 14-6); he is a painter of enchanted and refreshing still life; and he has a mind which has found material for fresh imaginative studies in the ancient themes of life and death. Some years ago (in 1950) when his large decorations of *Death* and *Resurrection*, executed for the music room of Mr. Henry P. McIlhenny of Philadelphia, were shown at the Museum of Modern Art in New York, they were rather ill received by New York studio opinion. A painter, it was felt, should not be interested in such themes in the twentieth century; or, if interested, should paint them in one of the accepted modern European styles, Expressionist, or Surrealist, perhaps. This reaction was a curious instance of how readily contemporary movements of revolt harden into new conventions; it was Watkins' individuality, his refusal to fit accepted patterns, that was complained of. What impressed me about these pictures was their eloquence and their extraordinary luminous color harmonies, of a clear soft radiance yet monumental power. They are the work of a highly personal imagination expressing itself in an exceptionally gifted style.

Charles Burchfield (born 1893) grew up in a small Ohio town called Salem, typical of the midwestern towns that are one of the norms of American life. Farming, the village and the factory meet in them. Architecturally undistinguished, culturally belonging to the lingering simple rural life of the past, they are also through their factories and stores linked to the mass production world of today.

As a boy he studied art in Cleveland and tried, briefly, to live in New York, but the big city bewildered and utterly defeated him. He went back after a few weeks to Salem, took a job in a local factory, and began to develop his own art, in water color, painting on week ends or at night. His aim was to paint nature, "not invent a quasi poetry and try to fit the facts of nature around it." But his response to nature was so deeply emotional that his first independent work was an art of visionary fantasy.

He had little command of tone or color at this period, but loved to play with the decorative and expressive qualities of line. To express the subject matter of the familiar scenes about him—the wooden houses, lawns and trees of Salem; the sun and moon; summer and winter; the sound of insects in summer, of winter wind in the trees, of the cawing of crows, the ringing of church bells—he invented a strange, calligraphic language of line.

Dissatisfied with the thinness of his early style, he settled down to master this world in terms of light and tone. His medium was water color but he came to use it with the power of oil. His art grew steadily more monumental, more objective and at the same time more deeply expressive, until he was able to paint, with great authority, the grandeur and power of modern industry in pictures like *Black Iron* (1935) (Plate III) or express in his landscapes the poetry of the sun and the revolving year.

In 1939 he began to rework some of his early, visionary water colors, enlarging, revising, enriching them with the authority and monumentality of style gained in his middle period. *The Sphinx and the Milky Way* (1946) (Fig. 14-7) is such a picture, a vision of a

14-7.   Charles Burchfield: *The Sphinx and the Milky Way* (1946).
(Munson-Williams-Proctor Institute, Utica, N. Y.)

night in summer, heavy with stars and the scent of flowers and filled
with the song of insects. A great moth in the foreground sips the
honey of a pale ghostly flower. Such a subject is part of the ordinary,
popular vision of the prettiness of nature—and Burchfield works best,
always, with ordinary, familiar materials. But he has turned the
subject into a vision of haunting mystery, filled with a sense of the
elemental powers in nature.

14-8.   Ivan Le Lorraine
Albright: *That Which I
Should Have Done I Did
Not Do* (1941). (Courtesy
of The Art Institute of
Chicago.)

In his most recent works, such as *Sun and Rocks* (1918/50, Albright-Knox Art Gallery, Buffalo), *Winter Moonlight* (1951), *Hot September Wind* (1953) or *An April Mood* (1946/55, Whitney Museum of American Art) this sense of awe-inspiring power and mystery in nature grows even stronger. Much of his most recent work strikes a note also of loneliness and chill. All his life Burchfield has had a vision of a phantom landscape. "Over the rim of the earth—to the North—lies the land of the unknown—it is windy, the ground is frozen, hard, barren—there is no snow—white wind clouds scud over a vast gray sky."[3] But whether he deals with the cold of March or November, or the heat of summer, Burchfield has created out of the typical, familiar, daily sights of his midwestern countryside a monumental, visionary art of "the big epic power of nature."

In Chicago there was Ivan Le Lorraine Albright (born 1897). Albright is a figure painter and one whose style expresses a pin-point vision of fierce intensity, of people and of their possessions in whose dusty, haphazard accumulation is told (to the artist's eye) the story of times and lives now dead. Of his haunting, melancholy visions of the beauty of decay perhaps the most poignant, certainly the most famous, is the one called *That Which I Should Have Done I Did Not Do* (Fig. 14-8) (1941), unique in subject, in style, and in a hallucinatory eloquence, as if of a vision in a dream.

Mark Tobey (born 1890), one of the artists who has given a voice to the Pacific coastland, is characteristic, in a way, because he did not originate there. He lived in New York, moved to the Northwest in 1923, was in Paris 1927-1929, spent a long time in England and the Far East 1931-1938; Seattle really became his home only in 1939. Influenced both by European abstraction and by the Orient, Tobey developed in 1935 his "white-line" style, a personal kind of calligraphic brush writing, interweaving on the surface in ceaseless movement over dimly discernible patches of color beneath. In his earlier works suggestions of natural forms come and go in this maze (Fig. 14-9); but recently those have largely disappeared, and the dance of color and direction alone create their music for the eye. "I am accused often of too much experimentation," he said in 1951, "but what else should I do when all other factors of man are in the

---

[3] This and the previous quotations of Burchfield's own words are taken from *Charles Burchfield*, by John I. H. Baur, published for the Whitney Museum of American Art by The Macmillan Company, New York, 1956.

same condition? I thrust forward into space as science and the rest do."

These five painters show the geographical and imaginative diversity of a continental culture in the thirties. Some (Hopper and Burchfield) use objective images; others (Watkins, Tobey, Albright) subjective, to express strong emotion. Some searched for the meaning of the familiar world about them; others transformed human personality into strange images, into a floating smoke of color, or into reflections as intense as a loon's feathers reflected in a mirror. They are not "regional" artists but they give a voice to regions of experience.

Thomas Benton (born 1889) was a "regionalist," in the sense that the nineteen-thirties understood by the word: a conscious reaction to the expatriatism of the twenties. This reaction began in the twenties: but the Great Depression killed the expatriate movement. When dividends from America were cut off, the intelligentsia drifted reluctantly home from Paris in the early thirties. Only a few die-hards clung to the Left Bank. Those who returned found the United States, under the New Deal, a much more lively and interesting place than the prosperous and complacent country they had left. The decade of the thirties was a time when the imagination of artists turned suddenly again to the United States, stirred by the feeling of crisis, by the dramatic national leadership provided by Franklin Roosevelt, and by the sense of great events taking place in our own land. It was a time of rediscovery for the nation as a whole of the importance, the vastness, the picturesque variety of the life, people, and traditions of their own country. Some of those who had once tried hardest to cut themselves off from the dull familiar prose of home in order to turn themselves into Parisians were also the most vehement in reaction.

Thomas Benton had left Missouri as a young man for New York and Paris. He was one of the first group of American art students to rebel against late Impressionism and turn to abstraction. He went through a long period of groping, described in an illuminating autobiography called *Artist in America*. Eventually he rebelled against a decorative abstraction alien to his vehemently positive nature, and turned first to painting historical murals, then realistic genre. His mural paintings in the library of the New School for Social Research, New York City (1930) and in the Indiana State Building

14-9. Mark Tobey: *San Francisco Street* (1941).
(Courtesy of The Detroit Institute of Arts.)

at the Chicago World's Fair of 1932 (now at Indiana University, Bloomington, Indiana) mark the high tide of his revolt against abstraction in favor of native subject matter.

Benton's mural style was an interesting invention. He filled his walls with figures in active movement, one scene overlapping and penetrating another in ingenious fashion. The scenes were separated by wholly arbitrary moldings, somewhat as overlapping photographs were separated in the pictorial sections of the Sunday paper. It is an original device and was used with imagination and effect. Benton has never seemed to me quite so happy in his easel painting. In a small canvas the restless movement of his drawing seems too insistent and mannered.

The revolt against the domination of French painting found in Benton and in the critic, Thomas Craven, two strident voices. Craven's eloquence, rather than any natural unity, grouped Benton and two other realists from the prairie states, Grant Wood from Iowa, and John Steuart Curry from Kansas, into a noisy crusade under the banner of "The American Scene." He attacked not only the contemporary French painters but American expatriates, and tossed in New Yorkers for good measure: they were all iniquitous and effete, compared with the artistic renaissance taking place west of the Mississippi.

Craven undoubtedly greatly overpraised these painters. (Wood and Curry, at least, died unhappy, haunted by the contrast between Craven's claims of greatness for them and their own knowledge of themselves.) Both he and Benton made many violently extravagant statements, yet can one blame them? For a generation, smart young wits in New York had used "Middle Western" as an omnibus term of contempt for all that they despised in the United States. I remember one instance of the sense of self-congratulation of the Easterner. It was in the twenties. A lecturer from New York, with a reputation as a wit, recited to his audience in a Midwestern city a verse which he said he had composed on the train, coming out to talk to them:

> O, pack my grip for a trip on a ship
> Where the scene at least is variable;
> For East is East, and West is West,
> But the Middle West is terrible.

Is it a wonder that the enraged natives of Kansas, Missouri, and Iowa, when their turn came, heaped insults upon the effete East and the colonials of the Left Bank, and claimed that art and virtue were to be found only in the prairies?

Grant Wood (1892-1942) grew up in Cedar Rapids, Iowa, in circumstances of extreme poverty and barrenness. At first his struggle was to break away from Iowa to Paris and to paint like an Impressionist. After a few years he came back to Cedar Rapids and, while teaching art, received a commission for a stained glass window in the local Legion post. Knowing nothing about the medium, he went to Munich to study this problem. There, among the early Flemish paintings and Gothic portraits of the Alte Pinakothek, the earnest, severe faces reminded him of his own people at home. It suddenly appeared to him that homely, simple things, seen with love and intensity, become both beautiful and important. He returned to Cedar Rapids determined to paint (if he could) his Iowan neighbors with all the fidelity and affection he admired in the pictures of the Alte Pinakothek. At first the fact that the memorial window commissioned for an American Legion Building had been made in Germany involved him in a hassle with the local forces. The window was rejected. The result was a memorable satirical picture, *Daughters of Revolution*. But the incident did not deflect him from his new purpose. Wood was a skillful and knowing figure painter, capable of the effective characterization shown in the two portraits of *American Gothic* (Fig. 14-10) (1930), which is perhaps his best work. He could paint the plain people of Iowa well. He was unsuccessful only in painting its landscape, for he tried to avoid the task of mastering the multitudinous forms of nature by using trivial stylizations from the landscapes in his mother's English china.

John Steuart Curry (1897-1946), born on a farm in Kansas, studied at the Art Institute of Chicago and the Art Students League, struggled for several years as an illustrator for pulp magazines, and managed to spend a year in Paris. On his return he settled in New York City where Mrs. Whitney gave him his first encouragement and support. His great ambition was to paint the life of his own state of Kansas, for he loved his native soil and wanted to make its prairie life a subject for art. He saw Kansas in a rather melodramatic way, choosing violent incidents—a tornado sweeping down on a farmstead, hogs fighting and killing a snake, or an emotional country baptism—and his melodrama helped to make his work popular. His weakness was that he really cannot be said to have mastered his medium: his drawing and color were weak and undistinguished;

14-10. Grant Wood: *American Gothic* (1930).
(Courtesy of The Art Institute of Chicago.)

although his sincerity was unquestionable, that is not enough to make great art. Only his murals in the Kansas State Capitol, though awkwardly placed and badly lighted, seem, by sheer force of their love for his homeland, to realize something of his dream.

To the three painters of the Corn Belt, Craven added a fourth master of the American scene, Reginald Marsh (1898-1954), who loved the tumultuous masses of humanity in lower Manhattan as Grant Wood loved his small-town Iowans. Marsh's pictures painted in the early thirties, showing depressed crowds in the Bowery and Union Square or exhausted sleepers on the Elevated, are the works by which he made his name; I am inclined to think they will also preserve it. They are somber pictures, grim in feeling, harsh in style, but they have emotion and power. He continued to paint the crowds on the streets of lower New York or at Coney Island; but his work showed an increasing coldness, so that ultimately his endless, teeming crowds came to seem like soulless automata writhing in the blast of some kind of mechanical twentieth-century inferno. This, too, may be called a vision of a sort, and perhaps Marsh may someday seem a kind of Fuseli of our times.

There are other painters whose subject is New York in this generation, chief of them, perhaps, Louis Bouché (born 1896), a painter of sharp eyes and witty intelligent mind; and Isabel Bishop (born 1902), whose world of New York shop girls is a little sad but well observed and truly felt.

The vital movement of the twenties had been to establish the new style of the century—the liberation of drawing and color from natural appearance, the creation of formal harmonies, and the expression of subjective emotions. The work of the thirties was to give form to a surge of national feeling which began to redress the balance between cosmopolitan and native strains in our culture, which had been out of balance for half a century.

The thirties did not create a "national" school of painting. Individualism is the core of American life and diversity its natural structure. (Our surface uniformities are the expression of our love of practical convenience and remain on that level.) There was a chorus of independent voices giving speech to the imagination in all parts of the country. The variety among the artists just mentioned—Hopper, Watkins, Burchfield, Albright, Tobey, Benton—is characteristic, then, of the decade: independent but not provincial; native, because deeply rooted in their own perspective upon life, but rarely chauvinist. The reawakening of the country to its own variety and wealth of imaginative material was, in the largest sense, the achievement of the thirties.

How large a part in this was played by the Federal Arts Project is difficult at this point to say. No adequate history of the New Deal's art projects has ever been written. Never popular with the general public, always severely criticized, they have never received the credit they deserved as a help to established talents or as a stimulus and training school for younger artists. What I can give here is not a history but an attempt to suggest the large, and I believe honorable, part the projects played in our artistic life in their time.

The Federal government entered the field of painting in 1933 on an unprecedented scale, in the form of work relief for artists, organized as part of the Public Works of Art Project under the general direction of Harry Hopkins, relief administrator. The first work relief program had two aims. One was strictly to give relief to the unemployed, but at the same time to maintain the self-respect of artists by giving them work during a period of disaster. The second aim was to provide works of art to decorate public buildings. In 1935 the second program was transferred from the relief administration to a newly formed section of Fine Arts under Edward Bruce in the Treasury Department. Assistance to the artist on relief was reorganized as the Federal Arts Project, under Holger Cahill, within the Works Progress Administration.

Holger Cahill's interest in popular art gave the Federal Arts Project a fortunate direction. Painters and craftsmen, under his direction, were put to work in groups that suggested the vanished workshops of the handcraft period. People with old-fashioned skills were set to work using them. The national heritage of skilled crafts and popular arts was studied and recorded on a regional basis. Local art centers were established, local skills fostered, local traditions revived and honored.

There were two other influential programs besides the creative projects. One was that of local art centers. At one time there were one hundred and three in operation, mostly in small communities, all over the nation. There is no question in my mind that these played a part in getting people all over the United States working in some medium—paint, wood, stone, textiles, clay—not as a livelihood but as a pleasant part of their daily lives. The second program was a historical research into our native inheritance of crafts and skills, which resulted in a monumental survey known as The Index of American Design.

The good that came from all this was an artistic activity diffused over the entire country in towns and cities where none had existed for two generations. Many young artists were given a start in their own communities who, in preceding decades, would have left home for New York or Paris, never to return. The interest in handcrafts was revived and refreshed, by both practice and historical study. If a greater degree of activity has been diffused all over the country since the thirties than had been seen there since the romantic period, the bitterly criticized WPA art projects must be given their share of the credit.

Unfortunately for the reputation of these projects, the activity most in the public eye at the time was also the least successful. A nationwide program of mural painting was set up to decorate the Federal buildings in Washington and the post offices, schools, and other public buildings rising all over the land. There were, among these murals, certain honorable exceptions to a general ineptitude. Boardman Robinson, Henry Varnum Poor, William Gropper, John Steuart Curry did creditable and pleasing works in the Federal department buildings in Washington. Ben Shahn's mural of the dreams and hardships of the immigrant, in the community center at Roosevelt, New Jersey, has artistic quality, like all his work. In Colorado, Frank Mechau (1903-1946) discovered himself in this program. His best work was the fresco of *Wild Horses* in the inner court of the Colorado Springs Fine Arts Center, which shows not only an intelligent use of local subject matter but a happy wedding of mural painting and modern architecture, unfortunately without descendants.[4]

[4] Of the Treasury Department murals, the most successful as architectonic decorations seem, understandably enough, to have been the last: Siporin's and Millman's post office decorations in St. Louis and Anton Refregier's Rincon Annex post office decorations in San Francisco belong to the artistic history of the forties. Both these murals have been heavily attacked by people who do not like their somewhat morose tone.

The most successful mural paintings to come out of the whole movement, in

But in general the mural paintings done at this time amount to rather unsuccessful illustrations, pasted on the wall with little understanding of architectural effect. Perhaps we should not blame the artists too severely. If you leave a horse in the stable for years, then suddenly, without exercise or preparation, set him to run a race, it is not surprising that the poor old nag is tied into knots before getting halfway round the track. The mural painting program was much like this. Nonetheless, it was a disappointment that American painters, given such an opportunity, and in spite of the example of Mexican painters over the border, were unequipped either to achieve monumental form or to put themselves in large sympathy with their fellow men. Regionalism in mural painting became identified with sentimental home-town subject matter, presented in a horrid melange of ill-digested modernisms.

During the years that saw the great bubble of prosperity swell and burst, the United States became gradually aware of a new school of painting in Mexico. The Mexican people had emerged from their long colonial sleep in the sufferings and triumphs of the Obregon revolution. In the twenties they produced a national school of painting. Its artists were vehemently national in spirit. They made a virtue of national and local subject matter and believed in the artist's identifying himself in spirit with the mass of people around him. They revolted against the abstract estheticism of the twentieth-century painting and its cosmopolitan thinness and wished to create instead an art at once monumental, national, and heroic. American artists saw Orozco's power to express the smoldering unhappiness of mankind and admired Rivera's epic narratives of Mexican history. The effect was electric, for here was an art of *meaning* which at the same time embodied the stylistic discoveries of twentieth-century painting.

No one can understand the developments of the thirties without remembering the influence of Mexico both on the painters of social protest and upon the mural paintings done under the Federal government projects. Rivera, Orozco, and Siqueiros all worked in the United States as well as in their own country. Orozco painted fres-

the opinion of many, were the frescoes representing *The Story of the Land Grant College*, executed by Henry Varnum Poor for the Pennsylvania State University at University Park, Pennsylvania (1940; 1948-1949).

coes at Pomona College, at the New School for Social Research in New York City, and at Dartmouth College, filled always with a somber awareness of man's suffering and his inhumanity to his fellow man. Rivera first celebrated *California* in the San Francisco Stock Exchange; then made the first serious attempt by an artist of the twentieth century to make modern technology and mass production the theme of mural painting, in The Detroit Institute of Arts; and having found the positive side of twentieth-century American life in Detroit's industry, found its negative side in the frenetic atmosphere of New York, that inspired his ill-considered murals in Radio City (afterward destroyed).

The Great Depression brought bitterness and despair in its victims that found expression in a wave of sharp, satiric art. Much of the social satire painted or written in the thirties has been forgotten. Its work is done. The advantage of such plain speaking is that it helps the country adjust its thoughts to hard problems. When the problems begin to be solved, the work that was merely propaganda for the day is forgotten. But some of the painted satire and social protest had more enduring qualities.

Philip Evergood (1901-1973) used the artist's new freedom from naturalistic drawing to achieve a vehement, angry expressionism. *My Forebears Were Pioneers* (1940), painted after the New England hurricane, was a cry of violent bitterness against what seemed the failure of the American dream. A witch-like old woman in black seated in a chair in front of a ruined mansion glares fiercely out of the canvas, seeming the very embodiment of the hatred of the past for the future.

William Gropper (born 1897) made the same use of dramatic exaggeration but, less gifted a painter than Evergood, did his best work in black-and-white.

Ben Shahn (born 1898) has now passed out of his stage of social protest. When he first made his appearance in 1932 he was a bitter, ironic draughtsman, a master of harshly expressive line, using color much as the colored comics do, to fill in areas with decorative tones. From 1935 to 1938 Shahn worked for the Farm Security Administration, as artist and photographer, traveling widely and learning to love the land to which he had come as an immigrant. In 1938-1939 he did a mural in the community center of Roosevelt, New Jersey, commissioned by the FSA, which is a vivid graphic statement, somewhat influenced in style by Rivera, of the contrasting facets of the immigrants' dreams of America and of the hard struggles of reality.

In his later development Shahn's drawing has grown more subtle, his color more luminous and imaginative, his feeling for his fellow man warmer. He has become concerned with individuals rather than types, with individuals who were lost and alone in the terrible bigness of modern cities and modern society. The sad, dramatic poetry of his art is still developing in new aspects and Shahn is now one of our most significant artists (Fig. 14-11).

While the American artists were suffering through the depression, another convulsion was spreading over Europe. In the thirties we began to receive refugee artists from Europe. George Grosz (born 1893) and Karl Zerbe (born 1903) fled from Germany to live in the United States. Feininger found Berlin no longer habitable and came back to New York. In the mid-thirties Pavel Tchelitchew (born 1898) and Eugene Berman (born 1899) came to America. Both had fled from Russia after the revolution and had attained fame as painters in Paris in the twenties. Amédée Ozenfant, the French painter and writer (born 1886), Kurt Seligman (Swiss, born 1900), and many others from Paris fled before or after the fall of France and sought refuge in New York; others, who survived the horrors of 1939-1945, came after the liberation. Some of these artists have remained and become a part of the artistic life of this country. George Grosz and Karl Zerbe, a gifted stylist, became influential teachers, as did Ozenfant and Hans Hofmann from Munich. George Grosz at first felt such a relaxation of tension after arriving in America that his work, once so savage, became mild and gentle until the onset of the war aroused him again to wild, hallucinatory fantasies. His autobiography, under the title *A Little Yes and a Big No,* is one of his major works of art in this country.

Transplanting to America has not affected the others so obviously. The mournful reveries of Tchelitchew and Berman found new subject matter during their stay here. Berman has added the Southwestern desert and Mexico to the inspirations of Italian landscape; Tchelitchew has studied the autumn colors of Connecticut and the world of medical science. Ozenfant has found the lighted city of New York at night a subject of poetry. All these men are essentially international in spirit. They have grown as artists and they enrich the artistic scene in America but their place of residence is the least aspect of their art.

The artistic tedium into which regionalism fell and the chauvinism of Craven and Benton were bound to provoke reaction. As Sinclair Lewis remarked, somewhere in America a pendulum is not a pendulum; it is a piston. In the later thirties the piston began to move

14-11. Ben Shahn: *Composition with Clarinets and Tin Horn* (1951). (Courtesy of The Detroit Institute of Arts.)

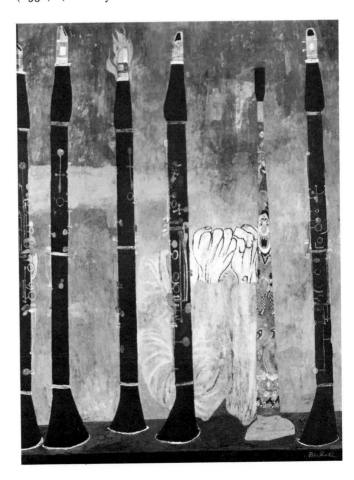

again. The school of Paris had by this time passed into a new phase. The flat, decorative colors and stylized drawing of the twenties were being combined with fantastic imagination in the work of painters like Miró, Yves Tanguy and, above all, Picasso. Their works inspired a new wave of abstract and fantastic art in America. The Society of Abstract Artists was formed in New York in 1936. Later a number of Surrealists, mostly refugees from the war, held an exhibition, encased in a vast expenditure of string, in an old building on Madison Avenue. More and more American painters began to follow their lead, turning away from a regionalism now become sentimental and banal to an art without anchor in space or time; resting on nothing except the artist's own self-consciousness.

The trend away from realism received a strong recruit in Abraham Rattner (born 1895). He had studied at the Pennsylvania Academy but went to Paris as a soldier in the 1914 war and returned afterward to live there for more than twenty years until the fall of France finally brought him back to New York in 1940. Rattner, adopting the idiom of Paris, had poured into it the intensity and Oriental richness of his Jewish heritage, creating an art of burning color and emotion.

The atmosphere of the 1939 war, with its international interests, and the awareness aroused in all men that they and their home towns were part of a continuum embracing the whole world, was seemingly favorable to the development of an abstract art. Many of the leaders of this second wave of abstraction and fantastic art were of the generation we are now describing, but they achieved recognition only with the postwar movement. Among those are Charles Howard (born 1899) of San Francisco, living recently in England, who has developed an eloquent art of color and moving shape: in New York there are Lee Gatch (born 1902), Bradley Walker Tomlin (1899-1953), Adolph Gottlieb (born 1903), Mark Rothko (born 1903), Clyfford Still (born 1904), Arshile Gorky (1904-1948), Balcomb Greene (born 1904), all painters of personal style. New York is the center of the movement and a second generation has come forward there since the war. Many of its best-known figures are painters now in their forties or early fifties who fall outside the scope of this chapter.

Fifteen

FROM THE END OF THE 1939

WAR TO THE PRESENT

THE PAINTERS of the second generation of twentieth-century paint-ing were born between 1885 and 1904. At the war's end they were at the height of their powers; while those who survived from the first generation were either the grand, or the forgotten, old men of painting.

When the battles against Germany and Japan ended, the tide of violence and death which had overflowed national frontiers and engulfed the continents began gradually to recede. One by one, now here, now there, the landmarks of the world as it had once been, began to reappear. But not all survived: some were gone forever.

Forty years had passed in the world of painting since the painters of the Ideal in the first generation had begun to introduce their rigorously stylized manner, their emphasis upon rhythmic pattern, their flat bright colors bearing little or no reference to what the eye sees in nature. This had now become the common vernacular of painting. A freely stylized, decorative manner, high keyed in color, two dimensional, emphasizing rhythmic structure of planes and out-lines, had taken the place of the effects of atmosphere, luminous tone and space with which American painters were working at the beginning of the century. The earlier, imitative talents, who had merely repeated watered-down variations of French Fauvism or German expressionism, were gone. The second generation had purged this style of its derivative elements and poured into it the vigor of remarkable artistic personalities.

One who wishes to renew his memory of how fresh and subtle were the perceptions, how elastic and varied the language of painting, as it was used by the leaders of this generation in the years immediately following the end of the war (and, although it may be unfashionable to look back, it is no bad discipline to renew one's awareness of the road we have traveled), can do so very easily. One need only glance again at the catalogues of the exhibition of Ben Shahn's work held by the Museum of Modern Art in 1947 or of the exhibits of Franklin Watkins at the Philadelphia Museum of Art and the Museum of Modern Art in 1950, to see how keen the sensibilities, how lively the language of expression were. These are two of the best painters but the country was full of others.

As a younger generation came back from the war or began to make itself known, it seemed for a time that Italy might play the role of inspiration and catalyst that France had played after the 1914 war. A generation of American soldiers had fallen in love with that beautiful, unhappy land in the midst of battle. As young painters returned there after the war, it was the drama and poetry of the cities of today and of the seventeenth- and eighteenth-century painters in the museums that moved them. A group of painters—of whom Carlyle Brown, Stephen Greene, Walter Stuempfig, and, a little later, William Congdon are the most conspicuous, perhaps—made a new and interesting direction out of this Italian figurative and landscape inspiration.

There were already, however, strongly divergent currents rising in both Paris and New York. The eagerness of the New York art world to renew its relations with Paris was shown when the Whitney Museum of American Art departed from its normal tradition and devoted its winter exhibition in 1947 to "Painting in Paris, 1939-1946." The Museum of Modern Art, that same spring, held an exhibition of large-scale modern paintings—Léger, Pollock, Siqueiros, Matisse, Carrà, Beckmann, Miró, Picasso, Lam, Chagall, Stella—heralding that interest in grandiose scale which was soon to become a major element in the artistic ambitions of the New York school. Art dealers with Paris connections held the first postwar exhibit of Picasso (and he at once began to reweave his hypnotic spell), and the new brutalism in French painting made its bow with the first

New York exhibit of Dubuffet. In the autumn the Art Institute of Chicago did an imposing review of surrealism and abstract art, with Rico Lebrun winning first prize.

The decorative, stylized but recognizable image of the world current in painting of the first and second generation was thus challenged from both within and without. Homer Saint-Gaudens had been in charge of the Carnegie International Exhibition since 1922; in 1949 the next to the last of his long series of reviews of contemporary painting was the last to feature the figure painters. It was for Saint-Gaudens a symbolical leave-taking of those artists whose work he had followed throughout his career: Max Beckmann, now resident in the United States, won the first prize; other prizes and honorable mentions went to Philip Evergood, Hobson Pittman, Alexander Brook, Robert Brackman, and Abraham Rattner; and Shahn, Hirsch, Hopper, Kroll, Gluckman, Isabel Bishop, Waldo Peirce, Louis Bouché, Robert Gwathmey, and Edwin Dickinson were also prominent. No such conjunction of representational painters was to be seen again in the fifties.

The major trend of the nineteen-fifties was toward abstraction. It had shown increasing strength through the forties, so much so that a review of the Whitney Museum's exhibition at the close of this same year, 1947, which announced so many major trends of the postwar period, could say "Abstraction continues to reign. . . . Baziotes, Bearden, and Pollock now better deserve the appellation 'Whitney regulars' than do Speicher, Alexander Brook and Bouché." But, although abstraction became the dominant trend, a remarkable diversity of styles and directions of thought existed within it.

One drive was toward a heightened stress upon the paint surface itself as a means of expression. Some of this came from the teaching of Hans Hofmann, whose emphasis on large, slashing strokes, spatterings of paint, and exploration of accidental effects was very influential in the formation of postwar painting.

Another was a stress upon total liberty of physical action, and of instinct, in the creation of a work of art. The influence of the Surrealists exiled from Europe by the war—Masson, Tanguy, Ernst, Duchamp, Matta, Kurt Seligmann—now flowed into abstraction; and a movement which had once seemed, in Paris, a rebirth of classicism by its rationalism, its insistence upon construction and upon order, now burst out, in New York, into a torrent of fluid

15-1. Mark Tobey: *Serpentine* (1955).
(Courtesy of the Seattle Art Museum.)

dynamism and subjective emotion. One of the first directions to emerge clearly, in fact, was the "automatic abstract art" of Robert Motherwell, who had come to painting by way of studying philosophy at Stanford and Harvard. Matta introduced him in the early forties to automatic drawing, originally developed by Miró. In Motherwell's art the creation of a picture was entrusted to the spontaneous movement of hand and brush, controlled only by unconscious inner forces.

Reliance upon the irrational, the accidental, the unforeseen, was a most important element in the formation of what has been variously called abstract expressionism, action painting, or simply the New York school. In 1948 Alfred Barr, speaking of the Museum of

Modern Art's recent acquisitions, observed judiciously, "Technically many of the artists seem to work with a high degree of spontaneity, even automatism, and some dependence upon accident."

Perhaps equally important, also, was the development of the element of calligraphy. Mark Tobey, of the preceding generation, had already begun his "white line" in the thirties. In the forties Jackson Pollock, by his invention of a new calligraphy and a new technique, more conspicuously than any other artist established abstract expressionism as a movement. Spreading big canvases on the floor, Pollock applied house paint and other pigments, sometimes pouring them directly from cans and letting them splash and run, sometimes spattering paint or dripping it from sticks. The method sounds like complete absence of control, and automatism. On the contrary, the rhythmic movements of his arm, combined with the beauty of his color sequences, gave his canvases an ordered complexity, a gaiety, and freshness which won him a unique and inimitable place in what now came to be called action painting. But many other painters—Adolph Gottlieb and his "pictographs" (which he began

15-2.   Jackson Pollock: *Convergence* (1952). (Courtesy of the Albright-Knox Art Gallery, Buffalo, New York.)

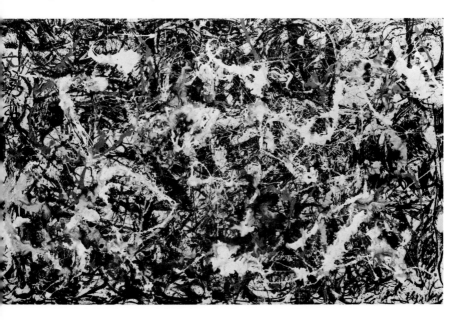

doing as early as 1947 and later abandoned for other themes), Bradley Walker Tomlin, later Franz Kline with his huge black-and-white hieroglyphs, for example—show the strength and variety of this drive toward the caligraphic.

Willem de Kooning, on the contrary, retained the conventional implement for applying paint to canvas—the brush—but used it with an unbridled violence that gave his canvases, even after he had given up pure abstraction and returned to some kind of recognizable

15-3.   Willem de Kooning: *Woman IV* (1952-1953). (Courtesy of the William Rockhill Nelson Gallery of Art, Kansas City, Missouri.)

15-4. Morris Graves: *Flight of Plover* (1955). (Courtesy of
the Whitney Museum of American Art, New York.)

image, a brutality of statement that shocked and fascinated. As a
world movement, abstract expressionism owes more of its popularity, perhaps, to de Kooning's ferocity in paint than to Pollock's
elegance.

Both in theory and in practice the entire movement was deeply
introspective. A "lyrical" abstraction was another major drive. It
may be typified by William Baziotes, with his poetry of shape and
color, on the one hand, and by the explorations of the mysterious
resonances of color and tone to be seen in various ways in the work
of Clyfford Still, Mark Rothko, Barnett Newman, and Philip Guston,
on the other.

In contrast to the vaporous, free-floating forms of lyrical abstraction, another trend explored the hard, pure geometry of shape and color. This had been a major theme of American painting from the time of Sheeler and Stuart Davis; but I. Rice Pereira (to whom the Whitney Museum gave a retrospective exhibit together with Loren MacIver in 1953), Lee Mullican, and Jimmy Ernst showed how possible it was still to create new and personal geometric styles.

There is no doubt that abstract art was the dominant movement in the postwar years and that it has had a great influence wherever younger painters are working in the Western idiom, from Paris to Tokyo. Its triumph was so overwhelming that it not only drew to it a larger number of able younger painters than I can name here but also, unfortunately, a host of feeble imitators who made it, in the words of Lloyd Goodrich and John I. H. Baur, "one of the most abused styles of our day, exploited by a multitude of inept paint manipulators who claim the privilege of the absolute freedom it offers in self-expression without accepting the discipline and rig-

15-5.   Andrew Wyeth: *Christina's World* (1948).
(Collection, The Museum of Modern Art, New York.)

orous self-examination which have been so plainly involved in the work of its leading practitioners."[1]

Toward the close of the nineteen fifties, a revolt against abstraction broke out on a very wide scale, which was recognized by the Museum of Modern Art's "New Images of Man," 1961. This revolt had been gaining momentum for some time. The "monster painters," such as Leon Golub, in Chicago, had begun to use the techniques of abstraction for quite a different purpose. A group of painters on the West Coast led by David Park and Richard Diebenkorn and others, had abandoned abstraction for figurative expression and had been acquiring followers during the later fifties. The painters who had created this revolution came from within the abstract movement: they returned to the human figure as a theme, but retained the traits of style—the scale, the physical surface, the violent touch—of abstract expressionism.

Finally, it must be added that, as one looks back upon the fifties, it is clear that the total dominance of abstraction was a dominance of critical enthusiasm and the art market, rather than of the actual practice of the arts or of significant achievement.

The representation of nature in the expressionist form continued to flourish. In the Pacific Northwest states of Washington and Oregon, Mark Tobey and two younger men, Morris Graves and Kenneth Callahan, created an art of lyrical fantasy. Graves' haunted imagery of birds, flowers, waves of the sea owed much to both the art and the mysticism of the Orient; Callahan's dreamlike world, on the contrary, is a tumult of human figures. Other painters of lyrical subjectivity, Loren MacIver in New York, Margo Hoff and Julia Thecla in Chicago, Jacob Lawrence speaking for the world of the Negro, created eloquent and moving work.

The school of sharp-focus realism (which had appeared with Peter Blume before the war) gained a new and potent leader in Andrew Wyeth and increased in members during the period, especially in the directions of satire (George Tooker, Henry Koerner, Robert Vickery, Alton Pickens) and *trompe l'oeil* (Aaron Bohrod, Kenneth Davies).

The "dark" school of enigmatic, hallucinatory images of nature,

[1] *American Art of Our Century*, New York, Frederick A. Praeger, Publisher, 1961, p. 216.

led by Edwin Dickinson, emerged strongly and gained younger recruits (Walter Murch, Ben Kamahira).

Social satire gained notable recruits in this generation. Jack Levine and Hyman Bloom appeared out of Boston's east side and Joseph Hirsch from Philadelphia to create an art of passionate protest against the imperfection of man and (in the case of Bloom) the moldering presence of death haunting the imagination.

Romantic realism declined in numbers from the prewar period but was never without distinguished exponents.

Why, then, did abstraction almost completely obliterate, critically speaking, the claims to attention of other kinds of painting? Among many possible explanations, two reasons suggest themselves in the history of those days.

Hope and fear, twin images of things to come, are close together in the human heart. The war had devastated two continents, had destroyed sixteen million people, had revolutionized the technology upon which modern populations live. The shocks of these giant changes fell not only upon those physically dispossessed but upon the old who had lost touch with the young; upon the educationally limited who found themselves in a world they could not understand and who saw intellectuals and research scientists, rather than familiar business types, being called in to manage the strange technology of this new age. Moreover, peace had brought no peace, only a struggle against a vengeful enemy who could not be met in the open but who fought a sinister war of subversion and stratagem. Out of the tangled net of human fears and frustrations produced by these overwhelming changes in the postwar world came explosions of resentment, capitalized upon by ambitious men in the national life, which had their echoes in the world of art. In the suffering days of the thirties, many artists had been vocal in protest movements; now their words returned to haunt them. At this moment, the abstract expressionists also were making their deepest plunge into the irrational. In a world where nuclear physicists and other intellectuals were assuming such frightening powers, the artists' incomprehensibility was only another pinprick—but pinpricks provoke sometimes violent reactions. The smoldering resentment against change, against intellectuals, against all aspects of the strange in modern thought burst out in a wave of political attacks upon artists and upon the unfamiliar and the irrational in modern art as "Communist subversion."

A series of episodes followed, irritating and insulting to artists. Anton Refregier was ordered to remove a portrait of Franklin D. Roosevelt surrounded by the Four Freedoms from a mural in a San Francisco post office. The State Department was forced to cancel the tours of two exhibitions of contemporary painting traveling abroad, to bring them home, and to sell the pictures which had been purchased for the purpose of national exhibitions. Individual artists were denounced in speeches before Congress and harassed in vari-

15-6.   Jack Levine: *Gangster Funeral* (1952-1953).
(Courtesy of the Whitney Museum of American Art, New York.)

ous ways. When *Look* magazine, in 1948, held a poll of museum directors, curators, and art critics to choose the ten best American painters, several of those chosen proved to be on the blacklist of the Congressmen who had appointed themselves to watch over art and therefore could not be included in any exhibition sent abroad by the United States Information Agency.

The Institute of Modern Art, Boston, chose this moment to change its name, becoming the Institute of Contemporary Art (1948). The change and the accompanying unlucky announcement were taken as a manifesto of opposition to the modern movement. Confronted by a statement from Boston which contained words like "an institution devoted to fostering contemporary art . . . must also proclaim standards of excellence which the public may comprehend . . ."; "Nature and mankind remain an inexhaustible source of inspiration. World chaos and social unrest, which prompted many of the excesses of modern art, are still with us, but the artist should not take refuge in private cynicism . . ."; ". . . he must come forward with a strong, clear affirmation of truth for humanity," the New York art world exploded. This, they felt, was an attack on the liberty of the artist: it was treason from within. The quarrel was soon over, and in the spring of 1950 the three institutions—the Museum of Modern Art, the Whitney Museum of American Art, and the Institute of Contemporary Art, Boston—issued a manifesto rejecting the assumption that modern art was antihumanistic, or un-American. "We believe," said the signers, "that the so-called unintelligibility of some modern art is an inevitable result of its exploration of new frontiers." But an irritable, controversial atmosphere continued to exist. When the Metropolitan Museum of Art made a vast effort to present a panorama of "American Painting, 1950," although the exhibition leaned heavily toward abstraction, an angry group of abstract painters boycotted the exhibition because they did not like the composition of the jury.[2] The inevitable war of generations was envenomed by political interference; and, in reaction to efforts at thought control by conservative artists and inartistic congressmen, the defenders of the liberty of the mind hardened their stand: they would defend the incomprehensible and unintelligible in modern art at all costs. We must honor those who fought for freedom of thought and expression on that battleground. Nonetheless, it may

[2] *Life* Magazine, however, published their photograph; which was even better (January 5, 1951, page 34).

be possible that extreme led to extreme and some breadth of critical sympathy was forgotten in the heat of battle.

The second factor was that for the first time American painters commanded a world reputation and a world market. When the Museum of Modern Art showed the New York school in Paris in its "Salute to France" exhibit (1955), the French critics were not enthusiastic; but the young painters were excited by the scale and violence of American action painting. And, on second thought, was not this, after all, the way in which the European intellectual preferred to see American culture—something powerful but raw and crude, vast but chaotic; in short, a formidable but still somewhat barbaric culture compared with their own elegant humanism? The *succès d'estime* of the action painters among the young in Europe was exploited with wide publicity and commercial skill by their New York handlers, leading to triumph where success can be most easily comprehended—in the market. Prices soared; and inflation of the size of canvases was outdistanced by inflation of their prices. The "young growth painter" appeared in our language and his prospects were passed along, like tips on the stock market, from gossip to gossip. American opinion was flattered to see American pictures being bought in Europe—and at such prices!

At the beginning of the 1960's the diversity of our complex, Continental culture seems once again to be reasserting itself, amidst a healthy debate of critical comment. On the one hand, Sidney Tillim in *Arts* (April 1961): "From exhibition to exhibition, the tremors in the crust of modern style are growing in intensity. Representational art is the mountain thrusting through the plain. For my part, it is the painting I am now most interested in. I find that it gives me more to look at and more to 'understand.' I appreciate its ring of familiarity and I believe it has a future." On the other hand, Sam Hunter, in the introduction to "American Art Since 1950" (Seattle World's Fair, 1962): "Pollock, de Kooning, Rothko and Smith, rather than the great European masters of modern art, remain the idols of the new generation. They and their fellow abstract artists have become the pre-emptive shaping force in our art. . . . The powerful leverage exerted by this group of artists in American cultural life, and the pluralistic character of their movement, have now quite altered the terms of the old dispute between representation and abstraction. It is no longer possible to assume that the opposing currents of realism, expressionism, a traditional romanticism, and abstraction are of equal validity."

It is evident from the whole of this book that the present writer sees the imaginative life of this country, as expressed in each of the arts, in terms of a sensibility woven of complex strands, developed out of an ancient and complicated past, rich by its innate diversity inherited from many gifted races, mingled by the slow development of centuries past into our many-sided awareness of life. I believe this still to be true. The creative life of this country is too large a phenomenon to be fitted into any one mold.

Painting in America is extraordinarily alive today, crowded with talents, immensely varied, ambitious, productive, undiscouraged by any obstacle—either poverty, overcrowding, war, the malice of decorators, the fury of architects, or the competition of all the protean amusements, distractions, and economic demands of the twentieth century.

But how could it be otherwise? This language of the eye, one of the noblest, most original, most ideal creations of Western man, has become part of our being; it is one of our instinctive forms of imaginative speech. In our branch of the Western world, in the United States of America, the mind and imagination are deeply stirred not only by the pressure of the terrible events and losses of our time but by passion to explore the whole world of sense and experience. The perceptive eye, the observing mind, the finely tuned emotions grow more, not less, significant. The language of the eye has only begun to tell its story in our civilization.

The things to look for are imaginative force and intensity. Each age brings its own novelties of subject and style; yet these are not necessarily important or lasting imaginative creations. Each life feels the oldest experiences as if they were new: and, indeed, they are new in each life. Creativity is part of the human spirit, and as varied, as manifold, as inexhaustible. It includes the daring mind grappling with the vast, new perspectives of our day and the Hopi Indian carving and painting the old, loved, unchanging image of his kachina. The novel and the traditional, the strange and the normal are equally its raw material. It proceeds by intensity of realization. The aim is freshness.

Selected Bibliography

THE BIBLIOGRAPHY given here makes no attempt to offer a complete documentation of 450 years of painting, nor to include all works of interest to the special student. It is intended to be useful to the general reader and the amateur, who wishes to go further than the present text can carry him—as it is the hope of both the author and the publisher that he will so wish. For those who desire to consult lists, many of the authors given below offer detailed bibliographies for their period. Among those most readily accessible, Virgil Barker's *American Painting: History and Interpretation* (1950); Flexner's *First Flowers of Our Wilderness* (1947) and *The Light of Distant Skies* (1954); and Larkin's *Art and Life in America* (1949) offer extensive and useful general bibliographies. Elizabeth McCausland's "Selected Bibliography on American Painting and Sculpture from Colonial Times to the Present" in the *Magazine of Art*, vol. XXXIX (November, 1946), pp. 329-349, is extremely useful. The *Dictionary of American Biography* does not always include the painters one wishes, but the biographies included give their own bibliographies. Finally, there is *The New-York Historical Society's Dictionary of Artists in America, 1564–1860* (1957), which is fuller and more accurate than Mantle Fielding's *Dictionary of American Painters, Sculptors and Engravers* (1926) and far more complete than the account of American painters given by any of the standard European dictionaries of artists.

The Archives of American Art, with its headquarters in The Detroit Institute of Arts, is engaged in a program of collecting the documents for the lives and activities of all American artists and craftsmen whom we can identify by name. (Only the anonymous household crafts and aboriginal arts are excluded.) It is, as of 1963, richest in documentation of twentieth-century artists, but it is growing rapidly toward a comprehensive national research collection.

The most extensive collection of photographs of American painting is in the Frick Art Reference Library, an institution to whose generous aid and hospitality the author, like every other student of art, is immensely indebted. The Waldron Phoenix Belknap Library of American Painting in the H. F. du Pont Winterthur Museum is also beginning a library of photographs, planned on the same noble scale but concentrated on the American field.

The aim of this selected bibliography is to offer current and easily available references. Special importance has therefore been laid on museum exhibition catalogs. In recent years, our knowledge has been advanced by many admirably thorough survey exhibitions and retrospective exhibitions of individual artists. Most of these catalogs are still in print and available from the museum that issued them, although not from general booksellers. The special student needs no guidance to the files of *The Art Quarterly* of which I have the honor to be one of the editors, to *Art in America*, the *Art Bulletin*, *The New-York Historical Society Quarterly*, the *Pennsylvania Magazine*, the *Journal of the American Antiquarian Society* and other similar journals; all periodical references are therefore eliminated.

No bibliography of American painting can, however, omit certain out-of-print but basic writers of the past, such as Dunlap (1834), Tuckerman (1867), or Isham (1905), whose work deserves our enduring gratitude and whose information cannot be replaced.

The exhibition catalogs and bulletins issued by the museums active in showing contemporary art are too numerous to mention; also, except in specialized libraries, difficult of access. Nonetheless, for the serious student the file of catalogs and bulletins issued by the following institutions is useful and indeed indispensable: The Museum of Modern Art, New York, *Painting and Sculpture in the Museum of Modern Art, A Catalog*, followed by annual supplements called *Painting and Sculpture Acquisitions*; the Whitney Museum of American Art, illustrated catalogs of its annual exhibits, as well as monographs; the Institute of Contemporary Art, Boston; the Pennsylvania Academy of the Fine Arts, Philadelphia; the Corcoran Gallery of Art, Washington; the Art Institute of Chicago; the Walker Art Center, Minneapolis; the San Francisco Museum of Art; the Los Angeles County Museum; the University of Illinois, Urbana, Illinois. All of these hold exhibitions of more than ordinary significance.

BIBLIOGRAPHY OF GENERAL SOURCES

BARKER, VIRGIL, *American Painting: History and Interpretation*. New York, The Macmillan Company, 1950.

———, *A Critical Introduction to American Painting*. New York, published by W. E. Rudge for the Whitney Museum of American Art, 1931.

———, *From Realism to Reality in Recent American Painting*. Lincoln, Nebraska, University of Nebraska Press, 1959.

BARR, ALFRED H., JR., *Fantastic Art, Dada, Surrealism*. New York, The Museum of Modern Art, 1947.

———, *Masters of Modern Art*. New York, The Museum of Modern Art, 1954.

BAUR, JOHN IRELAND HOWE, *American Painting in the Nineteenth Century; Main Trends and Movements*. New York, Frederick A. Praeger, Inc., 1953.

———, *The Eight: Robert Henri, John Sloan, William J. Glackens, Ernest Lawson, Maurice Prendergast, George B. Luks, Everett Shinn, Arthur B. Davies*. New York, The Brooklyn Museum, 1943.

———, *Landmarks in American Art, 1670-1950; A Loan Exhibition of Great American Paintings*. For the benefit of the American Federation of Arts, at Wildenstein. New York, Wildenstein and Company, 1953.

———, *Nature in Abstraction*. New York, Whitney Museum of American Art, 1958.

———, *The New Decade, 35 American Painters*. New York, Whitney Museum of American Art, 1955.

———, *Revolution and Tradition in Modern American Art*. Cambridge, Massachusetts, Harvard University Press, 1951.

BENJAMIN, SAMUEL GREENE WHEELER, *Art in America; A Critical and Historical Sketch*. New York, Harper & Brothers, 1880.

BIZARDEL, YVON, *American Painters in Paris*. New York, The Macmillan Company, 1960.

BOLTON, THEODORE, *American Book Illustrators; Bibliographic Check Lists of 123 Artists*. New York, R. R. Bowker Company, 1938.

———, *Early American Portrait Draughtsmen in Crayons*. New York, F. F. Sherman, 1923.

———, *Early American Portrait Painters in Miniature*. New York, F. F. Sherman, 1921.

BORN, WOLFGANG, *American Landscape Painting; An Interpretation*. New Haven, Connecticut, Yale University Press, 1948.

———, *Still Life Painting in America*. New York, Oxford University Press, 1947.

BOSWELL, PEYTON, *Modern American Painting*. New York, Dodd, Mead and Company, 1939.

BROWN, MILTON W., *American Painting from the Armory Show to the Depression*. Princeton, New Jersey, Princeton University Press, 1955.

BURROUGHS, ALAN, *A History of American Landscape Painting*. New York, Whitney Museum of American Art, 1942.

———, *Limners and Likenesses; Three Centuries of American Painting*. Cambridge, Massachusetts, Harvard University Press, 1936.

CAHILL, HOLGER, *American Folk Art; The Art of the Common Man in America, 1750-1900*. New York, The Museum of Modern Art, 1932.

———, *Masters of Popular Painting. Modern Primitives of Europe and America.* New York, The Museum of Modern Art, 1938.

———, *New Horizons in American Art.* New York, The Museum of Modern Art, 1936 (WPA Art Programs).

CAHILL, HOLGER, AND BARR, ALFRED H., JR., eds., *Art in America, A Complete Survey.* New York, Reynal and Hitchcock, 1935.

CHEW, PAUL A., AND HOVEY, WALTER READ, *250 Years of Art in Pennsylvania.* Greensburg, Pennsylvania, Westmoreland County Museum of Art, 1959.

CHRISTENSEN, ERWIN O., *The Index of American Design.* New York, The Macmillan Company; Washington, D. C., National Gallery of Art, 1950. (Folk art.)

CLIFFORD, HENRY; SLOAN, JOHN; SHINN, EVERETT, *Artists of the Philadelphia Press.* Philadelphia, Philadelphia Museum of Art, 1946.

DICKSON, HAROLD E., *Pennsylvania Painters.* University Park, Pennsylvania, Pennsylvania State University, 1955.

DORRA, HENRI, *The American Muse.* New York, The Viking Press, Inc., 1961.

DOW, GEORGE FRANCIS, *The Arts and Crafts in New England, 1704-1775.* Topsfield, Massachusetts, The Wayside Press, 1927 (Compendium of Newspaper Advertisements and Articles).

DREPPERD, CARL WILLIAM, *American Pioneer Arts and Artists,* with foreword by Rockwell Kent. Springfield, Massachusetts, Pond-Ekberry, 1942.

DRESSER, LOUISA, *Seventeenth-Century Painting in New England.* Worcester, Massachusetts, Worcester Art Museum, 1935.

DUNLAP, WILLIAM, *A History of the Rise and Progress of the Arts of Design in the United States,* 2 vols. New York, George P. Scott and Co., 1834. New Edition, edited by Frank W. Bayley and Charles E. Goodspeed, 3 vols., Boston, C. E. Goodspeed, 1918.

DWIGHT, EDWARD W., *American Painting, 1760-1960.* Milwaukee, Wisconsin, Milwaukee Art Center, 1959.

FIELDING, MANTLE, *American Engravers upon Copper and Steel* (a supplement to *American Engravers upon Copper and Steel by David McNeely Stauffer*). Philadelphia, printed for the subscribers, 1917.

———, *Dictionary of American Painters, Sculptors and Engravers.* Philadelphia, 1926.

FLEXNER, JAMES THOMAS, *America's Old Masters.* New York, The Viking Press, Inc., 1939.

———, *First Flowers of Our Wilderness, American Painting.* Boston, Houghton Mifflin Company, 1947.

———, *The Light of Distant Skies, 1760-1835*. New York, Harcourt, Brace & Company, 1954.

———, *The Pocket History of American Painting*. New York, Pocket Books, Inc., 1950.

———, *A Short History of American Painting*. Boston, Houghton Mifflin Company, 1950.

———, *That Wilder Image*. Boston, Little, Brown and Company, 1962.

FORD, ALICE, *Pictorial Folk Art, New England to California*. New York and London, The Studio Publications, Inc., 1949.

FRANKENSTEIN, ALFRED, *After the Hunt: William Harnett and Other American Still Life Painters, 1870-1900*. Berkeley and Los Angeles, University of California Press, 1953.

FRIEDMAN, MARTIN L., *The Precisionist View in American Art*. Minneapolis, Minnesota, The Walker Art Center, 1960.

GOODRICH, LLOYD, *American Watercolor and Winslow Homer*. Minneapolis, The Walker Art Center, 1945.

———, *A Century of American Landscape Painting, 1800-1900*. Pittsburgh, Pennsylvania, Carnegie Institute, 1939; New York, Whitney Museum of American Art, 1938.

———, *Pioneers of Modern Art in America*. New York, Whitney Museum of American Art, 1946. (Early twentieth-century artists who studied in Paris.)

———, *Young America; Thirty American Painters and Sculptors Under Thirty-five*. New York, Whitney Museum of American Art, 1957.

GOODRICH, LLOYD, AND BAUR, JOHN I. H., *American Art of Our Century*. New York, Frederick A. Praeger, for the Whitney Museum of American Art, 1961.

GOTTESMAN, RITA SUSSWEIN, comp., *The Arts and Crafts in New York, 1726-1776: Advertisements and News Items from New York City Newspapers*. New York, The New-York Historical Society, 1938.

GRIGAUT, PAUL L., *The French in America, 1520-1880*. Detroit, Michigan, The Detroit Institute of Arts, 1951.

GROCE, GEORGE C., JR., *1440 Early American Portrait Artists*. Newark, New Jersey, Historical Records Project, Works Progress Administration, 1940.

HAGEN, OSKAR, *The Birth of the American Tradition of Art*. New York, Charles Scribner's Sons, 1940. (From about 1670 to the revolution.)

HARTMANN, SADAKICHI, *A History of American Art*. Boston, L. C. Page, 1902; New Revised Edition, Boston, L. C. Page, 1932.

HASKELL, DANIEL CARL, *American Historical Prints*. New York, New York Public Library, 1927.

———, *American Historical Prints from the Phelps Stokes and Other Collections, 1497-1891.* New York, New York Public Library, 1932.

HEIL, WALTER, *Meet the Artist: An Exhibition of Self Portraits by Living Artists.* San Francisco, M. H. de Young Memorial Museum, 1943.

HESS, T. B., *Abstract Painting: Background and American Phase.* New York, The Viking Press, Inc., 1951.

HUNTER, SAM, "American Art Since 1950." *Art Since 1950.* Seattle World's Fair, 1962.

ISHAM, SAMUEL, *The History of American Painting.* New York, The Macmillan Company, 1905; new edition with supplement by Royal Cortissoz, New York, The Macmillan Company, 1937.

JANIS, SIDNEY, *They Taught Themselves; American Primitive Painters of the Twentieth Century,* foreword by Alfred H. Barr, Jr. New York, Dial Press, 1942.

JONES, AGNES HALSEY, *New-Found Folk Art of the Young Republic.* Cooperstown, New York State Historical Association, 1960.

———, *Rediscovered Painters of Upstate New York, 1700-1875.* Cooperstown, New York State Historical Association, 1958.

M. and M. Karolik Collection of American Paintings, 1815 to 1865. Cambridge, Massachusetts, Harvard University Press, 1949, published for the Museum of Fine Arts, Boston.

LA FOLLETTE, SUZANNE, *Art in America.* New York, Harper & Brothers, 1929.

LARKIN, OLIVER W., *Art and Life in America.* New York, Rinehart & Company, Inc., 1949.

LIPMAN, JEAN, *American Folk Decoration.* New York, Oxford University Press, Inc., 1951.

———, *American Primitive Painting,* New York, Oxford University Press, Inc., 1942.

LIPMAN, JEAN, AND WINCHESTER, ALICE, *Primitive Painting in America, 1750-1950, An Anthology.* New York, Dodd, Mead and Company, 1950.

LITTLE, NINA FLETCHER, *The Abby Aldrich Rockefeller Folk Art Collection.* Colonial Williamsburg, distributed by Little, Brown and Company, 1957.

———, *American Decorative Wall Painting, 1700-1850.* Sturbridge, Massachusetts, Old Sturbridge Village, in cooperation with The Studio Publications, Inc., New York, 1952.

LORANT, STEFAN, *The New World: The First Pictures of America.* New York, Duell, Sloan and Pearce, Inc., 1946. (Explorer artists.)

MC CAUSLAND, ELIZABETH, "A Selected Bibliography on American Painting and Sculpture from Colonial Times to the Present." *Magazine of Art* XXXIX (November 1946), pp. 329-349.

MC CAUSLAND, ELIZABETH, AND WILLIAMS, HERMANN WARNER, JR., *American Processional, 1492-1900*. Washington, D. C., The Corcoran Gallery of Art, 1950.

MC CRACKEN, HAROLD, *Portrait of the Old West*, with a biographical check list of Western artists. New York, McGraw-Hill Book Company, Inc., 1952.

MAC FARLANE, JANET R., AND WHEELER, ROBERT E., *Hudson Valley Paintings, 1700-1750*. Albany, New York, Albany Institute of History and Art, 1959.

MATHER, FRANK JEWETT, JR.; MOREY, CHARLES RUFUS; AND HENDERSON, WILLIAM JAMES, *The American Spirit in Art*. New Haven, Connecticut, Yale University Press, 1927 (Vol. XII in *The Pageant of America* series).

MENDELOWITZ, DANIEL M., *A History of American Art*. New York, Holt, Rinehart & Winston, 1960.

MILLER, DOROTHY C., *Americans, 1942: 18 Artists from Nine States*. New York, The Museum of Modern Art, 1942.

———, *Fifteen Americans*. New York, The Museum of Modern Art, 1952.

———, *Fourteen Americans*. New York, The Museum of Modern Art, 1946.

———, *Twelve Americans*. New York, The Museum of Modern Art, 1956.

MILLER, DOROTHY C., AND BARR, ALFRED H., JR., *American Realists and Magic Realists*. New York, The Museum of Modern Art, 1943.

MONRO, ISABEL STEVENSON, AND MONRO, K. M., *Index to Reproductions of American Paintings*. New York, H. W. Wilson Company, 1948.

MOTHERWELL, ROBERT, editor, *The Dada Painters and Poets: An Anthology*. New York, Wittenborn, Schultz, Inc., 1951.

MURRELL, WILLIAM, *A History of American Graphic Humor*, 2 vols. New York, Whitney Museum of American Art, 1933/1938.

NEUHAUS, EUGEN, *The History and Ideals of American Art*. Stanford, California, Stanford University Press, 1931.

PAGANO, GRACE, *Catalogue of the Encyclopaedia Britannica Collection of Contemporary American Painting*. Chicago, Encyclopaedia Britannica, Inc., 1945.

PEARSON, RALPH M., *Experiencing American Pictures*. New York, Harper & Brothers, 1943.

———, *The Modern Renaissance in American Art*. New York, Harper & Brothers, 1954.

PEAT, WILBUR D., *Pioneer Painters of Indiana*. Indianapolis, Indiana, Art Association of Indiana, 1954.

PIERSON, WILLIAM H., JR., AND DAVIDSON, MARTHA, *Arts of the United States: A Pictorial Survey*. New York, McGraw-Hill Book Company, Inc., 1960.

PLEASANTS, J. HALL, *Four Late Eighteenth-Century Anglo-American Landscape Painters*. Worcester, Massachusetts, American Antiquarian Society, 1943, reprinted from The Proceedings of the Society for October, 1942. Contents: George and Mary Beck, William Groombridge, Francis Guy, and William Winstanley.

———, *Two Hundred and Fifty Years of Painting in Maryland*. Baltimore, Maryland, The Baltimore Museum of Art, 1945.

PRIME, ALFRED COX, *The Arts and Crafts in Philadelphia, Maryland and South Carolina*. Topsfield, Massachusetts, The Walpole Society, 1929-1933; Series 1, 1721-1785; Series 2, 1786-1800.

RATHBONE, PERRY T.; RAVENSWAAY, CHARLES VAN; LEONARD, H. STEWART, *Mississippi Panorama*. St. Louis, Missouri, City Art Museum of St. Louis, 1950.

RATHBONE, PERRY T.; VOELKER, FREDERICK E.; FILSINGER, CATHERINE; EISENDRATH, WILLIAM N., JR., *Westward the Way*. St. Louis, Missouri, City Art Museum of St. Louis, 1954.

READ, HELEN APPLETON, *New York Realists, 1900-1914*. New York, Whitney Museum of American Art, 1937.

RICHARDSON, E. P., *American Romantic Painting*. New York, E. Weyhe, 1944.

———, *The Way of Western Art, 1776-1914*. Cambridge, Massachusetts, Harvard University Press, 1939.

———, *The World of the Romantic Artist. A Survey of American Culture from 1800 to 1875*. Detroit, Michigan, The Detroit Institute of Arts, 1945.

RICHARDSON, E. P., AND WITTMANN, OTTO, JR., *Travelers in Arcadia. American Artists in Italy, 1830-1875*. The Detroit Institute of Arts and The Toledo Museum of Art, 1951.

RITCHIE, ANDREW C., *Abstract Painting and Sculpture in America*. New York, The Museum of Modern Art, 1951.

———, *The New Decade*. New York, The Museum of Modern Art, 1955.

ROSSITER, HENRY P., *M. and M. Karolik Collection of American Water Colors and Drawings, 1800-1875*. Boston, Museum of Fine Arts, 1962.

SAINT GAUDENS, HOMER, *The American Artist and His Times*. New York, Dodd, Mead and Company, 1941.

———, *Survey of American Painting*. Pittsburgh, Department of Fine Arts, Carnegie Institute, 1940.

SLATKIN, CHARLES E., AND SHOOLMAN, REGINA, *Treasury of American Drawings*. New York, Oxford University Press, 1947.

SOBY, JAMES THRALL, *Contemporay Painters*. New York, The Museum of Modern Art, 1948.

SOBY, JAMES THRALL, AND MILLER, DOROTHY C., *Romantic Painting in America*. New York, The Museum of Modern Art, 1943.

STAUFFER, DAVID MC NEELY, *American Engravers Upon Copper and Steel*, 2 vols. New York, The Grolier Club, 1907 (supplementary volume by Mantle Fielding, 1917).

STOKES, I. N. PHELPS, AND HASKELL, DANIEL C., *American Historical Prints, Early Views of American Cities, etc., from The Phelps Stokes and Other Collections*. New York, New York Public Library, 1933.

SWEET, FREDERICK A., *The Hudson River School and the Early American Landscape Tradition*. Chicago, Art Institute of Chicago, 1945.

SWEET, FREDERICK A., AND HUTH, HANS, *From Colony to Nation. An exhibition of American painting, silver and architecture from 1650 to the War of 1812*. Chicago, Art Institute of Chicago, 1949.

TAFT, ROBERT, *Artists and Illustrators of the Old West: 1850-1900*. New York, Charles Scribner's Sons, 1953.

TUCKERMAN, HENRY T., *Book of the Artists: American Artist Life*. New York, G. P. Putnam's Sons, 1867, 6th impression, 1882.

WALKER, JOHN, AND JAMES, MACGILL, *Great American Paintings from Smibert to Bellows, 1729-1924*. New York, Oxford University Press, 1943.

WASHBURN, GORDON BAILEY, *Old and New England: an exhibition of American painting of Colonial and Early Republican Days, together with English painting of the same time*. Providence, Rhode Island, Museum of Art of the Rhode Island School of Design, 1945.

WATSON, FORBES, *American Painting Today*. Washington, D. C., American Federation of Arts, 1939.

WATSON, FORBES, AND BRUCE, EDWARD, *Mural Designs, 1934-1936*. Washington, D. C., Art in Federal Buildings, Inc., 1936.

WEHLE, HARRY B., *American Miniatures, 1730-1850, with a Biographical Dictionary of the Artists by Theodore Bolton*. Garden City, New York, published for The Metropolitan Museum of Art by Doubleday & Company, Inc., 1927.

WEHLE, HARRY B.; MAYOR, A. HYATT; AND ALLEN, JOSEPHINE L., *Life in America: a special loan exhibition of paintings held during the period of the New York World's Fair*. New York, The Metropolitan Museum of Art, 1939.

WEITENKAMPF, FRANK, *American Graphic Art*. New York, Henry Holt & Co., Inc., 1912; new edition, New York, The Macmillan Company, 1924.

WHEELER, MONROE, *Twentieth Century Portraits*. New York, The Museum of Modern Art, 1942.

WIGHT, FREDERICK S., *Milestones of American Painting in Our Century;* introduction by Lloyd Goodrich. New York, Chanticleer Press, Inc., 1949.

BIBLIOGRAPHIES ARRANGED BY ARTISTS

WASHINGTON ALLSTON: E. P. Richardson, *Washington Allston, A Study of the Romantic Artist in America.* Chicago, University of Chicago Press, 1948.

JOHN JAMES AUDUBON: Alice Ford, *Audubon's Animals: The Quadrupeds of North America;* New York, The Studio Publications, Inc., 1951. Alice Ford, *Audubon's Butterflies, Moths and Other Studies;* New York, The Studio Publications, Inc., 1952. Donald Culross Peattie (ed.), *Audubon's America, The Narratives and Experiences of John James Audubon;* Boston, Houghton Mifflin Company, 1940.

GEORGE BELLOWS: Peyton Boswell, *George Bellows;* New York, Crown, 1942. Art Institute of Chicago, *George Bellows; Paintings, Drawings, Prints;* Chicago, Art Institute of Chicago, 1946.

HENRY BENBRIDGE: David Sellin, "A Benbridge Conversation Piece." *Philadelphia Museum of Art Bulletin,* LV (Autumn-Winter, 1959-1960), pp. 3-9.

THOMAS HART BENTON: Thomas Hart Benton, *An Artist in America.* New York, Robert M. McBride, 1937.

GEORGE CALEB BINGHAM: Albert Christ-Janer, *George Caleb Bingham of Missouri;* preface by Thomas Hart Benton. New York, Dodd, Mead and Company, 1940. John Francis McDermott, *George Caleb Bingham: River Portraitist;* Norman, Oklahoma, University of Oklahoma Press, 1959.

CHARLES BURCHFIELD: John I. H. Baur, *Charles Burchfield.* New York, published for the Whitney Museum of American Art by The Macmillan Company, 1956.

MARY CASSATT: Frederick A. Sweet, *Sargent, Whistler, and Mary Cassatt.* Chicago, Art Institute of Chicago, 1954.

MARK CATESBY: George Frederick Frick and Raymond Phineas Stearns, *Mark Catesby: The Colonial Audubon.* Urbana, Illinois, University of Illinois Press, 1961.

GEORGE CATLIN: John C. Ewers, *George Catlin, Painter of Indians of the West;* Washington, D.C., Smithsonian Institution, Annual Report, 1955. George I. Quimby, *Indians of the Western Frontier: Paintings of George Catlin;* Chicago, Chicago Natural History Museum, 1954. Lloyd Haberly, *Pursuit of the Horizon, A Life of George Catlin, Painter and Recorder of the American Indian;* New York, The Macmillan Company, 1948.

CONRAD WISE CHAPMAN: Louise F. Catterall, *Conrad Wise Chapman, 1842-1910. An Exhibition of His Works in the Valentine Museum.* Richmond, Virginia, The Valentine Museum, 1962.

JOHN GADSBY CHAPMAN: William P. Campbell, *John Gadsby Chapman.* Washington, D.C., National Gallery of Art, 1962.

WILLIAM MERRITT CHASE: Wilbur D. Peat, *Chase Centennial Exhibition.* Indianapolis, John Herron Art Museum, 1949.

THOMAS COLE: Esther I. Seaver, *Thomas Cole.* Hartford, Connecticut, Wadsworth Atheneum, 1949.

JOHN SINGLETON COPLEY: James Thomas Flexner, *John Singleton Copley;* Boston, Houghton Mifflin Company, 1948 (a completely revised and enlarged version of the biography of Copley originally published as part of the author's *America's Old Masters*). Barbara Neville Parker and Anne Bolling Wheeler, *John Singleton Copley, American Portraits in Oil, Pastel and Miniature;* Boston, Museum of Fine Arts, 1938.

ARTHUR B. DAVIES: John Gordon and others, *Arthur B. Davies, 1862-1928, A Centennial Exhibition;* Utica, New York, Munson-Williams-Proctor Institute, 1962. Phillips Memorial Gallery, Washington, D.C., *Arthur B. Davies: Essays on the Man and His Art;* Cambridge, Massachusetts, The Riverside Press, 1924.

STUART DAVIS: James Johnson Sweeney, *Stuart Davis;* New York, The Museum of Modern Art, 1945. E. C. Goossen, *Stuart Davis;* New York, George Braziller, Inc., 1959. Rudi Blesh, *Stuart Davis;* New York, Grove Press, 1959.

WILLEM DE KOONING: Thomas B. Hess, *Willem de Kooning.* New York, George Braziller, Inc., 1959.

CHARLES DEMUTH: Andrew C. Ritchie, *Charles Demuth.* New York, The Museum of Modern Art, 1950.

FRANK DUVENECK: Norbert Heermann, *Frank Duveneck;* Boston, Houghton Mifflin Company, 1918. Walter S. Siple, *Frank Duveneck;* Cincinnati, Ohio, Cincinnati Art Museum, 1936.

THOMAS EAKINS: Lloyd Goodrich, *Thomas Eakins, His Life and Work;* New York, Whitney Museum of American Art, 1933. Fairfield Porter, *Thomas Eakins;* New York, George Braziller, Inc., 1959.

RALPH EARL: William Sawitzky, *Ralph Earl, 1751-1801.* New York, Whitney Museum of American Art, 1945.

SETH EASTMAN: John Francis McDermott, *Seth Eastman, Pictorial Historian of the Indian.* Norman, Oklahoma, University of Oklahoma Press, 1961.

PHILIP EVERGOOD: John I. H. Baur, *Philip Evergood*. New York, Whitney Museum of American Art, 1959.

LYONEL FEININGER: The Museum of Modern Art, *Lyonel Feininger . . . Marsden Hartley. . . .* New York, The Museum of Modern Art, 1944.

ROBERT FEKE: Henry Wilder Foote, *Robert Feke, Colonial Portrait Painter;* Cambridge, Massachusetts, Harvard University Press, 1930. Whitney Museum of American Art, *Robert Feke;* New York, Whitney Museum of American Art, 1946.

ERASTUS SALISBURY FIELD: Mary C. Black, *Erastus Salisbury Field, 1805-1900.* Williamsburg, Virginia, Abby Aldrich Rockefeller Folk Art Collection, 1963.

WILLIAM GLACKENS: Ira Glackens, *William Glackens and the Ashcan Group;* New York, Crown Publishers, Inc., 1957. Forbes Watson, *William Glackens;* New York, Duffield, 1923.

MORRIS GRAVES: Frederick S. Wight, *The Morris Graves Retrospective Exhibition.* Berkeley, University of California, 1956.

CHESTER HARDING: Margaret E. White (ed.), *A Sketch of Chester Harding, Artist, Drawn by His Own Hand,* edited by his daughter, Margaret E. White, new edition with annotations by his grandson, W. P. G. Harding. Boston, Houghton Mifflin Company, 1929.

MARSDEN HARTLEY: Elizabeth McCausland, *Marsden Hartley;* Minneapolis, University of Minnesota Press, 1952. The Museum of Modern Art, *Lyonel Feininger . . . Marsden Hartley . . . ;* New York, The Museum of Modern Art, 1944.

MARTIN JOHNSON HEADE: Robert G. McIntyre, *Martin Johnson Heade.* New York, Pantheon Press, 1948.

GUSTAVUS HESSELIUS: Christian Brinton, *Gustavus Hesselius.* Philadelphia, Philadelphia Museum of Art, 1938.

EDWARD HICKS: Alice Ford, *Edward Hicks, Painter of the Peaceable Kingdom.* Philadelphia, University of Pennsylvania Press, 1952.

WINSLOW HOMER: Bartlett Cowdrey, *Winslow Homer: Illustrator, 1860-1875;* Northampton, Massachusetts, Smith College Museum of Art, 1951. Albert Ten Eyck Gardner, *Winslow Homer, American Artist: His World and His Work;* New York, Clarkson N. Potter, Inc., 1962. Lloyd Goodrich, *Winslow Homer;* New York, published for the Whitney Museum of American Art by The Macmillan Company, 1944.

EDWARD HOPPER: Lloyd Goodrich, *Edward Hopper Retrospective Exhibition.* New York, Whitney Museum of American Art, 1950 (for a group of museums).

GEORGE INNESS: Elizabeth McCausland, *George Inness, an American Landscape Painter, 1825-1894.* New York, American Artists Group, 1946.

EASTMAN JOHNSON: John I. H. Baur, *An American Genre Painter, Eastman Johnson, 1824-1906.* New York, Brooklyn Institute of Arts and Sciences, 1940.

JOHN LA FARGE: Royal Cortissoz, *John La Farge, A Memoir and a Study.* Boston, Houghton Mifflin Company, 1911.

LOREN MAC IVER: John I. H. Baur, *Loren MacIver and I. Rice Pereira.* New York, Whitney Museum of American Art, 1953.

EDWARD GREENE MALBONE: Ruel Pardee Tolman, *The Life and Works of Edward Greene Malbone, 1777-1807.* New York, The New-York Historical Society, 1958.

JOHN MARIN: *John Marin Memorial Exhibition,* with a foreword by Duncan Phillips, appreciations by William Carlos Williams and Dorothy Norman, conclusion to a biography by Mackinley Helm; Boston, Museum of Fine Arts, 1955. *John Marin—Frontiersman* by Frederick S. Wight; Los Angeles, Art Galleries of the University of California, Los Angeles, 1955. *John Marin, Water Colors, Oil Paintings, Etchings:* "John Marin" by Henry McBride; "As to John Marin, and his Ideas," by Marsden Hartley; "John Marin—and Pertaining Thereto," by E. M. Benson; New York, The Museum of Modern Art, 1936.

SAMUEL F. B. MORSE: Oliver W. Larkin, *Samuel F. B. Morse and American Democratic Art;* Boston, Little, Brown and Company, 1954. Carleton Mabee, *The American Leonardo: A Life of Samuel F. B. Morse;* New York, Alfred A. Knopf, Inc., 1943.

ANNA MOSES: Anna Moses, *Grandma Moses; My Life's History,* edited by Otto Kallir. New York, Harper & Brothers, 1952.

WILLIAM SIDNEY MOUNT: Bartlett Cowdrey and Hermann Warner Williams, Jr., *William Sidney Mount, 1807-1868, An American Painter.* New York, published for The Metropolitan Museum of Art by Columbia University Press, 1944.

MOUNT BROTHERS: Bartlett Cowdrey, *The Mount Brothers: Henry Smith Mount, Shepard Alonzo Mount, and William Sidney Mount.* Stony Brook, New York, The Suffolk Museum, 1947.

GEORGIA O'KEEFFE: Daniel Catton Rich, *Georgia O'Keeffe.* Chicago, Art Institute of Chicago, 1943.

WILLIAM PAGE: Joshua C. Taylor, *William Page: The American Titian.* Chicago, University of Chicago Press, 1957.

CHARLES WILLSON PEALE: Charles Coleman Sellers, *Charles Willson Peale,* 2 vols.; Philadelphia, American Philosophical Society, 1947. Charles Coleman Sellers, *Portraits and Miniatures by Charles Willson Peale;* Philadelphia, American Philosophical Society, 1952.

JACKSON POLLOCK: Frank O'Hara, *Jackson Pollock;* New York, George Braziller, Inc., 1959. Sam Hunter, *Jackson Pollock;* New York, The Museum of Modern Art, 1956.

MATTHEW PRATT: William Sawitzky, *Matthew Pratt, 1734-1805*. New York, The New-York Historical Society, 1942.

MAURICE PRENDERGAST: Phillips Academy, Addison Gallery of American Art, *The Prendergasts; Retrospective Exhibition of the Work of Maurice and Charles Prendergast*. Andover, Massachusetts, Phillips Academy, 1938.

HOWARD PYLE: Charles D. Abbott, *Howard Pyle, A Chronicle*. New York, Harper & Brothers, 1925.

JOHN QUIDOR: John I. H. Baur, *John Quidor, 1801-1881*. New York, Brooklyn Institute of Arts and Sciences, 1942.

WILLIAM RIMMER: Lincoln Kirstein, *William Rimmer*. New York, Whitney Museum of American Art and Museum of Fine Arts, Boston, 1946-1947.

MARK ROTHKO: Peter Selz, *Mark Rothko*. New York, Museum of Modern Art, 1961.

ALBERT P. RYDER: Lloyd Goodrich, *Albert P. Ryder;* New York, George Braziller, Inc., 1959. Lloyd Goodrich, *Albert P. Ryder Centenary Exhibition;* New York, Whitney Museum of American Art, 1947.

JOHN SINGER SARGENT: David McKibben, *Sargent's Boston, With an Essay and a Biographical Summary and a Complete Check List of Sargent's Portraits;* Boston, Museum of Fine Arts, Boston, 1956. Charles Merrill Mount, *John Singer Sargent, A Biography;* New York, W. W. Norton and Company, Inc., 1955. Frederick A. Sweet, *Sargent, Whistler, and Mary Cassatt;* Chicago, Art Institute of Chicago, 1954.

BEN SHAHN: James Thrall Soby, *Ben Shahn*. New York, The Museum of Modern Art, 1947.

CHARLES SHEELER: *Charles Sheeler: Paintings, Drawings, Photographs,* with an introduction by William Carlos Williams; New York, The Museum of Modern Art, 1939. Frederick S. Wight, *Charles Sheeler, A Retrospective Exhibition,* with a foreword by William Carlos Williams and an appreciation by Bartlett H. Hayes, Jr.; Los Angeles, University of California Art Galleries, 1954 (for a group of participating museums).

JOHN SLOAN: Lloyd Goodrich, *John Sloan, 1871-1951*. New York, Whitney Museum of American Art, 1952.

JOHN SMIBERT: Henry Wilder Foote, *John Smibert, Painter*. Cambridge, Massachusetts, Harvard University Press, 1950.

CLYFFORD STILL: Gordon F. Smith and the artist and his wife, *Paintings by Clyfford Still*. Buffalo, New York, Albright Art Gallery, 1959.

DAVID HUNTER STROTHER: Cecil D. Eby, Jr. (ed.), *The Old South Illustrated,* by Porte Crayon (David Hunter Strother). Profusely illustrated by the author. Chapel Hill, North Carolina, The University of North Carolina Press, 1959.

GILBERT STUART: James Thomas Flexner, *Gilbert Stuart; A Great Life in*

Brief; New York, Alfred A. Knopf, Inc., 1955 (greatly expanded revision of the biography which appeared in the author's *America's Old Masters*). John Hill Morgan, *Gilbert Stuart and His Pupils; Together with the Complete Notes on Painting by Matthew Harris Jouett from Conversations with Gilbert Stuart in 1816;* New York, The New-York Historical Society, 1939. Lawrence Park, *Gilbert Stuart,* 4 vols.; New York, W. E. Rudge, 1926.

THOMAS SULLY: Edward Biddle and Mantle Fielding, *The Life and Works of Thomas Sully, 1783-1872.* Philadelphia, M. Fielding, 1921.

MARK TOBEY: Colette Roberts, *Mark Tobey;* New York, Grove Press, 1959. Edward B. Thomas, *Mark Tobey: A Retrospective Exhibition from Northwest Collections;* Seattle, Washington, Seattle Art Museum, 1959.

BRADLEY WALKER TOMLIN: John I. H. Baur, *Bradley Walker Tomlin.* New York, Whitney Museum of American Art, 1957.

COL. JOHN TRUMBULL: Theodore Sizer (ed.), *The Autobiography of Col. John Trumbull;* New Haven, Connecticut, Yale University Press, 1953. Theodore Sizer, *The Works of Colonel John Trumbull, Artist of the American Revolution;* New Haven, Connecticut, Yale University Press, 1950.

JOHN VANDERLYN: Marius Schoonmaker, *John Vanderlyn, Artist, 1775-1852.* Kingston, New York, the Senate House Museum, 1950.

FRANKLIN WATKINS: Andrew C. Ritchie, *Franklin C. Watkins.* New York, The Museum of Modern Art, 1950.

MAX WEBER: Lloyd Goodrich, *Max Weber;* New York, The Macmillan Company, 1949. William H. Gerdts, *Max Weber Retrospective Exhibition;* Newark, New Jersey, The Newark Museum, 1959.

J. ALDEN WEIR: Dorothy Weir Young, *The Life and Letters of J. Alden Weir.* Edited with an introduction by Lawrence W. Chisholm. New Haven, Yale University Press, 1960.

BENJAMIN WEST: Richard Hirsch, *The World of Benjamin West;* Allentown, Pennsylvania, Allentown Art Museum, 1962. Henri Marceau and Fiske Kimball, *Benjamin West, 1738-1820;* Philadelphia, Pennsylvania Museum of Art, 1938.

JAMES MC NEILL WHISTLER: Elizabeth Robins Pennell, *Life of James McNeill Whistler,* 6th edition, revised; Philadelphia, J. B. Lippincott Company, 1919. Frederick A. Sweet, *Sargent, Whistler, and Mary Cassatt;* Chicago, Art Institute of Chicago, 1954.

WORTHINGTON WHITTREDGE: John I. H. Baur (ed.), *The Autobiography of Worthington Whittredge.* New York, The Brooklyn Museum, 1942.

ANDREW WYETH: Gordon M. Smith, *Andrew Wyeth;* Buffalo, New York, Albright-Knox Art Gallery, 1962. Agnes Mongan, *Andrew Wyeth. Dry Brush and Pencil Drawings;* Cambridge, Massachusetts, Fogg Art Museum, 1963.

Index